"Few in hockey history have done more for The Game with less credit than Howard Baldwin. His leadership of the World Hockey Association led to the landmark merger with the NHL and grand expansion of the Ice Game. He was the man behind the Penguins' first pair of Stanley Cups and has vigorously — indefatigably — pursued more creative sports ideas than anyone I know. His story, automatically, becomes a must-read."

— Stan Fischler, Madison Square Garden hockey analyst
and author of more than ninety hockey books

"I've known Howard for over a decade. We've developed films together, some we made, some we did not. Regardless of the situation, Howard's always been an absolute gentleman, a great listener, a kind and curious human being, and a great guy to talk sports with."

— Matthew McConaughey

"Howard was one of the true leaders in ownership in the modern era of the NHL. He has always been a risk-taker and someone unafraid to fail. I am proud to call him my friend."

— Luc Robitaille

"It figures Howard would pick the toughest sport to fall in love with because he's a warrior who is all heart!"

— Sylvester Stallone

"It's an entertaining read!"

— Russell Crowe

SLIM AND NONE

My Wild Ride from the WHA to the NHL and all the Way to Hollywood

Howard Baldwin

with Steve Milton

ANANSI

This edition published in 2014 by
House of Anansi Press Inc.
110 Spadina Avenue, Suite 801
Toronto, ON, M5V 2K4
Tel. 416-363-4343
Fax 416-363-1017
www.houseofanansi.com

Distributed in Canada by
HarperCollins Canada Ltd.
1995 Markham Road
Scarborough, ON, M1B 5M8
Toll free tel. 1-800-387-0117

Distributed in the United States by
Publishers Group West
1700 Fourth Street
Berkeley, CA 94710
Toll free tel. 1-800-788-3123

House of Anansi Press is committed to protecting our natural environment. As part of our efforts, the interior of this book is printed on paper that contains 100% post-consumer recycled fibres, is acid-free, and is processed chlorine-free.

18 17 16 15 14   1 2 3 4 5

Library and Archives Canada Cataloguing in Publication

Baldwin, Howard, 1942–, author
Slim and none : my wild ride from the WHA to the NHL and all the
way to Hollywood / by Howard Baldwin ; with Steve Milton.

Includes index.
Issued in print and electronic formats.
ISBN 978-1-77089-363-4 (bound).—ISBN 978-1-77089-364-1 (html)

1. Baldwin, Howard, 1942–.   2. Hockey team owners—United States—
Biography.   3. New England Whalers (Hockey team).   4. Pittsburgh
Penguins (Hockey team).   5. Motion picture producers and directors—
United States—Biography.   I. Milton, Steve, author   II. Title.

GV848.5.B337A3 2014   796.962092   C2014-902716-8
C2014-902717-6

Library of Congress Control Number: 2014938680

Jacket design: Gordon Robertson
Text design and typesetting: Gordon Robertson

 Canada Council   Conseil des Arts
for the Arts   du Canada

 ONTARIO ARTS COUNCIL
CONSEIL DES ARTS DE L'ONTARIO

*We acknowledge for their financial support of our publishing program
the Canada Council for the Arts, the Ontario Arts Council, and the
Government of Canada through the Canada Book Fund.*

Printed and bound in Canada

Two roads diverged in a wood, and I —
I took the one less traveled by,
And that has made all the difference.

— ROBERT FROST

This book is dedicated to dreamers.

Contents

Part Three — The NHL: The Prosperous '80s

Part Four — The NHL: The Turbulent '90s

Preface

By Howard Baldwin

I am often accused of being a dreamer, but what people may not realize is that I have fed my dreams with hard work, perseverance and, yes, maybe a bit of luck, in order to bring my dreams to fruition.

For example, try this dream on for size:

It is May 6th, 1973. I am 30 years old and I am sitting in the famous Boston Garden, where practically every great hockey player in history has taken to the ice, from Eddie Shore to Bobby Orr.

I am watching the home team, my team, put the finishing touches on winning the first championship of the newly formed WHA. CBS TV is broadcasting the game nationally, and there is absolute bedlam in the arena. The final buzzer sounds and my New England Whalers are the first Avco World Trophy champions. The trophy is lifted, the champagne flows, and a dream has come true.

Still think I'm just a dreamer? Well then, here's another one for you:

It is June 1st, 1992. My wife Karen, Howard Jr and I are sitting with our partners Tom and Kathy Ruta and Morris and Sema

Belzberg in the famous old Chicago Stadium, where, again, practically every great player has jumped over the boards, from Bobby Hull to Chris Chelios.

My team is the Pittsburgh Penguins, a star-studded group that included "Le Magnifique" Mario Lemieux, Ron Francis, Joe Mullen, Tom Barrasso and hockey's heir apparent, Jaromir Jagr. We are in the process of sweeping the Chicago Blackhawks to win Pittsburgh's second straight NHL championship. The clock ticks down to zero, and the next thing you know I am standing on the ice, hoisting Lord Stanley's Cup over my head, and Karen and I are only a few minutes from sipping champagne out of the sacred chalice.

If that's not enough, how about one more?

It is February 27th, 2005. It is the night of the Academy Awards, the most important date of the year in Hollywood, and our film *Ray* is nominated for Best Picture.

It is pretty surreal. Karen and I have attended many events that draw significant national attention, including All-Star Games and Stanley Cup finals, but nothing could compare to this night.

We have completely enjoyed being showered with all kinds of perks that go to the nominees. Karen has been asked to wear $1.5 million worth of Neil Lane diamond earrings, on loan for the night. They were delivered earlier in the day by two young women who pulled them out of a valise loaded with carats and carats of baubles intended for other nominees and stars, just as casually as if they were delivering pizzas. We were picked up by a stretch limo provided by Universal, the studio that distributed *Ray*, and made the slow crawl in bumper-to-bumper Los Angeles traffic to the Kodak Theatre, where we ran the Red Carpet gauntlet. It is something you just have to experience to believe. The flash bulbs are so numerous that by the time you've walked from one end to the other, it feels as though you have spent a few hours in the midday sun.

Rubbing elbows with every imaginable celebrity, we tried to do a reality check as we found our assigned nominee seats — in the fifth row, front and center. I had to take a moment to breathe deeply and take it all in. It was star-watching at its best, up close and personal.

To my left sat Karen and the rest of our *Ray* entourage. To my right sat Adam Sandler. I was wearing my New England Whaler Avco World Trophy championship ring for good luck, not thinking anyone would notice it. I was fiddling with it because I hardly ever wore it and it was just too darn big for my liking, as most of these sports rings are. Adam saw the ring and commented on how great looking it was and that, incredibly, he had been a big Whaler fan.

Adam asked me how I got the ring, and I explained that in my late twenties I had started the Whaler team in the WHA and we had won everything that first season. He seemed amazed and wanted to know how I had gone from winning a WHA championship to being in the room, nominated for an Academy Award. I laughed and said he wouldn't believe me if I told him. He wanted me to tell him the whole story, but I assured him it was a mighty long one — way too long to tell him there in one sitting — but that one day I might just write a book and send it to him so he could have his answers. He told me he would hold me to that, and I guess that is how I got here.

All three nights were the stuff of dreams, but they had become my incredible reality. Here is the story of how it all happened. Maybe by the end of my story you will agree that being accused of being a dreamer isn't such a bad thing — if you are willing to work hard and persevere to see those dreams come true.

Who is Howard Baldwin?

By Steve Milton

I think a more appropriate question might be, "Why isn't Howard Baldwin in the Hockey Hall of Fame?"

True, his name may be only vaguely familiar to the general sports public, but who, other than his mentor Ed Snider of the Philadelphia Flyers, personifies post-expansion-era hockey more completely than Howard Lapsley Baldwin? Through nearly five decades he has been heavily involved, and highly influential, in almost every aspect of the professional game.

Howard started his hockey business career in 1966, the final year of the "Original Six," working in the Eastern Hockey League, the league that inspired *Slap Shot*. His first year in the National Hockey League, as ticket manager for the newly minted Philadelphia Flyers, was also the first year of the fastest expansion in NHL history.

He was a founding owner in the World Hockey Association — the legendary rebel league that forced the NHL out of its medieval stupor — after obtaining the rights to the New England Whalers, essentially on a bluff. When the WHA and NHL eventually "merged" to end hockey's Seven Years War, Howard Baldwin was not only the president of the WHA, he was the one person in the room who had also been at the "outlaw" league's first formal meeting.

Still only in his mid-30s, Howard had come a long way in the seven years since a leading Boston sports columnist had snootily dismissed his chances of successfully establishing a WHA team in New England as "slim and none."

Howard's highest public profile came as the managing partner of the New England (then Hartford) Whalers in the WHA and in the NHL, and later of the NHL's Pittsburgh Penguins. Gordie Howe, Bobby Hull, Dave Keon and Mario Lemieux all played their last hockey game in one of his sweaters before being inducted into the Hockey Hall of Fame (although Lemieux would later "unretire").

Most people, even some hockey people, don't know that it was also Howard Baldwin who was primarily responsible for the birth of the San Jose Sharks, arguably the most consistently successful of the warm-weather franchises, and a team he should have owned and technically did own for the first half-hour of its existence. He also briefly owned the Minnesota North Stars.

Not content to limit himself to a single level of hockey, Howard, with his partners, engineered one of the most unusual experiments in modern hockey history when they bought 50 per cent of the famous Moscow Red Army hockey team in the mid-1990s. He exported North American hockey marketing and off-ice organization to Wild West Russia two decades after his Wild West WHA had imported European players and on-ice strategies to North America. There is a lot of what-goes-around-comes-around in Howard Baldwin's business life.

Howard was also responsible for one of the most successful franchises in the American Hockey League, when he plugged the Penguins farm team into Wilkes-Barre, Pennsylvania. He later took a dormant AHL franchise and turned it into the Manchester

Monarchs, which he then sold to the Los Angeles Kings. He also helped bring AHL hockey to Des Moines, Iowa.

Although Howard was never the majority owner of any of his major league teams, the hockey fans assumed he was, because he was so clearly the "face" of the franchise. Inspired by Ed Snider, he listened to fans and valued their input, and unlike most owners, he had an affinity for the game itself because he'd grown up skating on frozen ponds and had dabbled in playing college hockey.

Both traits made him more of a populist owner than most of his peers, never too far removed from the game or the people who pay to watch it. He was a working owner, counting tickets, hammering out difficult contracts, courting local politicians, doing whatever it takes, with no task beneath him, to help his club. He ran his teams the way a "character" hockey player plays the game.

Howard Baldwin is an American who has had a dramatic impact on Canada's game. The hockey landscape has changed vastly because of some of the things he's been integrally involved with. Without the WHA, it's unlikely that Canada would have seven major league hockey teams today, that American players would be as highly regarded as Canadian ones, that the game would have been as European-like fluid or that players could have earned enough to buy their own teams. Howard was ticket manager of the Philadelphia Flyers when the first computerized box office came to hockey, and the marketing knowledge his group brought to Russian hockey has been adopted by the KHL, helping ensure its survival, and more jobs for players.

Howard was decades ahead of his time in gender equality: Stan and Shirley Fischler became the first male-female broadcast team in history when his Whalers hired them in 1972; during his brief tenure as a World Football League franchise owner, he made Dusty Rhodes the first female general manager in North American pro sports; and the Whalers provided Colleen Howe with an office and a marketing-management job when Gordie, Mark and Marty played in Hartford.

Since moving into movie production in the 1980s, he has used film to bring broader audiences to his favorite sport with *Sudden Death*, *Mr. Hockey* and, most notably, the classic *Mystery, Alaska*.

Howard was already the only owner with his name on both the Avco World Trophy (WHA) and the Stanley Cup when he almost completed a most unlikely Triple Crown. *Ray*, his production company's biopic of Ray Charles, was nominated for the Academy Award for Best Picture and did win two other Oscars.

Just as many of hockey's legends eventually found themselves playing for Howard's teams, so Academy Award winners have appeared in his films. Jamie Foxx was named Best Actor for *Ray*, and some of Howard's other films have included Best Actor winners Geoffrey Rush, Russell Crowe and Matthew McConaughey, and Best Supporting Actress winner Penelope Cruz.

Howard is a Renaissance Man of entertainment, and has chosen two of the businesses just about everybody thinks they could succeed at themselves: movies and sports.

Howard is the first to tell you that he grew up in an affluent, deep-rooted Eastern family, and that that background had its advantages. They weren't the advantages you'd immediately assume. For one thing, he chose a career path — more correctly, two of them — which veered dramatically from the traditional family blueprint. His family never provided, nor did he ask for, the capital to fund any of his hockey projects.

However, his upbringing did imbue him with a strong work ethic, a rigorous sense of responsibility to those who have shown faith in him, a fierce loyalty and the social graces to ease his way through the most treacherous business situations. There can be no disputing that the large circle of successful people he, and his family, knew provided him with lots of initial contacts.

Because he's a people person, Howard maintains and nourishes those contacts. People from one era of his life keep popping up in others, the most notable example among many being the Kelley family: Howard tried out for Jack Kelley's hockey team, later hired him to coach the Whalers and, even later, to be president of the Penguins; hired Jack's son David as a Whalers stick boy and later combined with David to make the iconic hockey movie *Mystery, Alaska*; and had Jack's other son, Mark, as a scout with the Penguins and general manager of the Red Army team. While we were writing this book, I used to joke that Howard's life is a huge Venn Diagram, that if it were possible to have negative degrees of separation, he would.

For a high achiever, Howard is very sensitive about other people's feelings — sometimes to his own detriment, says his wife, Karen. He responds better when someone doesn't raise their voice with him because yelling is too reminiscent of his days in the Marine Corps. When they were first married, Karen Baldwin had to remind Howard that she was only raising her voice because she was in the other room and wanted to be sure he heard her, not because she was mad. That helps explain the calmness with which Baldwin can approach bitter negotiations.

"It's hard not to like Howard, even if you're on the other side of the table," says Bob Caporale, a renowned sports-investment advisor who was a young lawyer when he met Howard during the very earliest days of his WHA adventure, and who has remained a close friend.

"He never raises his voice. If things go bad, he doesn't slink away. He'll try to think of another way it'll work for everyone. During the negotiations for the merger of the NHL and WHA, he had perseverance and commitment. I was involved over those couple of years, and it's my view the merger would never have happened without Howard. The way he approached it was not adversarial."

Howard's close friend John Coburn, with whom he founded the New England Whalers, also speaks highly of his business intuition. "He may not be a highly educated person," Coburn recalls warmly, "but Howard has the most street smarts of anyone I know."

Because he had difficulty reading, Howard struggled academically, but his people and communication skills have always more than compensated. He loves to laugh and is a terrific storyteller, as you'll see from the anecdotes in this book.

No wonder he gravitated toward the ultimate storytelling neighborhood: Hollywood. Or, as we've often referred to it in his case, Hockey-wood. While Karen was a movie nut when she was growing up, Howard says he wasn't. But in casual conversation he often compares people to film characters and situations to movie plots.

Theirs is a hand-in-glove marriage: each has the perfect skill set to complement the other, and their combined output in a day is staggering. This is my 23rd book and their first, but they were the ones who really took the reins, so I'm not surprised that they've been able to successfully guide more than two dozen films onto the screen. The Baldwins are an impressive couple.

Howard not only succeeds, he puts others in the position to succeed. When someone has failed him, Howard rarely sees it that way: he usually thinks he didn't help that person enough. Some around him, for instance, complained that for their biggest-budget film, *Sahara*, he and Karen favored a director who'd never done anything quite that large before, but they insisted he get his chance. Just as, you might infer, someone once gave Howard his chance.

During the early days of the WHA, Bob Caporale was talking to Bob Schmertz, whose investment had allowed the New England Whalers to become the best-financed WHA team from the first puck-drop. Caporale was surprised to learn that Schmertz had never even seen a hockey game before he met John Coburn and Howard Baldwin.

"He said, 'But I listened to Howard, and I was impressed with his enthusiasm and how it should be run,'" Caporale recalls. "To me what Bob was saying was, 'I am investing in Howard Baldwin, not the team.'"

Schmertz was a very smart man, so he knew that with Howard Baldwin, his chances of success were much better than "slim" or "none."

PART ONE

From the Ground Up

"Howdy"

On a misty night in May of 1942, Howard "Howdy" Lapsley, one of my father's closest friends from Harvard, took off in a two-seat observation plane to watch the rendezvous of some naval planes and a torpedo boat squadron.

An errant plane dove down and struck Lapsley's plane, completely destroying it and killing him instantly. My father was devastated.

Two days later — May 14th, 1942 — I was born, and my parents named me Howard Lapsley Baldwin after my father's deceased friend. From day one his nickname, "Howdy," became mine too. My name has meant so much to me because its original "owner" meant so much to my father. I have worn it proudly because there is history and meaning to it.

I am the third of four sons born to Rose and Ian (Mike) Baldwin. My brother Ian is the eldest, Michael came next, and Philip is almost five years younger than I am. We grew up in Mount Kisco, in Westchester County, New York, and had the privilege of spending all of our summers in a place called Wareham, Massachusetts, located on the gateway to Cape Cod. In the winter, we had the frozen ponds and rivers around home to skate and play hockey on.

I can't remember a point when I did not have hockey in my life. I'll never forget putting on double-runner skates for the first time when I was two or three, and skating on the ice in the driveway ruts. I quickly became a good skater and a pretty good player.

My dad had been a great hockey player at Harvard, and the five consecutive goals he scored against McGill in the first period of their 1933 game is still a school record for most goals in a single period. Nicknamed "Iron Mike," he was extended an invitation to play in the 1936 Olympic Games and had an opportunity to try out with the Boston Bruins, but couldn't because his father wanted him to join the American Dye Wood Company, the family business, as soon as he graduated. At that point in time, playing professional hockey was not a viable profession for a young man graduating at the top of his class from Harvard.

My father was the youngest of nine children and had grown up in tremendous affluence. His father made a fortune in business, only to lose much of it in the Great Depression, but my dad was always proud of his father's courage and integrity in trying to pay back every debt that was incurred. That has served me well, as honoring obligations was one of my early life lessons. My dad, an executive recruiter, may not have ever made the money my grandfather did, but he always provided well for my mother and their four sons. We always had everything we needed, and frankly, much more than most families.

My mother was one of six children — five girls and a boy — of a well-to-do, old-line Boston family. She was the product of a union of the Welds and the Saltonstalls, two very well-known Massachusetts dynasties. While my father was in the Marines and away at war, she did a remarkable job of raising us alone while she herself was still quite young. Later, while she was working during the day at the Harvey School, the boarding school my brothers and I attended, my mother completed her college degree in New York

City at night, which I considered pretty extraordinary, and still do.

My parents and siblings always loved and supported me. There were certain traditions in my family, though, that did create some pressure and expectations. We were meant to go to a prestigious New England prep school — St. Paul's in New Hampshire—then to Harvard, then off into the business or banking worlds.

I was not going to be able to follow that path, because I was not a great student. Today, the diagnosis might be dyslexia or ADHD, but back then I was just a slow reader and had difficulty concentrating for a length of time. I learned to adapt to the problem and not attempt to fight it when it happened. The times when I was able to read, I did have incredible retention. At the Harvey School they had a horrible weekly tradition of posting our grades for the whole school to see. It made me hate school even more to be publicly humiliated, as I often failed or just barely passed.

After the Harvey School my two older brothers went to St. Paul's, which was the crème de la crème of hockey prep schools, but St. Paul's was not in the cards for me. Instead, my parents found Salisbury, an up-and-coming prep school in the northwest corner of Connecticut, and I was enrolled there in 1956. I loved Salisbury and I thank God for this experience. I made great friends and excelled in sports. I made the varsity hockey team in Grade 9, and it became clear that if I wanted to, I could play college hockey some day. While I continued to struggle academically and knew it would be hard to keep up at college, that served as my motivation. I even took a post-grad year at Salisbury to try to raise my marks, but that didn't work out too well. My average went up only one point!

I was aware that "What do we do about Howdy?" had become a common question in my family. I knew that if I didn't start to make some decisions for myself, I would start to sink. It was time to establish my own path, whatever that might be, or my self-esteem would suffer. I was not fitting into the family career mold, and I knew that in order for me to make that mark, I had to do something distinctive.

So I signed up for the Marine Corps.

Parris Island: Basic Training

In September of 1961, at the age of 19, I took a train out of Boston bound for Parris Island, South Carolina, where I would undergo 13 rigorous weeks of basic training for the Marine Corps.

I chose the Marines because it was the hardest service branch that I was aware of, and my father and other family members had served in the Marine Corps. My parents had accepted and supported my decision because I had committed to something and was following through. For me, this was a way of achieving my own identity.

My father and my first cousin Lou Preston, who was like a fifth son to my dad, had been in the Marines during World War II. Lou was at Iwo Jima and eventually became chairman of J.P. Morgan and later the World Bank, but sadly died far too young, in his early 60s.

I wasn't really sure how much the Marines meant to my father until after he died and I was going through his desk and found four or five thick files full of everything that had to do with him and the Marines. Since he had three children, my father wasn't required to go to war, but he wanted to do his duty. He didn't see action as such, but had gone to Officer Candidate School, served as a drill instructor at Parris Island, and served in Guam. One of my earliest memories is of my mother dressing me and my two brothers up to go to the train station to meet my dad.

I had plenty of warnings prior to enlisting that Parris Island was going to be tough, so when the train pulled into Beaufort, South Carolina, I was ready for anything. I stepped off the train and the whole town was out there to greet us. It was a little town with dirt streets and as soon as we got off the train the drill instructors started screaming, and I mean screaming, at us.

The instructors marched us down the street and into a restaurant for a meal. This was 1961, when segregation was still entrenched in the South, and running right down the middle of the restaurant was a chicken-wire fence. "No Colored" were allowed on the one side. It was not a nice place.

It was about an hour-and-a-half bus ride from the town over a natural causeway to the island. On the way, they made it clear that there would be no going AWOL, because the water was full of nothing but alligators and water moccasins. I remember saying to myself that I might have made a mistake, but this would be the first one where I couldn't call home. I would have to see it through.

It was 13 weeks of harassment and living a Spartan life. We were yelled at for 13 weeks, and we soon realized that there was no talking back. I was six feet, 190 pounds, and in good shape, so I had no trouble with all the physical demands like some of the guys did. And once I got into the groove with the stuff they were doing to us mentally, I just said, "Okay, that's the way it is." But they really did bust our balls for the whole 13 weeks. The whole methodology of this kind of training is to absolutely break you down then build you back up the way they want you, so that when you're told to do something, you don't think about it. You just do it.

When people ask about Parris Island, I say, "Imagine the worst . . . and double it."

They pushed us to the maximum, and every one of us had our individual tests we had to face. There had been some bad accidents at Parris Island in previous years, and even a couple of deaths.

Times were a little different when I got there. Technically, they were no longer allowed to rouse us in the middle of the night on a whim and they weren't supposed to touch us, although they still did both.

I loved drill practice, but once I made a mistake during it and the sergeant hit me in the stomach and again in the jaw. I was so surprised that I actually started to laugh. But he never bothered me again: that was my test.

By sheer coincidence a friend of my brother Ian's, Ted Ross, was in our platoon, and so were some really promising major league baseball prospects. I had always loved baseball, and on Parris Island I got hooked on it again because Bob Meyer, Pete Mikkelsen and Gene Alley were all in my platoon.

Meyer, a relief pitcher, was what was then referred to as a "bonus baby" for the big signing bonus he got from the Yankees. When he made the team in 1964, his very first strikeout victim would be Carl Yastrzemski. Mikkelsen would go on to pitch for the Yankees and four other teams in a 10-year big-league career, and Alley was the Pittsburgh Pirates' starting shortstop for a decade, beginning less than two years after we took our basic training.

Meyer made the mistake of complaining about the hard conditions in a letter he wrote home. The drill inspector opened it and read it, and after that they just rode Bob hard for three or four weeks. They'd call him a spoiled brat and they'd go to him at night and punch him repeatedly on his right arm and say, "You'll never pitch for the Yankees!"

Then he'd head to the shower, wink at me and say, "They still haven't figured it out."

They didn't realize that Bob was a southpaw.

After I came out of Parris Island I was confident, and maybe a little arrogant, because I survived physically and mentally. People sometimes think I'm embellishing how tough it was, but I'm not.

Although I never had any combat experience, Parris Island gave me an enormous respect for the military, what they do, how hard it is and how committed they are. I did things that I would never think of doing without being ordered to, and it gave me a sense that I could get through anything. It gave me great confidence to realize, "I can do it — there isn't anything I can't do."

So now it was time to pick what path I would follow in my adult life.

Boston University, Jack Kelley and My Baseball Career

With the confidence and experience I'd gained from the Marines, I decided I would try to get my college education. In the fall of 1962 I enrolled at Boston University. I applied late and there wasn't room for me at the dorms on the main campus, so I lived downtown on Beacon Hill in an apartment-like building that was the law school dorm.

The Boston University Terriers had just hired Jack Kelley as coach to turn the hockey program around. The team had had some success in the late 1950s, but had only been to the NCAA final tournament once in nine years and was coming off two straight losing seasons. It was going to take Jack a couple of years, but he would develop BU into one of the great hockey schools in the NCAA. By 1964 the team was winning at least 20 games a year in a 30-game schedule, and in 1971 Jack's Terriers won their first NCAA championship, and then repeated the next year.

I tried out for the freshman hockey team because in those days, first-year students weren't allowed to play varsity sports. Bob Crocker was the freshman coach and also the chief talent recruiter for Jack Kelley, finding the players who would form those championship teams.

At prep school, I'd been an offensive defenceman with a good shot and stickhandling ability and would occasionally move up to play some left wing. After more than a year off skates, however, my skills were a bit rusty. I practiced with the team for a week but I realized that, after the Marines, I wasn't up for another rigid fall of getting up at four in the morning for practice. I just wasn't going to do it and Crocker knew it, and he cut me from the team.

In my sophomore year I started tryouts again, but it was almost as if I'd grown out of playing hockey, and I also knew I wasn't going to excel at it, so I went to see Jack to tell him that. He said he wasn't going to cut me, but I knew I was finished with it.

In that short meeting, Jack and I made an impression on each other. He was very strict but very fair. I greatly appreciated, and loved, that he was a strong disciplinarian. He was, and is, just a wonderful guy.

I wasn't sure what impression I made on Jack — somebody who was not afraid to say what I thought, I guess. Rather than drifting into a situation I wasn't sure I wanted, I had been proactive.

That started a strong personal and professional relationship between Jack and me that continues to this day. When John Coburn and I started the New England Whalers in 1972, we hired Jack as coach and general manager, and Jack hired Bob Crocker as his assistant. Bob is now with the Los Angeles Kings and is still one of the most respected scouts in the NHL.

I have always loved baseball, so with hockey no longer in the picture I decided I would try out for BU for the fall season and made the team as second-string catcher. I was proud of that, because I hadn't even played baseball in high school.

Things weren't going quite as well in the classroom. I started out in business administration and knew right away it wasn't for me. With my love of sports, I went into physical education but didn't look at it closely enough. When I started classes, I found out that, oh my lord, you've got to study chemistry, biology and anatomy. I hadn't counted on that.

I was barely getting by and, being impatient, also wanted to see if I could play baseball at a higher level, so after the fall semester, I decided to leave school to take shot at professional baseball. I realized that it was very unrealistic, as I had played only one year of organized baseball, and I played very little in that one year. If I was going to leave BU, I needed some reason, and baseball was it. I said to my mother and father, "There are better things you can do with your money than have me burn it here at BU."

To finance my trip to a two-week baseball camp in Bradenton, Florida, where major league scouts were supposed to attend, I took a painting job, then became a guinea pig for high-paying medical experiments on withstanding pain. They'd wire me up, jolt me with electricity, and the further I could go, the more they would pay me. They said that I'd shown the highest tolerance for pain to date. I didn't know exactly why that was, but then I *had* just come from Parris Island.

When I got to Florida, wouldn't you know it, my old friend Bob Meyer from Parris Island was there too, a week away from his training camp with the Kansas City Athletics, so we worked out together. My roommate was a pitcher from Springfield — a city which would later play a major role in my hockey life — named Dave Motyka, who had played the year before for the Giants farm team in the Appalachian League, the lowest of the minors.

After a couple of days in camp we realized that although we had paid, we weren't going to get the advertised scouts. So Dave and I went up to Lakeland to try out for the Detroit Tigers. We just walked in. I had only a modicum of baseball credentials from BU, but Dave had real credentials so they decided to give both of us a look and I got to play a couple of inter-squad games at the double-A level.

The Tigers camp was a great experience but they didn't have any openings in their system for us. A Washington Senators scout who was there said we could come to Pompano Beach for a tryout. Dave went home and I continued to Pompano Beach, but after running into another old friend, Henri David from Salisbury School, I decided not to go to the Senators camp. Henri and I went up and down the state, attending car races and watching jai alai games. Deep down I knew I was not going to make it in professional baseball, but I'm glad I gave it a try.

When I came back north, my anxious parents felt it was time for me to do something, so I got a job with Alex Taylor and Company, a sporting goods company in New York, at $75 a week. I started as a clerk in the store, but Mr. Taylor put me on the road to go to schools and sell them equipment and uniforms. I hated the job. I have no trouble selling a concept, but I don't like selling products, and there were many days when I wouldn't go to work. After I commuted in from home in Bedford, New York, I'd just sit in Grand Central Station and read.

Meanwhile, my Marine status had changed because of the time I'd taken to try my luck at baseball, so I had to do another 30 days at Camp Lejeune, North Carolina, in the fall of 1965. My third week there, we were playing touch football, and after I caught a pass, I turned and snapped my Achilles tendon. The medical staff had gone home for the weekend, so a corpsman looked at it and said I had a sprained ankle. They gave me some crutches and I wrapped the ankle with an Ace bandage, but the pain was incredible. I went to the doctor on Monday and he misdiagnosed it as a sprained ankle too. I flew home, and my shocked parents immediately took me to a doctor. Within hours they were performing a very difficult surgery that would require a long recovery period.

My father was angry and sent letters wondering how the injury could have been misdiagnosed. The Marines paid for everything, and even though I had another year of duty left, I never heard from them again until I got my honorable discharge a year later.

I went back to work at Alex Taylor's, but I was living in Hell's Kitchen and had to take the uptown bus, then the cross-town bus, while on crutches. I couldn't get around like that, and I knew I'd have to leave.

New York Shenanigans, and a Big Break

I had come to the realization that I wanted to get into the sports business in some capacity, and I had been putting out feelers to friends and family about my future.

My initial connection to the business came from a family friend named Bill Putnam, who was a lending agent at J.P. Morgan, a company my family had ties to. I met Bill at his office to ask him to keep his ears open for me. Bill was close to the Philadelphia people, Ed Snider and Jerry Wolman, who would eventually get an NHL franchise there.

I didn't know at the time that Bill was angling to get into the sports business himself. He soon went to Los Angeles to work with Jack Kent Cooke and was part of the application process to get an NHL expansion team, which they were awarded in 1966, to start play in the fall of 1967.

One day early in 1966 I was in my New York apartment, still laid up on crutches, when the phone rang. It was Jack Kent Cooke, and in his great big booming voice he informed me that he was coming to New York and would try to squeeze me in for a quick meeting.

I told him how excited I was to get his call, but that I had a cast on my ankle and couldn't go anywhere, so I wouldn't be any good to him for the next six months.

"Oh dear," he said. "Well, let me know when you get it off."

Soon Bill Putnam had left Los Angeles because Cooke was evidently a hard guy to work with, and he went to Philadelphia to work with Wolman and Snider, who now had their expansion franchise.

Nothing was happening in New York for me, so when the headmaster of the Harvey School called to offer me a job as interim baseball coach while the regular coach recovered from an emergency appendectomy, I jumped at it. The headmaster knew me well because I had gone to the Harvey School — which had since moved from Hawthorne to Katonah, about 20 minutes away — and by then my mother was the head of the lower school and my father was a trustee. It was a great experience coaching and working at the same place as my mother. However, when summer came that job ended, and I returned to New York.

I went back to being a laborer for a construction company I'd worked with the previous summer. I worked on a skyscraper on Central Park West at 74th Street, and spent most of the time leaning out over the edge, sometimes 40 floors up, passing lumber up to the next floors. I drew the line when they put me on the last floor being built and there was no ceiling you could hang on to as you passed the lumber. I said I wasn't going to the top of the building ever again, and they put me on the cleanup crew, still on the edge, but not on the top floor.

Then my youngest brother, Philip, with whom I always had a great time, came to work with me. We were working in the Bronx to clean up a construction-lumber yard. If you've ever seen *Fort Apache, The Bronx*, this was it. Right in the absolute bowels of the Bronx.

It was about a six-week job, and the foreman, Paul LeDuke, couldn't grasp that these two privileged young men were driving in from Bedford in a yellow Mustang (mine) to the Bronx to work for him. Philip was mischievous and drove Paul crazy with all kinds of shenanigans.

At the time, Philip was friends with the daughter of John Lindsay, the mayor of New York. After work one day, he had to go to Gracie Mansion, where the mayor lives. We rigged up a bucket by poking holes in it with a screwdriver so Philip could take a shower. When Paul asked where he was going, Philip replied that he was headed to Gracie Mansion for a date with the mayor's daughter. It was inconceivable to Paul that anyone working in the Bronx for him would be dating the daughter of the mayor of New York, and he never believed that the story was true.

We managed to stretch the job out into August, and then I got my first big break.

Bill Putnam called from Philadelphia to tell me that the new Flyers franchise had bought one-sixth of a team in the lowest minors called the Jersey Devils, and that there was a job for me there as operations manager. It was a real turning point. I felt I was finally going to get my chance. I was ecstatic.

The Flyers were building a new arena, the Spectrum, but it was just a hole in the ground at the time, so I met Bill at his temporary office at 15th and Locust Street in Philadelphia. We had a wonderful visit and he offered me $7,500 for the job in Jersey. I would hold out hope that they then might take me up to the Flyers when they started in the NHL the following year.

Bill could have offered me 10 cents and I would have found a way to work there. So I packed my car and headed for New Jersey, feeling that the right door had finally swung open.

Jersey: A Devil of a First Year

So in the summer of 1966, at the age of 24, I began what I call my college undergraduate education in sports. And it was all four years rolled into one.

On a hot, humid day in August, I arrived in Cherry Hill, New Jersey, for my first day on the job. I went over to the Cherry Hill Arena to meet the other five partners, the businessmen for whom I'd be working directly. Bill Conway co-founded the Mister Softee ice cream company, Bud Meier was a builder, Cal Silver was an accountant, Harold Aranow was a roofer and I was never exactly sure what the fifth partner, Rex Van Zant, did for a living.

Obviously I felt my future in hockey, if I had one, was going to be eight miles to the northwest, with the Philadelphia Flyers when they started playing in the NHL. But I wanted to please these five men, who were all well-intentioned guys but who knew about as much as I did about running a hockey team . . . which was nothing. I wanted to learn everything I could about the hockey business, and Cherry Hill turned out to be exactly the right place to do that.

The Cherry Hill Arena was decaying and seemed ancient, even though it had opened only eight years earlier. Some of the cooling pipes were defective, and when you were playing near center ice you had the sensation of skating over a gully. The dressing rooms were small and, if we're being kind, "rustic."

The fans sat in wooden theater seats and the press box was a gondola, small and kind of perched out over the stands. To get in, you had to climb up a ladder like a fire escape. The arena was already on its third name and it looked like an old Stop & Shop, a warehouse almost, with a peaked roof over the front entrance. It was set into a very large parking lot; after it was torn down in the

16

'80s, the space became a shopping plaza. The arena seated 4,500 and had been home to the Eastern League Jersey Larks in 1960–61, and didn't host pro hockey again until the Devils brought EHL hockey back to town in 1964.

I could not have guessed that six years later I would be back at the Cherry Hill Arena with my own team, in a league that nobody had even yet thought of, to play the WHA's New Jersey Knights. *Sports Illustrated* called it the worst arena in the WHA, while others called it the worst hockey rink in pro hockey. Anywhere.

To me, the Cherry Hill Arena was a shrine. It was the greatest thing I'd ever seen, and oh my God, I loved it, because it was a rink, because it was pro hockey.

The Flyers already had their general manager (Bud Poile) and coach (Keith Allen) in place for the following year, and it was up to them to oversee the hockey operations in Cherry Hill. To coach the Devils, they brought in Vic Stasiuk, who had just finished his terrific 19-year pro career a few months earlier. Vic played for the Chicago Blackhawks, had his name on two Stanley Cups with the Detroit Red Wings and then became left winger on the Bruins' famed "Uke Line" (they were all of Ukrainian descent) with Bronco Horvath and Johnny Bucyk, and scored 20 goals — a major benchmark for the 1950s — four times. He was brought back to the Detroit organization for the final half-dozen seasons of his career. He was really, really bitter at the Wings because they sent him all the way down to Memphis of the Central Professional Hockey League for the 1965–66 season, his last, to make room for Gerry Abel, the son of Detroit coach Sid Abel.

I rented an apartment in Haddonfield, and when Vic got there he suggested that he and I "batch" it together.

Vic was a great big powerful man with one of the warmest and most engaging smiles I'd ever seen. In all my four decades in hockey, there are few people I've met who had more passion and love for the game than Vic did. He had left his wife and four children back in his home town of Lethbridge, Alberta, during the hockey season, because he knew he'd only be in Cherry Hill for the one year. The next year he expected to become the coach of the Flyers' top farm team in the American Hockey League, which eventually turned out to be the Quebec Aces. The Flyers bought the team in May of 1967 and, true to their word, would send Vic there to coach.

We set up a bed for Vic in a little area off the kitchen, split the monthly rent ($150, as I recall) and drove to work together every day. To be more accurate, I drove to work every day. I didn't know it yet, but Vic had a reputation in the hockey world for being "tight with the dollar." So it turned out that one of my jobs was to be Vic's chauffeur, since he didn't have a car with him. But I didn't mind that, because for me it was a big thrill. Here I was working for a team, batching with a real NHL guy, and by living and spending all my time with Vic, I knew I'd meet more great hockey people and learn a lot more about the league than I would have otherwise. I was only 24 years old.

Vic and I shared a small single office. If we stood up straight, we'd smack our heads on the concrete tiers on which the stands sat. And we had two other employees in there with us too: our secretary/office manager, Jeannie Verlandin, who was a jack-of-all-trades and, thank God, was very familiar with the area; and a local celebrity named Stu Nahan.

Stu was a real character and, like Vic, became a great friend. The Flyers hired him as a PR consultant to get him on the payroll and, frankly, to kiss his ass hoping for a little publicity and to establish some validity in a town that was already loaded with high-profile pro teams and great college basketball. He had his own kids' show called *Captain Philadelphia* on a UHF channel and also did the weather. He was known as the voice of the Philadelphia Eagles locally and on CBS nationally, so he had a high profile.

Stu worked maybe all of half an hour a day for us. He'd come into the office, make some calls to his agent, and then leave again. So in reality, the front office was Jeannie and me.

I was the operations manager but quickly became a one-man band. I organized all the tickets, handled the PR, did finance, sales and marketing, wrote the game-night notes, sold advertising on the back of tickets, got the players in and out of town and organized their working visas, and even drove the team bus once in a while.

I did everything, but 90 per cent of my job was ticket sales. I think we had only 200 season tickets, so it was all gate sale and advance tickets. We had a little reception desk to sell "hard" tickets. Hard tickets were literally that. They weren't printed off on a computer right as you buy them, like they are today. We played 36 games at home, and had 4,500 seats, so we had over 160,000 tickets that arrived in a box, each one standing for a specific seat on a specific night.

We were doing the games on the radio, with Gene Hart — who became the voice of the Flyers, forever — making the calls. The Flyers also got their longtime trainer, Frank Lewis, from the Devils that year. Walt Schumann of the Camden *Courier-Post* covered the team and even went on the road with us. And because the Flyers were soon going to start up, we got some coverage from the three Philadelphia daily papers too.

We worked at it 24/7, and although I don't know if we ever filled the building completely, we never fell below 1,500 to 2,000 fans a night, and near the end of the year we were nearly selling out.

The Eastern Hockey League:
The Real *Slap Shot*

I was familiar with the NHL from going to Rangers and Bruins games with my father and friends, but until Bill Putnam offered me the job, I didn't even know there was such a thing as the Jersey Devils and had no idea what the Eastern Hockey League was. I just knew they were minor league guys. It was pretty close to the bottom rung on the pro hockey ladder, and the best that most of the guys could hope for was to make it to a higher minor league like the AHL. The team was heading into its third season and had finished last in the northern division the previous year, so Vic had his work cut out for him.

We had players like Benny Greco, who played six seasons in the EHL, and Wayne Caufield, who played seven, then another seven in leagues ranked even lower. There was the odd player who had played a few games in the NHL, like our goalies, Marcel Pelletier and Norm Defelice. Marcel was a career minor leaguer, pushing 40, who had played a half dozen NHL games and was brought in to help coach and sometimes fill in for Normie, who had played 10 games with the Bruins exactly a decade earlier and didn't see the NHL again. This was the 15th of Normie's 16 years in the EHL, and he played for seven different teams in the league. He was a tough customer and foul-mouthed, really foul-mouthed. Almost every word he spoke began with an F and ended with a K.

EHL legend Reggie Meserve, our highest-paid player, probably making only about $7,500 for the year, was in his third year in Jersey and 13th in the EHL. Except for one solitary game in the AHL, his entire 15-year pro career was spent in the EHL, and at that level he could score, set up goals, and really mix it up. That year he had 106 points in 72 games for us, and 94 minutes in penalties, one of the few times he didn't top 100. Reggie couldn't really open his hands out flat. His fingers were really curved from gripping the stick and from punching, because the shape you make with your hand is kind of the same in both actions. I found out later that Meserve had once played for the Toronto Argonauts of the Canadian Football League, as did another one of our tough players, Bobby Taylor. Bobby spent a number of years in the CFL and was a fierce-looking guy. He had almost no neck. He wasn't that great a hockey player, but Vic needed a tough guy and Bobby always kept coming back for more. I remember thinking at the time, "There's a movie in that guy!" Once he was running to catch the bus and Vic said, "Have you ever seen a guy with that much power?" He was just fascinated with Taylor's athletic prowess.

The league was all guys playing on the way down, and none on the way up, except for the one year I was there, when a couple might hope to make it because of the coming expansion. One was our 21-year-old rookie, Rosaire Paiement, who had been a junior star in Niagara Falls the year before. Rosaire was from a northern Ontario family of 16 kids and was naturally tough, which helped him carve out a decent pro career. It was his only season in the "E," a rarity, and he scored 61 goals and 126 points for us, and spent a whopping 175 minutes — nearly three hours — in the penalty box. He made the Flyers within two years and eventually played in the WHA for six years, one of them for me in Hartford.

If you couldn't fight you couldn't play in the Eastern Hockey League of that era. I didn't know that when I arrived there, with my main exposure to hockey coming at high school and college games, where fighting is rare.

We scheduled our first exhibition game against our biggest rivals, the Long Island Ducks, who had the notorious John Brophy on defence. Five minutes into the game, I'm in the office with

Jeannie counting the meager gate receipts and I can hear all this screaming and yelling from the stands, which were right above us. I said, "My God, there must be a riot out there! Watch the cash, I'm heading out to see what happened." I run into the arena and into total bedlam. Every single player from both teams is on the ice; they're all punching one another, and the fans are screaming in joy. I look over at our bench, and there's Vic standing there with arms folded across his chest and a big smile on his face, giving me the thumbs-up sign. He was loving it. "Holy mackerel," I'm thinking, "this is going to be some wild ride."

The Johnstown Jets, the team the movie *Slap Shot* was based on, were also in our division. Eventually Steve Carlson, Jack Carlson and Dave Hanson — Steve and Dave were two of the "Hanson Brothers" goons in *Slap Shot* — would all play for us in New England. That movie came out in 1977, just 10 years after I was in the Eastern League and people had no idea how accurate it was. They assumed it was only a parody, but that's the way it was. The games would go on for three and a half hours. In Clinton, New York, where the Comets played, most of the seats in the arena were fold-up chairs, and during fights the fans would throw their chairs right onto the ice. Now that's audience participation.

In the Stands and on the Road

Later in the season, we were going on the road to play the Ducks again, and since we had family on Long Island, I said to my father and mother, "Why don't you join me for the game?" They hadn't seen us play yet. They did and, naturally, there's a brawl right away. Right away. I could see my father getting madder and madder because he came from the college game, was a hockey traditionalist and never believed in fighting. And some time later, but still in the first period, Vic leaned over to the penalty box to yell at the referee and the Ducks player in the box. Unfortunately that was also where the P.A. announcer sat . . . and he didn't have his mike off. So out of all the arena speakers you could hear a series of really juicy expletives directed at the referee. He threw Vic out of the game, of course, and the police came to the bench to escort Vic out through the stands. They took him right past our seats and he stopped, one cop on each arm, and proceeded to introduce himself to my mother and father. "Mr. and Mrs. Baldwin!" he said. "Sorry I can't stay longer . . . but nice to meet you." And down to the locker room he went, still held by two cops. And my dad said, "Well, what a unique introduction to your roommate."

I learned a lot about hockey that year, besides fighting, because I spent so much time with Vic. If we didn't have a game at night, we went to one somewhere, sometimes driving for hours. All in my car, of course. We used to go up to Madison Square Garden, and one time when my car was in the shop, we drove the team bus up to see the Rangers. The bus had been renovated with bunks — it was a 10-team league and we had to travel all day and night to places like Nashville and Charlotte. Vic was always anxious to get to the arena in time for the pre-game warm up, and when I asked him why that was so important he said, "I can tell how everybody's going to play by the way they warm up. I've gotta see if they have bounce in their legs."

It was on one of those bus trips up to New York that I first met Gordie Howe. Vic loved Gordie—and who didn't? — and after we watched the Red Wings play the Rangers, my favorite team when I was growing up, we went to the locker room to meet Number 9. For me, it was a huge event and Gordie didn't disappoint — he was very witty and gracious. I had no idea how our paths would cross so dramatically a few years later, but I never forgot that initial meeting.

I was meeting hockey people and steadily increasing my hockey knowledge, so I guess Vic figured I could probably handle another assignment. He had to go back to Lethbridge for a while because he was buying a golf course, his lifelong dream. We didn't have a game until Friday, when we were hosting our big rivals from Long Island, so Vic said he would fly back home on Monday, do the business deal, then be back in time for the game, and he wanted me to run the practices while he was gone. Plus he didn't want Bud Poile, Keith Allen or anyone in the Flyers organization to find out. I was worried about it, but agreed, as long as he wrote everything down that he wanted me to do.

Onto the ice we go on Monday for practice and the players are all there with condescending smirks all over their faces. They're humoring me. We have a good practice until I see in Vic's notes the dreaded words, "Make them do 20 wind sprints at the end." I hold my breath and then say, "Okay guys we're doing wind sprints." Up and down they go, but after a just a few I feel a stick hit my ass and it's Reggie Meserve. "Howard, we've done enough wind sprints today. Okay?"

I might not have excelled at school, but I know when to listen to a big guy with a hockey stick whose fingers are permanently curled into a fist. "Okay, Reggie," I say, as if it was my idea.

Friday comes and a big blizzard is supposed to hit. I'm suddenly worried Vic won't make it back in time. And it just so happens that Bud Poile calls me looking for Vic. I told him he wasn't in, and when he asked why, I had to tell him. Bud was not pleased at all. He mentioned the blizzard then said, "Howard, you coached the team this week? Okay, if you two schemers are thinking like this, if Vic doesn't get in you're going to have to coach the team tonight. So get ready for it." I was in shock — not only at having to be behind the bench but also because I wanted to please Bud and all the Flyers personnel. I desperately wanted a position with them the next year. I'm in there writing out the lines just in case, but I figured the guys would do whatever they wanted to anyway. I was absolutely praying that Vic would get back, and he did . . . about an hour before game time. Bud and Keith came to that game, and Bud said to me afterward, "Well, Howard, now you can add 'coach' to your resume."

Blizzards are a recurring theme in hockey stories. One day we were heading up to Clinton, New York, through a raging snowstorm, with Vic driving the bus. The defroster was broken and Normie Defelice was standing beside him, wiping down the windshield occasionally, and I'm in the front seat, praying we'll get there.

About an hour outside of Clinton, this car comes at us out of nowhere, and Vic has to swerve sharply to the right. We go right through the guardrail, and I figure we're dead. Down an embankment we go, the bus rolls, and all I can hear is Normie saying, "Hang on, Vic, keep the wheel until we turn right side up." Of course, because it was Normie, it was more colorfully stated and peppered with words that all began with F. We end up in a field, but we have all four wheels on the ground. The players have all been tossed around badly and Vic is still gripping the steering wheel hard, stunned beyond belief. But Normie doesn't miss a beat and tells Vic to open the door. He goes outside, looks around, and says, "We can get out of here! Drive right across the field." By now, cars are stopped all along the road and people are running down the hill toward us to help out. But Vic starts driving, crosses the field, goes through a little gate in a stone wall, and we continue all the way to the game. We were an hour late and lost the game 6–1, but who cared? All that mattered was that we were alive. Believe it or not, we all jumped on that same little red bus and drove back to Cherry Hill.

We ended up in second place in the Northern Division, and who do we play in the first round but the Johnstown Jets? The series went the limit, with the deciding game in Johnstown. The place was packed, and their fans figured they were going to win. And if I thought the regular season was fight-filled, it was nothing compared to the playoffs. I drove to the game with Stu Nahan in his brand new Cadillac, and neither of us was too optimistic. But we won 6–1 in a real upset. As the game ended, Defelice flipped a puck into the stands, trying to do a nice thing for a fan. It was an innocent gesture, but as luck would have it, the puck hit the face of a woman who wasn't looking in that direction. It turned out to be the team owner's secretary, and the fans immediately assumed it was a deliberate action.

While we were in the dressing room celebrating, there was a loud knock on the door and I told Vic not to go out there, but he's a tough guy and opened the door anyway. There's the team owner in front of a lynch mob of hundreds of fans. He said the police were on the way "and they're going to arrest Defelice because my secretary had two teeth knocked out." Vic came back in the locker room and said, "You gotta get Normie out of here." Stu immediately assumes the role of Captain Philadelphia, sees a small window in the dressing room, tells me to crawl through it and go get his Cadillac and back it up as close as I can to the window. I did as instructed, and there was Stu — a Philadelphia celebrity, the guy who does the CBS football game of the week — stuffing himself and Normie through the window. Normie's still got his helmet on and every second sentence out of his mouth is, "Howard, what the fuck?" or simply, "What the fuck?" We stuffed Normie into the trunk with his full goalie gear on, and he's hysterical with laughter. We told the guys we'd meet the bus 30 miles out of town, and just as we were leaving the parking lot, I swear to God the cops arrived with sirens blaring. They flooded into the dressing room looking for Normie, but Vic acted all innocent and said, "I guess he got scared and ran."

We ended up winning two playoff rounds and losing the final to the Nashville Dixie Flyers in five games. They were a good team and defending champions, so it was a pretty impressive first season for us, and the franchise just about broke even too.

I hoped to be with the Flyers five months later, but to this day I feel that the season with the Jersey Devils, as crazy as it got, was my favorite year in hockey.

And it was a pretty good prelude to another crazy league which would start in only five years.

The Move to Philly

I had crammed all four years of my hockey undergraduate degree into just that one season with the Jersey Devils, but I earned my MBA at the Philadelphia Spectrum.

I spent the first few weeks of the summer of 1967 on the edge of my seat, antsy and just waiting for the phone to ring. I expected the Flyers would eventually call, and in mid-July Bill Putnam finally did, asking me to a meeting in midtown Philadelphia.

The Flyers rented temporary office space while they were waiting for construction of the Spectrum to be completed, hopefully in time for the home opener. The team was meant to play their first three games on the road, to provide a little cushion for construction delays, then open at the Spectrum on Thursday, October 19.

When I walked into Bill's office, I would have signed on as a janitor if that's what they wanted, but Bill offered me the job of ticket manager at $7,500 per year. There was no raise from what I'd made with the Devils, but that was fine with me. After learning to skate on the ponds of Bedford, and playing a little college hockey, I was going to be working in the NHL. The league might have doubled in size from the Original Six to 12 teams, but there still weren't that many jobs available in the game and I felt really lucky to have one.

I want to emphasize how small front offices were in the first year of expansion. Each might have had a staff of 8 or 10 people, while today there are more than that in just the sales and marketing departments of most teams. So you could really learn a lot if you were willing to commit yourself, which I was, because you had to do a little bit of everything, no matter what your actual job title was. It was great training for me, and I was really lucky to be able to watch Ed Snider. He can be an intimidating guy, but I realized that if I paid attention I would learn how a good owner can operate. I was there to learn, learn, learn, and for the rest of my life in hockey I have used many of the principles and tactics I picked up from Ed.

The Flyers have been such a profitable and model franchise for so long, people forget that initially their success was far from a sure thing. There was a lot of financial turmoil around the team in the early years, even before they dropped the first puck. The franchise was originally owned by the wealthy real estate developer Jerry Wolman, who also owned the NFL's Philadelphia Eagles. His good friend was Ed Snider, who was also the executive vice-president of the Eagles at the time and had a minority interest. A contractor named Jerome Schiff also had a piece of the franchise, and Bill Putnam got a piece for doing the behind-the-scenes politicking that helped land the expansion franchise, even though Philadelphia wasn't among the favorites to get one of the six new teams.

But Joe Scott, who had just retired from the beer distribution business after making Ballantine one of the most recognized brands in the area, still had to help the group arrange the extra financing when they fell short of the $2 million NHL expansion fee. Snider knew Scott from his dealings with the Philadelphia Eagles, which Snider was helping run.

Although it was Wolman who financed the arena, Ed was the one who saw the potential in hockey and led the drive to build the Spectrum. Ed had seen the huge lineups at the Boston Garden a couple of years earlier to buy tickets for the then-last-place Bruins. He figured that if people would line up to see a team in last place, then the NHL must be on to something. The promise of the new arena, and the prestige of having high-profile NFL people such as Wolman and Snider involved, was probably why the NHL chose to put an expansion team in Philadelphia instead of Baltimore, despite the fact that Baltimore had a far more successful minor league hockey history and was considered by most people in hockey to be the front-runner to land a franchise for the area.

People forget now that the day before the Flyers' home opener, Wolman fired Ed from the Eagles. It was a huge falling-out. Wolman was having financial difficulties with a building in Chicago that had problems with the foundation and was costing him millions, so he went to Eddie and Bill and said, "Look, I gave you your stock in the team, and I need your interest to collateralize this." Eddie wouldn't do it. Eddie was right too; he had earned that stock. So Wolman soon sold out to Ed, and Ed brought in Joe Scott for 15 per cent. Ed had 60 per cent, and Bill, who was running the team as president, had 25 per cent.

Right away it was clear there were going to be some interesting dynamics around the Flyers, because Bill and Ed couldn't have been more different personalities. Eddie is a very strong and aggressive Easterner, and Bill is a laid-back Texan. Bill is a dear, dear guy, but he wasn't aggressive enough for Ed. From the start, he blended into the old boys' network which had run the NHL for years, and there were even a few newspaper columns over the years that suggested he might be the next president when Clarence

Campbell retired. Bill ended up lasting only three years there and left the Flyers in 1970, not long before I did, when he lost a power struggle with Ed to buy the team. I will always be indebted to Bill for opening the door for me to get into the world of professional sports. I was pleased years later when (in Hartford) we started our own regional network called PRISM, later renamed SportsChannel, and I was able to hire Bill in an executive capacity to work for me.

So all that was going on — not that it would really affect me, because I was pretty low on the totem pole.

I shared an office with Bill's executive assistant, Ken Blackburn, a great guy who was a jack-of-all-trades and master of none. Blackburn was very helpful to me with my department. He loved Bill Putnam, and he worshipped Branch Rickey, the famous baseball pioneer who had signed Jackie Robinson to break the color barrier. For years, Ken had been the male secretary to "Mr. Rickey," which was the only way he ever referred to him. A couple of times I called him "Branch" and was admonished for it.

Ken had a multitude of great baseball stories which I, of course, loved to hear. He had a very dry wit, and one time he told me how he was chauffeuring "Mr. Rickey," who was always a terrible back-seat driver, and his wife to training camp in Florida. When they came to a railroad crossing, Rickey told Ken to slow down, look both ways and make sure no train was coming. He'd already been at his back-seat driving best that day, and out of sheer frustration, Ken stopped and, to the shock of the Rickeys, got out of the car, walked over to the track, bent his ear to the rail just like in the Old West and came back to the car and announced to Rickey, "It's safe to cross."

Who could have guessed that 40 years later I would be working as a producer with Branch Rickey Jr. and Robert Redford on a Jackie Robinson movie? Life is like that — a nature walk with many paths that keep crossing.

The Flyers also hired a consultant to work with me, a guy named Leo Carlin, who was the Eagles ticket manager and came from an old Philadelphia ticket family. To this day Leo still works with the football team, and in 2012 he was inducted into the Eagles Hall of Fame. Leo taught me the fundamentals, one of which was to understand the importance of what I was in charge of. Tickets were the absolute lifeblood of any franchise. In those days they made up at least 95 per cent of a team's income. Teams didn't have electronic advertising in the stadium. The ice and boards were all white — no advertising. In-arena advertising was modest at best because there wasn't the electronic/TV coverage which drives so much of sponsorship revenue today.

So I had my hands full, figuratively and literally too. We had 600,000 tickets at the start of the year to cover the whole season. Eventually we would put in the first computerized ticketing system in sports, but that year it was all hard tickets. (The computerized ticket system for which we became guinea pigs was called Ticketron, which morphed into the giant company Ticketmaster). I got all the tickets printed by Globe Ticket or by National Ticket, and Leo told me that I had to learn to count them by hand. I just had to, and I did. To this day, if you give me a pile of tickets, I can fan them out in one hand and count them quickly and accurately. I used to do that with a deck of cards to impress my kids.

Hockey was a hard, hard sell in Philadelphia. We were selling, then giving, selling, and giving. Joe Scott liked to take a handful of tickets and go out to a bar and give them away.

Joe Scott, who was used to it from the beer business, really loved the direct sales. He was a guy who would drive me crazy . . . in a good way. He had tons of contacts in old Philadelphia, and as a new owner he really rolled up his sleeves and went at it. He'd say to me, "Come on, grab 200 or 300 tickets and we'll stop in a bar or a restaurant." He gave a lot of tickets away, but he really worked it. He exposed the product to thousands of new fans, and hockey is a game that people turn on to once they see it live. Ed, Joe and Bill Putnam taught me that ownership that's willing to roll up its sleeves and actually work will be successful.

The Philly experience would be invaluable to me later, when I ran the New England Whalers. Our ticket manager, Chris Gallagher, was inexperienced, and 24 hours prior to our opener at Boston Garden I got a panicky request from him for help. I went down to the basement ticket office and saw piles of tickets for opening night on a large table. Chris was overwhelmed and didn't know how to deal with it all. I told him I'd work through the night with him and together we'd get the job done. And we did, counting every single ticket by hand and arranging them for the next night's game. It wasn't beneath my dignity to do this — I'd had the training in Philly.

The Flyers Get off the Ground

We couldn't possibly have thought it then, couldn't even have imagined it, but the Flyers would become the most iconic of all the new franchises, and one of the most iconic in the entire sport.

Philadelphia is a fantastic sports city, but the history of hockey there was not a vast one — and what there was, was atrocious. Every team there had folded except the Jersey Devils, who were playing about seven miles from the Spectrum. Fans were already locked into the Philadelphia Phillies, the 76ers and the Eagles. It was also the best college basketball city in the country, and those teams had nearly the following that the pro teams did. And Flyers games with Stu Nahan and Gene Hart were on Channel 48, a UHF station that didn't have great penetration. Only the road games were on TV, and they didn't do the seven games from the West Coast. The home games were only on radio, but during that first year the broadcast wouldn't start until the third period, because the airtime cost too much.

So the Flyers were the classic underdogs in terms of future survival, and people were scratching their heads wondering about them, especially when you had other places with a long history of hockey, like Buffalo, Vancouver and Seattle, which didn't get expansion teams. And probably should have.

The Original Six hadn't helped very much either. The $2-million expansion fee seemed high for that era, and for that the six new teams were rewarded with the chance to select from a pool of players from the very bottoms of the rosters of the existing six. The new teams got really young players or ones that were way past their prime. But Bud Poile, the general manager, and Keith Allen, the coach, did a brilliant job of drafting for the Flyers and managed to get a few, like Bernie Parent, Joe Watson, Ed Van Impe, Gary Dornhoefer and Brit Selby, who would become Philadelphia fan favorites for a long time. And when they bought the Quebec Aces of the AHL that May, they also got a couple of dozen players there, including Andre Lacroix, Serge Bernier, Jean-Guy Gendron and Simon Nolet, who became stars and gave the Flyers a bit of a French feeling the first few years.

Another surprise for fans who think the Flyers have always been the Broad Street Bullies is that we weren't a very tough team at the start. Actually, we were kind of bland.

I wasn't involved with the on-ice stuff, but I was a real fan and followed it closely. We began our first season on the West Coast, and it didn't go well: we lost 5–1 in Oakland (for the record, Bill Sutherland scored the first goal in Flyer history) and 4–2 in Los Angeles. Our first win came in the third game, a few days later, a

2–1 victory in St. Louis on the night before the home opener.

Meanwhile, we were going balls-out to get ready for the opening bell. We had our seating manifest, and were selling tickets based on it. But in a new arena you never really know, until all the seats are put in, what you actually have and whether the manifest matches up with the seats available. Ownership had made up their minds, thank God, that they weren't going to open the Spectrum with a hockey game. Instead, the Quaker City Jazz Festival was the first official event, a couple of weeks before the Flyers were scheduled to open. Everybody in ticketing, whether we were working in hockey or for the 76ers, agreed that we would all work the jazz festival that night to help out and learn, and it's a good thing we did, because 350 tickets were printed and sold that didn't have corresponding seats in the building. And that became a recurring nightmare all season long.

Our first home game was against the Pittsburgh Penguins, a no-brainer piece of scheduling because Pennsylvania had suddenly gone from zero NHL teams to two. It was a defensive battle, which became our style that year, and the only goal came from Sutherland three minutes into the third period for a 1–0 win, with Doug Favell getting the shutout. Sutherland was one of the players Philadelphia acquired when they bought the Aces. He and Leon Rochefort were the only Flyers to reach 20 goals that year, and they had only 20 and 21, respectively.

Back then, so much of our gate was driven by the walk-up crowd. We had only 1,500 season tickets, about 10 per cent of the Spectrum's seating capacity.

How did we do that first night? There were 7,812 people in a new building that could accommodate 14,646 for hockey, and the gross gate was about $21,000. I didn't know how to judge that, because we didn't have any other games to compare to, but I remember that everybody was disappointed. One fan walked right through a window because they didn't have the signage on it yet. He's lucky he wasn't beheaded.

So we went along from game to game, taking in 13 grand here, 17 grand there. It was really, really tough, money-wise. If I were Ed and Joe, I would have been scared shitless. And I'm sure they were. Ticket sales were the way you had to make your money, and I think the whole year we grossed only about 750 grand at the gate. Remember, there were no box seats then; there were no club seats then, no dasher-board advertising.

We always had an eye on the weekend of February 3 and 4 — this is weird how I remember the dates but that's how important it was — when we had back-to-back home games with Chicago and Toronto. The Leafs had just won the Stanley Cup, the last one of the Original Six era and, since then, the last for the franchise. And the Blackhawks had Bobby Hull, who would lead the NHL with 44 goals that year, and Stan Mikita, who would finish first in overall scoring.

There was a capacity crowd for both those games through sold tickets and "comped" tickets. And when I say that, understand that there were a good two or three *thousand* comps at each one. But it was worth it. We beat Chicago 5–3 behind Bernie Parent on Saturday night, and Toronto 4–1 on Sunday with Doug Favell in net. (It wouldn't be the last time that a team I was involved with would take something important from the Leafs. Only with the Hartford Whalers, it wouldn't be two points, it would be three young defencemen.)

That weekend was when things turned the corner for the Flyers, and the team really started to take hold in the city.

I was learning everything I could about the ticket end of the business from Leo and Joe and also a lot from simple trial and error. The system wouldn't be computerized for a couple of years, and we couldn't process credit card orders over the phone yet either. We had 16 ticket windows spread around the Spectrum concourse, and I would allot 400 or 500 hard tickets to each one.

One of those was Gate 9, the Will Call Window. We used to do what today is a cardinal rule of don't-dos: if someone called up the day before the game and said, "I'd like to have you hold the seats in my name and I'll pay for them at Will Call," we did it, just for customer service. But we never had a 100 per cent pickup. After those two games against Chicago and Toronto, there started to be a huge demand for tickets and we had massive numbers at Will Call. I usually had young guys in there because it was hectic and they could handle it better. But one day when I had to use an older guy, Harry Crumlish, in the booth, this friend of Ed's showed up and his tickets weren't there. The guy found Ed and Ed comes down and the door is sealed — remember just about everything was in cash those days — and Eddie demands to be let in but Crumlish said he couldn't do it. Eddie started kicking the door. I was downstairs in my ticket "bunker" and a stretcher came by with Harry Crumlish on it. We thought he might be having a heart attack, but thankfully it was just stress-induced chest pain. I was convinced I was going to be fired, but Ed just said, "I'll see you tomorrow." To this day Ed and I have a good chuckle over that story.

The First of My Missing Roofs

That first year we started out really slowly, but none of the six expansion teams were a bang-out success at the beginning. Certainly Oakland wasn't, and Minnesota didn't make an impact right away. L.A. was a question mark, but at least it was backed by big bucks. And Pittsburgh had a lot of problems, even though it was a good hockey town. Every one of us struggled. And then, slowly, across the league, things started to build for the new teams. St. Louis probably started the quickest because they made the Cup finals in the first year and the next two as well before the divisional format was changed. They were the hottest of the expansion teams.

Although the established teams hadn't given the expansion teams much in the way of proven players, they did guarantee them some success by lumping all six newcomers in the West Division, while the Original Six formed the East. That meant that one of the new franchises was sure to play in the Stanley Cup final. In year one, the Flyers finished first in the west, one game under .500, but with Parent and Favell we allowed the third-fewest goals in the whole league, which was a positive sign heading into the playoffs.

But, in keeping with the hardscrabble theme of the Flyers' first year, naturally we couldn't finish the regular season without one more major stumbling block.

On March 1st, 1968, a massive wind blew a huge section of the Spectrum roof right off. There were 11,000 people in the arena, waiting for an Ice Capades matinee to begin, and they suddenly found themselves gazing right up at the sky. The Spectrum was located in a wind tunnel, and a huge patch of tar paper and shingles measuring 100 feet by 50 feet was torn off and crashed to the ground outside the arena. Communication wasn't instant back then, and I learned of the situation when I arrived at work the next morning. Everybody was already standing around with long faces. When the mayor, James Tate, went up on the roof to take a look, the wind almost carried him off too. The mayor declared the building closed, and we're all looking at each other saying, "What do we do now?" We had a home game two days later against Oakland, and five other home dates to finish the regular season.

The Flyers were carrying loss-of-business insurance, and Bill Putnam came to me and said, "Howard, take about 10,000 of those tickets and lose them so we can claim the loss of business."

"Really?" I said, a little nervous about the order.

But what was I going to do? So I bundled the tickets up, threw them into the trunk of my car, and just left them there.

We hastily arranged to play Oakland at Madison Square Garden, then a few days later we rented Maple Leaf Gardens to play the Bruins, and then we moved into Le Colisée in Quebec, where we owned the Aces, for our final five home games. (And how's that for foreshadowing? I've got to be the only hockey guy who's ever been through losing two arena roofs, and when it happened in Hartford 10 years later, where would I be at the time? In Quebec City.)

A week or so after our conversation about the 10,000 tickets, Bill asked to see me. "Just curious," he said. "What did you do with those tickets? Did you throw them out?" And I told him I hadn't. I just knew it — I knew it wasn't the right thing. Bill knew it wasn't the right thing too. He was under tremendous pressure, so I had figured not to take him literally when he told me to lose them.

When I told him I still had them in the trunk of my car, he said, with obvious relief, "Thank God! Go get 'em and put 'em back in your ticket racks."

We were both lucky I hadn't followed his orders.

We got the Spectrum back in time for the playoffs. Even though we had home-ice advantage against St. Louis in the opening round, we fell behind three games to one. But we forced a game seven when Don Blackburn, later to become a Whaler player and our first NHL coach, scored in double overtime in game six, right in St. Louis. Then we lost the deciding game 3–1 at home, and St. Louis went on to their first of three straight appearances in the Stanley Cup finals, all losses.

End of the Apprenticeship

In my second year with the Flyers, Bill added "sales manager" to my portfolio, and I was learning things rapidly by watching Ed Snider at work. Ed included me in all the sales and marketing decisions, which was great because I thirsted for the knowledge. I couldn't have been given a better gift than working for Ed. It was like studying for my PhD in hockey ownership.

Ed was incredibly charismatic and incredibly aggressive. He didn't have a lot of experience with the sport of hockey, but he knew business and marketing. Ed was about as smart and creative a guy as you would ever want to meet. The Flyers were his calling, and Ed had the vision to understand that through the Flyers would come many other opportunities for him, such as the Spectrum and many of the wonderful companies he has built since then. He did intimidate people — I was actually a bit afraid of Ed, although not physically. Still, he was always good to me, and to this day he's a friend. I learned so much from Ed and one of the things in my life that has made me most proud was that when he was inducted into the Hockey Hall of Fame in 1988, I was the one who nominated him.

During those few years in Philly, I saw what went into the process of doing it the right way: how to move seats around, how to raise prices, how to make decisions based on economics.

The team slumped after the first year, dropping from 73 points to 61 in 1968–69, and to 58 points in 1969–70, missing the playoffs completely. But while the team struggled on the ice, each year our season ticket sales progressed and the dollars went up. The Flyers were gaining popularity, but part of the revenue increase was also because we knew how and when to raise ticket prices. What I learned in Philadelphia was that the way you price a house, and scale a house, is everything. I carried that on to my Hartford years. When we got to the NHL, I was most proud of the fact that in the smallest market in the league and in the smallest arena, we had the third-highest gross gate.

What I loved about Ed and Joe Scott was that we didn't make a decision on a price change without thorough and thoughtful study, walking up into the seats and really looking at what the impact would be. It's really a judgment call, so we would climb into the stands and study whether the price could change from, say, $3.25 to $4.50 starting at Row 10 instead of at Row 11. Those prices may sound way too low, but they were real. I can still tell you, to this day, which section of the Spectrum cost how much in the first year of expansion. The tickets were colored by price: red was $2.00 per game; yellow, $3.25; green, $4.50; blue, $5.50; and orange, $6.50. Not exactly today's face value!

When we made price changes, we tried to offend as few people as possible, and that was a little easier if we didn't already have season ticket holders in that area, because they'd sure let us know about it. I was blessed to have that time in Philadelphia — it taught me that you had to listen to people, because we just had to try so goddamned hard!

The whole time in Philly, I was like a kid in a candy factory. The executive offices were right across the hall from the ticket offices, so whether you were a basketball player or a hockey player, you had to come into the back end of the Spectrum, walk down the corridor, down the hall and past my office. I had a Dutch bay door, so I saw everybody. I had chats with Wilt Chamberlain and Bobby Orr when they'd pop their heads into my office. One day during the first year, Bud Poile yelled over, "Howard, get your ass in here," and I had to be the legal witness to Bernie Parent signing his first contract. It wasn't the only one I witnessed either.

One night that year, I was working late while the Philadelphia Indoor Tennis Championships were being played at the Spectrum.

I went out to the arena floor and there was Althea Gibson, all alone, practicing her serve. For those who don't know, Althea was one of the greatest female athletes in history. She broke the color barrier in two sports — international tennis and the LPGA. Althea was the first person of color to win a Grand Slam event (the 1956 French Open), and she won 11 Grand Slam titles in all. She was about 40 when I met her that night, and still playing on the tennis circuit.

Thinking I'm the hot-shot tennis player, I asked her if she wanted me to hit some balls back to her so she didn't gave to chase them around the arena. She said she'd love that, and I'm thinking, "I'll show her."

Her very first serve just about took my head off. I ended up getting only a few back to her, but what a thrill it was.

In the Flyers' third year, Vic Stasiuk had taken over as coach. Bobby Clarke had arrived as a rookie, and Keith Allen was promoted to GM after Ed Snider fired Bud Poile. Bud Poile and Bill Putnam were close and Ed didn't tell Bill before he fired Bud, and that created a deep rift. Ed was a dominant owner, so you could see him wanting to get the front office to his liking, not to Bill Putnam's liking. And Keith was absolutely the perfect GM for Ed, as easygoing and mild-mannered a fellow as you'd ever want to meet. Bill had never really stood a chance there. He lost the power struggle, sold his stock and was gone from the Flyers by June of 1970.

I wouldn't be far behind him.

Instinctively, I felt like I had to move on. Not that I was unhappy — in fact, it was quite the opposite. But I am by nature restless, then as now.

I had actually begun to have stirrings the previous year. I used to car pool with Bill Henderson, who worked in sales with us and would later become the first sales manager for the Hartford Whalers. One time as we drove home, we were talking about our goals in life. Just as we came onto the Walt Whitman Bridge, which is right outside the Spectrum and runs over the Delaware River, I suddenly blurted out, "One day I want to own a team."

Bill looked at me like I was completely nuts. "How are you going to do that?"

"I have access, contacts, through my family," I said. "And I hope one day that I can put a deal together to get a team."

I think that was probably the first time that thought had come out of my mouth, and maybe even the first time it went from the back of my brain to the front. I don't know why I had decided I wanted to be an owner. I've never really thought about it. I guess I always thought it was prestigious to own something, to own something you love and that you can work with and that you understand. I knew I was never going to be a banker, which a lot of people in my family became, or get into a job that had anything to do with tradition. But I had to do something that would get me recognition and give me a career.

Strangely, in 2013, when we were clearing up my mother's estate, I found a letter to my dad that I don't even remember writing. It was written that same year, and I was telling him my goals about maybe someday owning a team, so it was obviously more on my mind than I realized. My parents never gave me any money to invest in ventures — I wouldn't have expected them to — and although my father had contacts, I wasn't asking him in that letter to set me up with those people, nor would I ever dream of that. It was just a fantasy, really; a pipe dream. Now, having a dream of owning and actually owning are two very different things. Remember, I was only 28 then, and hadn't had the time to accumulate any of my own money.

I got the 1970–71 season organized that fall, but one day I woke up and realized it actually was time to go. NHL front offices were very small, and I sensed that I'd gone as far as I could. I felt that if I stayed in Philly I might have still been there 20 years later, but I also might have still been ticket manager and sales manager. Nothing wrong with that, but it's not what I felt I wanted to do or be. Plus I wanted to get back into the New England area, and I really wanted to have my own thing going, whatever that would turn out to be.

People in that environment had been so good to me, and I had learned so much from Ed Snider and Joe Scott. I was thankful for it, and I left on good terms. I knew that you don't ever burn bridges because you're never sure when you might be crossing over them again.

My decision to leave the Flyers was crazy. It was insane. I had a good position, the company was very happy with me, and I was in hockey management. Even talking about it now, I know that it was a stupid decision on paper. However, all of my instincts were leading me in the direction of taking that next step, which would have to be bold if I were going to achieve the goal of ever getting my own team.

So in November I left the Philadelphia Flyers. I was taking a big chance, but in the early 1970s, a lot of people were taking big chances and I would soon become involved with quite a few of them.

As I pulled away from the Spectrum in Philly for the last time, I realized I was taking one hell of a risk in leaving what was then a very tight-knit fraternity of an NHL team's front office. I knew the minute that I hit "home shores" I would be second-guessed about taking this big chance. Somehow, however, I knew that it was my time and the right decision to make.

For the NHL, storm clouds were on the horizon. The league had doubled in size and in doing so had created a much greater awareness of the passion people had for the sport, but had also created an awareness that there were flaws in the league as it related to their player relations. The good news in the expansion was that the league doubled in size and stoked widespread excitement for the sport. The bad news was that other markets that were on the outside looking in now wanted to get into the game, which created a demand that the WHA would meet. Hockey was about to experience the 1970s — the decade of revolution. Who would have thought as I left Philly in 1970 that within a year and a half there would be a rival league with twelve new teams, and I would have one of the twelve?

As they say: gentlemen, start your engines, because here comes the WHA.

PART TWO

The WHA Years:
The '70s

Winging It

I t was the spring of 1971, six months since I'd left the Philadelphia Flyers. I'd taken a gamble in leaving a steady job in hockey, and I was searching for my next career opportunity in sport. I was starting to get worried. My expenses were mounting and I was borrowing from family and friends to make ends meet. I had two children to support. All I knew was that I wanted to get back into pro sports, and in the New England area.

My old friend Johnny Coburn and I had taken over his parents' clothing store in Wareham, Massachusetts, and we had an office for ourselves in the back of the store.

While running the store, Coby and I also put together a business plan for building a small rink somewhere in Cape Cod, because the area didn't have one. We thought maybe we could attract an Eastern Hockey League team, or maybe a franchise for the North American Hockey League, which was just about to start up. We had started to raise money when Vince McMahon — yes, the wrestling guy — beat us to the punch. He broke ground later that year for the Cape Cod Arena in South Yarmouth, which would seat 4,500 people and become home to the Cape Cod Cubs of the EHL in October of 1972.

One typical weekday morning in our store, I was reading the *Boston Globe* when I saw a brief article about the two founders of the American Basketball Association, Dennis Murphy and Gary Davidson, who were apparently at it again and were forming a league called the World Hockey Association to compete with the NHL. And they had already been talking to potential investors.

I showed the article to Coby, and he seemed to be as excited as I was. So I made a suggestion which would turn a small newspaper story into a major event in our lives:

"Let's call these guys."

We knew from the *Globe* article that they were in Newport Beach, California, so we dialed Long Distance Information and, just like that, got a number for the World Hockey Association. Dennis Murphy himself picked up the phone and I got right to the point.

"Hi, I'm Howard Baldwin and I have a partner, John Coburn. I worked with the Philadelphia Flyers but am currently in the Boston area and we're extremely interested in learning more about the WHA and are interested in putting a team in the New England area. We feel we have the financial backing for this type of venture, depending upon what the deal is."

The WHA had a great interest in Boston because it was the hottest market in hockey at the time. The Bruins had just won their first Stanley Cup in 39 years on the famous overtime goal with Bobby Orr flying through the air, the AHL Braves were drawing really well in the Garden and college and high school hockey were still as popular as ever in the city. But so far nobody had expressed an interest in having a WHA team there. Dennis was excited about the idea.

"I'm going to fly out there in the next 30 days and meet you two guys!" Dennis said.

"What do we do now?" we asked ourselves, a question that we'd find ourselves repeating quite regularly over the years. We were young and fearless, with nothing to lose. All our instincts told us this could be the brass ring we were looking for. So why not go for it?

And that began our quest for a WHA franchise, with us fully cognizant of these facts: we didn't have any money, and we didn't have an arena. But we both felt we could "pull this off," as we described it, and we should try. We knew the ABA and the American Football League had worked, and now it was hockey's turn, and these were the same two guys who had started the ABA!

I knew enough from my three years with the Flyers that presentation is half the battle. So Coby and I put together a really nice brochure articulating the history of hockey in New England and listing the compelling reasons why the WHA should establish a foothold in the New England marketplace. We also put together an impressive board of directors consisting of friends and family who were in prominent positions.

Of course, we had to have an office that gave an impression of legitimacy — not extravagance, but understated elegance. We rented a small office, and then went to our friend Albert "Guppy" Ford, an antique dealer, who let us borrow some really good antiques to make the office look like it had substance and that we were established. For that we gave him 1 per cent of the "team."

Gary Davidson and Dennis Murphy were kindred spirits and hustlers of a sort, and were seasoned pros at attracting investors after their years promoting the ABA. Physically they were polar opposites. Davidson had movie-star good looks — think Robert Redford — and tremendous charisma. Murphy was a short, roly-poly Irishman who also resembled a movie star — but unfortunately that star was Mickey Rooney.

Davidson didn't come to Boston, just Murphy. We picked him up at Logan Airport. This was before the jet-way was installed, so he had to come down from the plane on the portable stairway. He stumbled, hit the tarmac and sprained his ankle. So we started our first meeting with the WHA in the hospital emergency ward. There was probably some kind of symbolism in that. Dennis scouted out our "operation," including the new and improved office, and was impressed.

A few weeks later, Davidson and the league's attorney, Don Regan, came to visit us too, and as part of their tour we drove them past our parents' homes. Neither of us mentioned the fact that our families weren't about to invest one red cent in a crazy hockey venture, but we wanted to give them the impression we had access to money by showing them our family homesteads. They clearly believed that we were entrepreneurs with access to money, based on what they had seen, and that this would be good for the league. Keep in mind that, without question, they were selling us and we were selling them. We didn't know what they had and they didn't know what we had. Both sides had a silent commitment to find out, though.

They said, "Here's what you're going to need. You have to show us you have a suitable arena to play in, and that you have the financial backing, and you must come to the first league meeting with the $25,000 entry fee and another $10,000 for league dues."

Coby and I just looked at each other, shrugged and agreed. Sounded reasonable to us.

That wasn't a lot of money, even back then. We thought we could come up with it, but I'll emphasize this: at the time we did not have it. That said, they didn't have a league yet, either.

Eventually we were able to borrow the $25,000, and we gave 1 per cent of the action to a fellow named Peter Leonard for putting up the 10 grand for the league dues.

The first WHA organizational meeting we attended was in October of 1971 at the Hotel Americana in New York City. The league was going to be formed that week, and we were showing up with almost no business experience, without an arena to play in and with our financing limited, and all borrowed. It seemed overwhelming but we felt we had come this far and we were up for the rest of the ride.

We had expanded our little group to include Godfrey Wood, a great friend of Coby's and a former all-American goaltender at Harvard. Woody's role was to work with us on raising capital. We also had our lawyer, George Perkins, from a small New Bedford law firm, who was willing to roll the dice with us regarding his legal fees.

In New York, we were invited up to the presidential suite to meet the league brass and the rest of the owners. Murphy was there and so were Davidson and Regan. Davidson and Regan were Californians, real surfer types who seemed to find everything slightly amusing. We quickly nicknamed these two "the Laughing Boys" — and it stuck.

When Coby, Woody, George and I walked in, everybody looked up at us and the room went silent. Three icons of western Canadian hockey — Ben Hatskin of Winnipeg, Bill Hunter of Edmonton and Scotty Munro of Calgary — were in there, and we could easily see that in their minds we didn't fit the profile at all. Hatskin was in charge of league finances, Hunter was running the hockey end of things and Munro was the great ideas man. Visualize *Goodfellas* and you get what we saw when we walked in. Ben eventually became a dear, dear friend, but he was a very tough guy. And all of them were looking at us like, "Who are *these* young upstarts?"

The idea was for the WHA to come out of the New York meetings with 12 franchises that they could announce to the hockey world, which would develop publicity and momentum. Murphy and Davidson were brilliant: for most of the three days that we were in New York they kept everybody, all the potential franchisees, separate from each other. I don't think they wanted us to compare notes and figure out that the team investors were the important ones, not the league founders, because without franchises there is no league. Gary and Dennis were making it sound like people were lining up to get into the league, when in fact they weren't. Far from it: they were lucky to get 12 applicants. But they had the credibility of having started the ABA, so people felt that there was at least some substance there. Gary was the charismatic one, with a winning smile, while Dennis worked his ass off all the time. They were a good team. But they didn't know a thing about hockey, which became evident when we had a chance later to read through the league by-laws — in many instances the ice surface was referred to as "the court."

I would be remiss if I didn't point out here that the $25K each franchise put up would go directly to Mr. Murphy and Mr. Davidson.

When it was our turn to appear to make a pitch, the entire process was testimony to the theory that sometimes when you have nothing to lose, you can achieve great success. Bottom line, we were clear to them: we didn't have an arena but could get one, and we felt the financing wouldn't be an issue.

We were able to convince them that we had the potential to be a stable ownership group. We didn't tell them we had the money, and we remained steadfast in our confidence that we would be able to find a place to play. We mentioned the new rink being built in Providence, Rhode Island, as well as the old Boston Arena, which we thought we could get, and the Boston Garden, which was a long shot. We were earnest and committed, and because of that, and of the appearance of wealth behind us, they agreed to give us 30 days to do what we said we were going to do.

They said, "We're having a second meeting in November at the Fontainebleau Hotel in Miami. Come back then."

The WHA was announced to the world as 10 franchises — the Miami Screaming Eagles, the Los Angeles Aces (owned by Murphy), the Chicago Cougars, the New York/Long Island Raiders, the Dayton Arrows, the San Francisco Sharks (owned by Davidson), the Calgary Broncos, the Alberta Oilers, the Winnipeg Jets and the Minnesota Fighting Saints.

We went back home and started going a hundred miles an hour looking for financing and for an arena. The Bruins owned the Garden and weren't really taking us seriously. The Boston Arena was old and misshapen. And we got scammed in Providence, which I'll tell you about later. When it was time to go to Miami 30 days later, we knew we could get the Boston Arena but also knew that it wasn't adequate, although at least it was a place to play in New England.

We decided to go to Florida because Dennis and Gary were encouraging us to come and we felt strongly that they needed a New England presence — besides, the weather in Miami in November is nice.

Then fate stepped in or, rather, sat down behind us. Coby and I went to the airport to catch a plane to Florida, and who should get on with us but a fellow named Phil David Fine, whom I'd met once with my father. He was the brains behind getting the New England Patriots' stadium in Foxboro built and he also knew the lawyer for the Boston Garden, Charlie Mulcahy. By sheer chance, Phil was sitting right behind me on the plane, and I re-introduced myself to him. He remembered me and asked why we were going to Miami. So I told him about the WHA, the meetings in Miami, our bid to get a hockey franchise for New England and that we were hoping to find a place in Boston to play our games.

Phil loved a challenge, and when I finished telling him about our plan, he said, "I'll tell you what, son, you get the franchise, come back to me, and I'll get you a place to play, but for doing that my firm will represent you."

We got to the Fontainebleau, charging it to Coby's American Express card, which was pretty close to maxed out. Murphy and

Davidson were playing the same game they did in New York: keeping the franchise applicants apart from each other, waiting in their rooms for their appearance before the league brass. They were trying to create a charged and competitive atmosphere around the meetings, leading everyone to think that there were six other applicants at the hotel who were bidding for the two vacant franchises. The hotel just happened to be next door to Miami's Playboy Club, though, and at least we were able to watch the nude sunbathing on the roof while waiting in our room.

As Coby and I began to meet some of the other franchisees, the Playboy Club seemed like a perfect neighbor for a WHA meeting. We come from conservative "blue blood" backgrounds, so we were really taken aback when, as we were having a drink with Paul Deneau, who owned the Dayton franchise, he leaned over to the next table and stage-whispered something very, very inappropriate in the ear of an attractive young lady. Our first thought was, "Okay, how do we get into this league . . . but never let our families meet any of these characters?"

Almost all of the people we were exposed to in the WHA were interesting characters, but to a man were actually great guys, no matter what their background. They were all there in the spirit of adventure, creating something new and exciting for their respective cities. Some were visionaries, some were just mavericks, but the common denominators were to have some fun, to make some money and to establish the WHA as a successful business.

When we were summoned into our meeting, we embellished a few things. "We're just about there. We're this close to finishing it off. You just have to take a chance with us."

I admit we also made the connection with Fine and the Boston Garden seem a little more concrete than it actually was. They told us to go back to our rooms again, and wait. In an hour, they called us down and said, "Okay, boys, you got the franchise.

You've got two months to get a place to play . . . but you're in."

Then they paused and delivered the big "but": "By the way, the franchise fee is now 250 grand, not 25 grand."

They said the price had soared because the new league was attracting a lot of attention from potential buyers. That one really threw us for a loop, and we asked for a five-minute break to talk it through. They agreed and added, "You don't have to come up with the $250,000 now — take a few months to get it. Just have it at our next meeting in February in Quebec."

At this point, there was little that could faze Coby and me. We just looked at each other out in the hallway and said, "Well, we're too far down the road to pull back now. Let's agree to it." We didn't even have the $25,000 on our own, let alone 10 times that much, and we didn't have a rink, and we didn't have an owner. "So let's just say okay and get this show on the road."

I should point out that, by now, there was a considerable amount of media attention for our efforts and, of course, a huge amount of skepticism. We were already out on the ledge, so might as well keep on walking.

We went back in, told them that we'd pay the $25,000 now and the other $225,000 at the first WHA player draft in mid-February and said, "Guys, we're in."

"Great," they said. "Congratulations. You are now members of the World Hockey Association."

At the meeting Ottawa was also granted a franchise, bringing the new league up to 12 teams.

We went down there with nothing and were coming back with a hockey franchise. We had return tickets in coach, but when we arrived at the Miami airport Coby said, "No more coach for us, we're OWNERS now," and took what was left on his American Express card and upgraded us to first class. We may not have had first-class funds, but at that moment we felt rich.

I remember that Coby had one of those silly laugh machines with him for some reason. We had way too much to drink on the flight and he kept playing the laughs. Rather than get annoyed, the other passengers got into the spirit of it all and we had a great time celebrating all the way home.

The next morning I was still riding a little high and feeling pretty good about myself and I went to the Sippican Shop, the little diner where I always had my coffee, and extended cordial greetings to such luminaries as Chet the plumber, Ernie the builder and Jay the TV guy.

Sitting next to me was a guy who had his *Boston Herald* open to the front page of the sports section. The famous hockey columnist D. Leo Monahan was covering the WHA and said that these two New England kids had two chances of making it with this league. And those chances became the headline over his column.

"Slim and None."

The fellow who was reading the paper looked over at me and said, "Are you sure you know what the hell you're getting into?"

Actually, I didn't. It was at that moment that reality set in and I realized the fun was over and it was Game On.

Game On

When I think back on it, it was overwhelming. Coby, Woody and I had to raise money, find a place to play, get a hockey team put together, and *then* get a marketing and business group together. And you couldn't get numbers two, three or four without getting number one. You had to have the capital. That would make the difference between "none" and at least "slim."

Woody was working in New York for the investment firm Shearson Hayden Stone, run by Sandy Weill, someone who would become a well-known financier and the eventual CEO of Citibank. Hence, Woody was the perfect guy to raise the money.

As well, we brought in Bill Barnes, who became the point man in marketing. Bill ended up being one of my closest and dearest friends. He was vitally important throughout Whalers history as a stabilizing influence on the franchise, and as a marketing expert. Being about 10 years older, Bill also gave us some much-needed maturity. As part of the seed group, Bill was also an equity holder. Peter Leonard had put up the 10 grand for league dues, so he got 1 per cent. George Perkins got 1 per cent for doing all the legal work. Guppy Ford got that 1 per cent for giving us those antiques for the office. Woody would get a couple of points if he found the money, and Sandy Weill would get a point too. That was the group that owned 100 per cent of the New England hockey team, which didn't have a place to play, or even a name.

One day Sandy Weill said to Woody, "Why don't you call up this guy Bob Schmertz? He's been looking to put a Canadian Football League franchise in Yankee Stadium, and he might be interested in hockey." Schmertz, a real estate developer from New Jersey, was also part-owner of the NBA Portland Trail Blazers. So Woody cold-called him and told him about New England, and Bob said he'd be interested and would fly into New Bedford, the closest airport to Marion, Massachusetts, where we were.

It was a cold Saturday morning in December, 1971 when Coby and I drove out to the airport in Coby's jeep to wait for Schmertz's private plane. It didn't show up and we were getting nervous, thinking, "Oh my God, we've been stood up." Then there was a call for me at the airport desk — there were no cell phones in those days — saying they had the two airports mixed up and had landed at Bedford.

Bob arrived with his lawyer, Jack Giordano, who was a tough guy. We could tell the minute he opened his mouth that he was the bad cop. We got in the jeep, we pulled away from the airport and the first thing that happened was my door flew wide open. Giordano didn't bat an eye, and said to Coby, "Just keep going. We don't know him, and we haven't made a deal yet."

We got to George Perkins' law office, there was a little bit of small talk, and Bob said, "What are you fellows looking for?"

We said we needed a million and a half dollars and we wanted to go 50-50 with him, with his money always coming out first, as it was the risk money. Bob didn't bat an eyelash.

He said, "This is what I'll do. I'll give you a million-dollar line of credit and $300,000 in working capital. I want 60 per cent, you guys have the other 40, and I really don't care how you divide that up amongst yourselves."

So just like that we had our capital. Coby, Woody and I were stunned that it was that quick and that easy. The whole thing took maybe half an hour and suddenly, after months of bluffing about money, we were the best-financed team in the entire league.

Things started falling in place quickly from there. The way it broke down was that Bob owned 60 per cent, Coby and I each owned 12 per cent — mostly sweat equity, but we did put a little money into it — and the other 16 per cent was chopped up among all the aforementioned others.

Before he left, Bob asked how much Coby and I were paying ourselves and when we said $18,000 each, he said it wasn't enough and to raise it to $20,000. The other thing he said was, "By the way, I am going to come to the next league meeting with you and we are going to make it clear to Murphy and Davidson that we are only putting up 25 grand, not 250 grand." Sounded fair enough to us. We shook hands, took him back to the airport and then had a nice night out.

Schmertzie, from day one, was a fabulous partner. He would soon acquire the Boston Celtics with the help of Phil David Fine, and it gave us huge credibility to have our primary owner also owning the Celtics. I had no great interest in basketball, but Red Auerbach, the Celtics president and general manager, was an iconic NBA figure, so it was a big thrill for me to become friends with him and some of the other old Celtics, such as Tommy Heinsohn. During the first year of the WHA, Bob married Phyllis Kane, a terrific lady who to this day is a very dear friend of ours. Sadly, Bob died prematurely in 1975, at the age of 48, just three years after we first met him. When I left Hartford in 1988, they wanted me to be in the first class of the Whalers Hall of Fame, but I said that I wouldn't go in until two other gentlemen were inducted first: Bob Schmertz and Jack Kelley. WHA trophies were eventually named after six of the founding members, of which I was one, but I insisted that they take my name off of it and put Bob Schmertz's on. I did this for two reasons: one, he deserved it, and two, I was too damn young to have a trophy named after me.

I've often been asked why I thought Bob bit on our proposal. The best answer I can give you is that I think he believed in the notion of a rival league because he had seen the AFL vs. the NFL, and he saw the ABA vs. the NBA while he was one of the owners in Portland. I also think he saw something in us that made him believe we might just make this work.

So I think that Bob believed, "Hey if I make money, great. If I don't make money, it's just a loss. Let's roll the dice and see what happens."

Fortunately, I'm proud to say, we came through for him big time.

I don't want to get on a pulpit here, but I think the sad thing in business today, at least the businesses I'm in, is that there is not enough eyeball-to-eyeball contact. If we had tried to do the

Whaler financing with e-mails — "my lawyer will meet yours," that kind of thing — it never would have happened. Sitting down face-to-face with Bob enabled us to work it out. We looked each other in the eye and established a rapport. There is not enough of that any more — in any business.

Now we had our working capital, and heading into the first week of January all we had to do was hire a full front office, find an arena to play in, name the team, et cetera, et cetera, et cetera.

We only interviewed two people for the combined position of GM and coach that first year. One was Jack Kelley, who had turned the hockey program at Boston University completely around. The other was Harry Sinden, who had coached the Bruins to the 1970 Stanley Cup and would soon be the coach of Team Canada in the famous Summit Series with the Soviet Union. Harry had had a falling-out with the Bruins that dated back to the '70 championship season, when they refused to give him a raise, and now he was working at Stirling Homex, a construction firm in Rochester, New York.

Coburn and I used to play ping-pong for hours, and one night, in the middle of one of the marathon matches, when we were slightly hammered, the phone rang. It was Harry Sinden. He said, "Understand you've been trying to reach me." I told him we'd like to talk to him about the new WHA team, and we agreed to meet him at the Westbury Hotel in Toronto, which was Toronto's "hockey hotel," right behind Maple Leaf Gardens. It was also owned by an uncle of mine. Harry was really terrific and after our meeting said, "Look, I'm really interested." But within 48 hours he called and said, "No, I can't do it. I think I've got a chance back in Boston." I think he leveraged us to get back to the Bruins, and he stayed there forever.

Would we have hired Harry if he'd said yes? I honestly don't know. But I will tell you that after we met with Jack Kelley, I remember saying to Coby that if push came to shove, if we had to make a decision, we'd be leaning toward Jack.

Jack had just won the 1971 and '72 NCAA championships with Boston University. Nobody in hockey was hiring out of the college ranks, but we felt that for Boston we had to make a splash and get ourselves on the front pages of the sports section. We just thought that with our backgrounds — and I've kind of done this all my life — we should go against the grain. Jack had local branding and our instincts were that the game was changing and that it was going to be opened up to college players. So we said, "Let's make a courageous choice."

Jack had both titles, GM and coach, and did a great job for us. What I loved about Jack was that to two young guys starting something new, he could appear to be very fierce. He was like a drill-instructor personality. We were a little intimidated — make that more than a little — but we also knew he'd take charge and would put a competitive team on the ice. He was very clear-cut about what he wanted in personnel. He wanted Ron Ryan, who had played for him at Colby (where Jack was the first-ever small-college coach to be named NCAA hockey coach of the year), as his assistant GM, and he wanted Bob Crocker, the BU freshman coach, as his assistant as well, and Jack Ferreira as his chief scout. Jack was intensely loyal and I really appreciated that. But there were, over time, certain people who weren't as loyal to him as he was to them.

We signed a three-year contract with Jack, averaging about 30 grand a year, with bonuses for winning. And that's where Bob Schmertz went way above and beyond the call of duty. One of the things Coby and I had misjudged was the impression that people had about the highly speculative nature of the league, and Jack wanted his contract guaranteed. He was leaving the security of college and had a young family — wife, Ginny and children, Paul, Nancy, David and Mark — to provide for and couldn't be gambling with his career. Bob guaranteed Jack's contract and almost every single player's contract for that first year. That went a long way toward securing the success of the Whalers franchise.

Jack was coming to work for us at the end of the school year, and shortly after hiring him we attended a testimonial dinner at BU for all the great work Jack had done at the university. It was there that I first met Ginny Kelley, who had a great spirit. I'll never forget her leaning over to me halfway through the dinner and saying, "Howard Baldwin, you better know what you're doing. My husband is leaving a pretty stable gig here." I thought, "Oh great, more pressure on me."

Thank God I was used to the pressure coming at me from everywhere.

Finding a Rink, the Hard Way

We had our hockey office and now it was time to be nervous about the rest of the league until we actually dropped the puck. We had a lot of meetings, and a lot of things were changing rapidly in the new league. But the league knew there wasn't a shred of doubt about our ability to perform now that we had Bob Schmertz. Every team was supposed to put up a $100,000 performance guarantee, and we were one of only two or three to do it. We had gone from having people wonder whether we could pull this off to being one of the top teams in the league in terms of financial stability.

We were going to have to play our first season in two different arenas. One was the old Boston Arena. That was a done deal. We also wanted to play some dates in the Boston Garden. Philip David Fine felt he could deliver that despite the fact that three teams — the Bruins, Celtics and Braves — were already in there, playing the same six months of the year that we were. We had to take the worst dates, which we opted to do for the credibility of being in the city's major arena.

One of the great benefits of associating with Phil David Fine's law firm, Fine and Ambrogne, was the introduction to a young associate named Bob Caporale. "Cap" had joined the firm recently and had a great passion for sports. Cap and I formed a business association and friendship through this experience. He was at my side every step of the way and is still a friend and integral part of my life.

We could have gone to the Arena for all our games, but that would not have sat well with the league. The Arena was a famous local landmark, but it was decrepit. It was located near Northeastern University and was used for college hockey and fights. It had seating for only about 5,500 and the ice surface was oval, shaped like a football. If you shot the puck along the boards hard enough, it probably would have gone round and round all day, just like pinball. When I called my father and said, "Dad we've got a place to play," and told him it was the Arena, he said, "You're kidding aren't you? Let me tell you, I played there in 1933 for Harvard and it was a dump then. You can't play there."

I told him it would get fixed up, and it did. They made the ice regulation-size and built locker rooms for us and the visitors. We had to build another dressing room when we landed games in the Garden, because the existing rooms there were all taken. In the end, we played 19 of our home games in the Boston Arena, and the other 20, plus all the playoffs, at the Boston Garden.

The most interesting prospect we explored was the brand new arena in Providence, Rhode Island — the Providence Civic Center. Going to Providence seemed logical. It would have been a perfect fit, and Providence could have become what Hartford eventually did.

We tried to get into Providence, but there was tremendous corruption and we got scammed. For some reason the Civic Center authority, which consisted of some of the leading business-people in the city as well as a politician or two, were protecting George Sage, the owner of the Providence Reds in the AHL. Then, through Jack Kelley, we met a local businessman named Bob Reid, and he said, "I believe I have somebody that will be able to help you get into Providence." Bob came up to lunch with us in Boston with a business associate named Jimmy and a "consultant" named Ray Badway. And if the last name wasn't enough, all you had to do was look at Ray and you'd start thinking, "This may not work." He looked like a real tough guy.

They asked for $15,000 for "expenses" to get us into the arena. We gave them the money with high hopes that this might work. Of course, we never got in, never got our money back and never asked for it, either. We took a chance and it didn't pan out and we wound up in Boston in the Arena and the Garden.

However, there is a postscript to the Providence experience.

After our second WHA season, I got a telephone call from an assistant attorney general in Providence named Bud Cianci, saying that he'd like to come up and see me. Bob Caporale helped me deal with the issue. He is a very creative lawyer who would always find a way to solve a problem no matter what the size.

So Bob and I met with Cianci, and Cianci asked some questions about what we went through in Providence and why we thought we didn't get into the new arena. I answered them truthfully. After Cianci finished questioning me, I asked for a short recess so Cap and I could go into another room to talk. I said "Cap, he didn't ask the right questions. Why don't we just tell him the truth, that we were scammed?" Cap said, "Okay, but I want to make sure you can't get in any trouble and that I can get you immunity." So Cap goes in and talks to Cianci and Cianci says, "Fine, I'm not after

Howard, I'll give him immunity." So I come in and tell him about the 15 grand that was given to the group we lunched with in Providence. His eyes lit up like a Christmas tree. As a result, the corruption in the Providence Civic Center became his whole political platform when he ran for mayor. He won . . . and he became a legend. He's actually gone to jail himself for corruption, but he did a lot of good things for Providence and helped rebuild the city.

So flash forward to two years later, and the trial's going to start. Nobody cared about it except the three people who were in trouble — Jimmy Howe, Bob Reid and Ray Badway. And who's the key witness, but me? By then I had become WHA president and the league All-Star Game was in Edmonton right when the trial was to start, so I said to the lawyer who prepared me, "It's not going to take long, right?" "Oh no, it's just going to take a day, Mr. Baldwin." So I go to this courthouse in Providence, knowing that at the end of the week I had to go to Edmonton. I'm on the stand Monday. Then I'm on the stand Tuesday, then Wednesday, then Thursday. I'm totally frustrated as I needed to leave for the All-Star Game. During the recesses, Ray Badway had all his boys with him out in the hall and they'd come up to me and say, "Now, Howie, you don't want to testify against us do you?" I'd say, "I don't want to do anything, but I have to tell the truth." Bob Reid's daughter would come up to me crying, asking why I had to testify against her dad. I explained to her that she might be better off asking her father that question.

Now Friday's session ends, and they say they need me back Monday. I said to Cap when we left the courthouse, "Enough already with this trial, I am going to Edmonton." He said, "Write the judge a letter and say you'll be in on Tuesday when you get back from the All-Star Game." So I do just that and off to Edmonton I go. I arrived back at court on Tuesday and testified for another hour, after which they thanked me and said I was finished. But when I start to get off the stand, the judge says, "Mr. Baldwin, please stay right here." She dismissed the jury and everybody else except for me and Cap. Then she starts telling me why I'm in contempt of court because I didn't show up on Monday.

Bottom line: I had to write out a $350 check for Monday's court costs. Meanwhile, within two weeks they dropped the case, because nobody cared about it. I have since learned that the $15K went into the pockets of one of the three businessmen and was used for the education of his kids.

Well, at least somebody got something out of the experience.

Building the Whalers

We had our arenas, we had our coach and GM, and it was already pretty clear that we were going to be one of the better-financed teams in the league. So now we needed a name.

We all came up with ideas and lists of names and various color combinations for the logo. It was actually Ginny Kelley who came up with the idea of "the Whalers." We all loved that idea, and when it came to picking the colors we felt that there was already ample black and yellow for the other Boston hockey teams. So we went with green and white.

Then the question was: would it be the Boston Whalers or New England Whalers? That problem was easily solved for us as "Boston Whalers" was already taken by a successful boat-manufacturing line. And we preferred the New England designation anyway, as we wanted to reach out to the entire region, not just to Boston.

Next on our docket was dealing with the $250,000 franchise fee. It was February of 1972, and the league meetings were in Quebec. As promised, Bob Schmertz flew to the meetings with us. By now, everyone knew we had the highest-profile owner in the league and everyone was excited to meet him, until he stood up and said, "I'm glad to be in this room. I'm excited about the league. However, I want to make one thing clear: we aren't paying the 250 grand for dues. You'll find we will be great partners in the league, but just because we came in 30 days after the original 10 franchises doesn't mean we are going to pay 10 times more than what they paid. Particularly when three or four of them are no longer in the room. We'll pay the 25, but if you think we're paying the 250, throw us out right now." We didn't have to pay it.

A couple of weeks later in Newport Beach, California, we had the first WHA player draft. Jack couldn't be there, as he still had his coaching duties at BU, so he was in Boston, running our draft by telephone (not unlike the NFL did for years). Ronnie Ryan, Godfrey Wood, John Coburn, Bill Barnes and myself were at the draft table in Newport, with Ron connected by phone to Jack.

Before the draft officially began, Bill Hunter, the flamboyant owner from Edmonton, was really fired up. He was the classic P.T. Barnum type, and he said, "Now we're going to introduce somebody, one of hockey's most famous and influential people. And if he doesn't support this league, we are going to send him back to Toronto in a hearse." He was introducing none other than Alan Eagleson, the head of the National Hockey League players' union. Of course Alan loved this league — as did every hockey agent in the world — as it did nothing but drive up the prices for the players. Alan only signed a couple of dozen players to our league, but he used the WHA to get better deals for his players in the NHL.

And here's a very, very important point. At that time the NHL was not proactive in dealing with any outside threats to their player contracts. They were in a strictly reactive mode. They chose to believe that their reserve clause was valid. If the NHL had been smarter when they did their first expansion in 1967, they would have looked more closely at their contracts. Once the NHL realized the WHA was on the horizon, they then reacted by doing only the obvious, which was to announce further expansion, thereby enticing potential WHA markets to hold out hope for the NHL. Over the next several years the NHL went into Buffalo and Vancouver, Atlanta and Long Island, Washington and Kansas City.

But what the NHL missed was that no rival league can possibly start without the credibility of labor. If we were going to bill ourselves as a major league, we had to have major league players. But rather than look at their players' contracts and ask themselves, "Do these guys have any chance at getting our players?" they were just arrogant and *assumed* their contracts would be held up in court. In hindsight, which admittedly is 20-20, they should have immediately collectively bargained a standard player contract that didn't violate the anti-trust laws so blatantly. If Joe Blow signs a $10,000 one-year contract with the Toronto Maple Leafs, that shouldn't bind him for life. It's just common sense. But that's what the reserve clause said: once you were with a team you were with them essentially until they traded you or officially let you go. In the WHA we felt strongly that the standard contract as written by the NHL at that time violated every existing anti-trust law, especially in the United States. None of us were going to sign a player if they had another year of their NHL contract, but if that contract was up, we believed the players became what we now call "free agents."

Those were the principles that the WHA was luring players with. We would offer them more money, creating a competitive market for labor for the very first time. We would outlaw the reserve clause in our contracts and we would also argue that the NHL reserve clause was illegal, and that when the term of a player's contract ended, he was free to sign anywhere. We had to win that battle in court, several times, because the NHL kept coming at us on several fronts.

We wouldn't have had a league if we lost those cases. But we won them all, starting with a huge victory in the summer of 1972 in Boston, after the NHL filed an injunction to prevent Gerry Cheevers and Derek Sanderson coming to our league. Cap and I were in the courthouse when the decision was announced, as were Sanderson (in his suit and tennis shoes) and several other players. The case lasted about 10 minutes before the judge ruled in the WHA's favor. Later that year in Philadelphia, with Bobby Hull and John McKenzie, we won another landmark case that settled the reserve clause for good. The judge spoke very harshly against the NHL, ruling that the reserve clause had not been bargained in good faith and was in fact illegal, and that the restraining order the NHL had obtained to prevent Hull from playing in the WHA was totally invalid. Hull immediately got on the ice with the Winnipeg Jets, and the war the NHL thought couldn't possibly happen was on, full scale.

When we held the first WHA player draft, we thought all of this would eventually happen and that the courts would rule in our favor, so we went about our business as if we were going to win. But there was still a variety of drafting approaches from the 12 original teams. Several franchises went for the splashy signings, but we went for guys we thought could play right away, and whom we could sign.

Jack did a great job for us in the draft. His approach to building our team was based on realism. He didn't want to pick guys he knew were unlikely to leave the NHL, but instead picked players who were not real fixtures with their NHL teams. Our first signing was Larry Pleau for three years at $30,000 a year. He'd been making $15,000 for the Montreal Canadiens. He was a New England guy, from Lynn, Massachusetts, and Jack was smart that way: we would go after players with New England roots. So we took Kevin Ahearn of the U.S. Olympic team, a Boston College player, and Tim Sheehy, also a Boston College player. They were Irish names too. We had a real Boston flavor to that team, starting with Jack Kelley.

Jack also had the courage to sign U.S. college players, a group that had traditionally been looked down on by NHL old-liners. Obviously the NHL couldn't challenge the college players in court because they weren't under contract to the NHL, and that was part of the reason to take them. So Jack signed Bobby Brown, Jake Danby, Ric Jordan, Guy Smith and John Cunniff, who were all good, solid players coming out of New England college hockey. He also made some good choices up front with Pleau, Tommy Webster (our first scoring star), Terry Caffery, Brit Selby, Mike Byers, and Tommy Williams, who had been the first American skater to play regularly in the NHL (with the Bruins). These were good players who were like third- and fourth-liners in the NHL — well, they didn't really have fourth lines then — but who weren't getting enough of a chance with their teams.

Our marquee signing was Ted Green, and it really helped that he had played so long for the Bruins. He had come back to play after suffering that horrible head injury in the fall of 1969, when Wayne Maki of the Blues swung his stick at him. He needed a two-and-a-half-hour operation for a skull fracture and was partly paralyzed for a while, but fought back to play and won the Stanley Cup with the Bruins in 1972. We signed him for 60 grand, probably twice what he was making in Boston, but he added instant legitimacy to our blueline and was a great veteran to have on the team.

We didn't have a lot of identifiable names — Ted was the only player on the team who made more than $35,000. We had Al Smith in goal, from the Red Wings, and Bruce Landon from Springfield in the AHL. We had a good young defence, with Teddy, Paul Hurley (another New Englander), and three kids from the Toronto Maple Leafs — Ricky Ley, Brad Selwood and Jim Dorey. Those three were going to be mainstays for the Leafs, but because the Leafs didn't

believe the WHA would get off the ground, they lost all three of
them, and along with them most of their future on the blueline.

We didn't specifically target Harold Ballard and the Toronto
Maple Leafs, although when I look back at what happened, maybe
I shouldn't be so firm in saying that. The WHA probably ended
up picking on the NHL teams that were rigid. It wasn't smart to
go against Ed Snider, because you knew that he was progressive
and smart. And of course I never would have done that, on prin-
ciple. And Ed proved he was progressive. Somebody in our league
signed Dave Schultz and Bill Flett, and Ed said "Screw that" and
within the next 48 hours he went around and signed them both
back again. He said, "I'll see you in court," and nobody took him
on. Ed got it real quick, but some of those other guys didn't. The
Leafs didn't. The Islanders didn't. They were an NHL expansion
team and the WHA took seven of their expansion draft choices.

Then there was the Adams family in Boston. Look who they
lost: we signed Ted Green; Cheevers went to Cleveland; Philadelphia got Johnny McKenzie and Derek Sanderson. The Bruins
had just won two Cups in three years, and they just didn't get it.
The Rangers got it, though, and they had the money to spend so
they locked up their players so we couldn't get them. Interest-
ingly enough, most of the Original Six had enjoyed the benefits of
the restrictive reserve clause for so long that they were the teams
which struggled the most in losing players to the WHA.

Some of the other teams had splashier signings and drafts than
we did — Sanderson, McKenzie, Cheevers, for example, and Winnipeg drafting Bobby Hull, which I thought was far-fetched at the
time. The Miami Screaming Eagles drafted and signed goalie Bernie Parent, the league's first big catch. Although Bernie became
better known for winning two Stanley Cups for the Flyers, he was
Toronto property in 1972, and the Leafs were refusing to negotiate with any player who used the WHA as a bargaining chip. So

Toronto lost three of their young defencemen, and a franchise goalie.

Miami was supposed to be a cornerstone franchise of the league, securing us a toehold in the southern states while the NHL was trying to do the same thing with Atlanta. Because Miami was a new, non-traditional market, there were even plans not to use the traditional black puck. In fact, the WHA used a blue puck for the first week or two of all games. This was a natural extension of what Murphy and Davidson did in the ABA when they introduced the red, white and blue ball. (They never trademarked that ball, and that miscue cost them millions.) They did trademark the blue puck, but its chemical makeup created a harder texture and the puck tended to shatter the glass more. And the players hated it anyway, so the innovation was quickly abandoned.

Herb Martin, the Screaming Eagles owner, decided he would keep us all in the loop on the great things he was going to do in Miami, including building a fancy arena. He sent us black-and-white 9-by-11 photos of the arena, and it was Alan Eagleson who first noticed that something wasn't right. He thought he could see palm trees through the front doors of the building in the pictures. "What kind of arena is this?" he said. "They've got a wall up and all you see inside is palm trees?" What the guy had built was a facade, and finally somebody had taken a moment to examine it. Al said all this in public and suggested that somebody check on the Miami franchise. The WHA did, found out the owner was a fraud, and moved the franchise to Philadelphia, where it became the Blazers.

There were some crazy bastards in that league. The Minnesota Fighting Saints, for instance, used one of their later picks in the first WHA draft to select Wendell Anderson, who was the governor of Minnesota and hadn't played hockey since the 1956 Olympics. And the Winnipeg Jets chose Soviet premier Alexei Kosygin in the 70th round, as their final pick.

At that time in the WHA we were breaking new ground almost every day of the week. It was exciting. It was stimulating. It was fun.

And let's be candid: it can't be done that way any longer. For a new league to work, you need a labor pool, and there is no incentive now for any player to go league to league when they can already go team to team as free agents.

A lot of WHA people have said that they had a strategy right from the start to create a merger with the NHL, but there really wasn't a strategy. We were all just trying to get a league going and make some money and we were having a lot of fun doing it.

It's interesting that some of the owners in the early WHA clearly didn't know hockey. The Canadians — Benny Hatskin, Bill Hunter, Scott Munro, Johnny Bassett when he joined the league — they knew the game. The guys in America were not as well-versed, but they understood the concept of a new league and the business of sports.

Those who instinctively knew enough to hire hockey guys did okay. But in Chicago, Jordan and Walter Kaiser were the original owners of the franchise and they hired Ed Short, the former GM of the Chicago White Sox. After the draft in Newport Beach, everyone went home to their respective markets and began the task of signing players. We would do weekly conference calls updating each other on the signings. On each call, Ed Short announced no players had been signed. Finally someone fearing the worst (that the franchise had no money) said to him, "Why haven't you signed any players?"

Ed then told us that he had had his secretary type up 50 contracts, each with a salary number on it that he thought a player should earn, and he mailed them to the 50 players. He couldn't understand why none of the players responded. In baseball this was the way it was done, but at the time, of course, baseball had the reserve clause and you either signed or you stayed home. The

WHA was signing players all over the place and we were looking at Chicago and they hadn't signed anybody. They finally ended up getting hockey people in there and they stumbled their way through that first year, and in the second year they actually took us out of the playoffs.

Right from the start, franchises were moving around, and it continued that way for seven years. Before the first puck dropped, San Francisco moved to Quebec to become the Nordiques (proving to be one of the great franchise shifts, ever), Miami moved to Philadelphia to become the Blazers, the Dayton Arrows moved to Houston to become the Aeros, and the Los Angeles Aces took San Francisco's original nickname, the Sharks. Everybody was nervous about one another, but everybody was also starting to feel confident that the league would be launched successfully. Everybody was apprehensive about the future, and that never changed until we did the merger with the NHL seven years later. Every year in June, when we would have the end-of-the-year annual meetings — I called it Russian Roulette — we'd be wondering who would be in and who would be out.

The "W-Hull-A" and the Whalers' First Season

Very early on, Benny Hatskin came to the board and said, "I think I can sign Hull." Hatskin had grown close to Bobby Hull's agent, Harvey Wineberg, and although Hull would score 50 goals in the NHL in the 1971–72 season, his contract with the Blackhawks was set to run out in October. And I've already told you what our league thought about the reserve clause that the Blackhawks believed would keep Hull in Chicago as long as they wanted him.

"It's going to cost a million dollars signing bonus, plus his salary," Ben said. "And I'm asking everybody in the league to chip in, because you're all going to make money on it when Winnipeg comes into your building."

We knew enough to know that you needed a star to make a new league work. A lot of owners think people want to look up at them in their private box, but I'm a great believer that the athletes are the stars, so we — the Whalers — immediately voted to chip in our share for Hull. We trusted the people around the table and we assumed that when they said they were going to chip in, they were going to come up with the money. Hull was going to be great for the whole league. A million bucks divided by 12 teams, so call it about $100,000 each for the signing bonus. And the Jets would pay the salary, about $250,000 a year. Remember, Gordie Howe had retired then, so Hull was the most charismatic player (along with Bobby Orr) in the NHL.

I don't think people, including me at the time, ever thought that Ben could sign Hull, but he was able to do it. You could make the case that it was one of the biggest signings in sports history. It solidified our league, gave us legitimacy and, once Hull was joined in Winnipeg by Anders Hedberg and Ulf Nilsson a couple of years later, it set a new style of play for the game that the WHA eventually took with it into the NHL.

When it came time for people to pay for Hull, only three or four of us did. Three of us, as well as Winnipeg, added another $150,000 to our original contribution of $100,000 because we recognized the enormous value that this held for the league.

Hull signed, and the WHA had two big press conferences. The first one was in Winnipeg, where he signed the contract under Canadian law. We presented him with an oversized check for a million bucks, and that picture made it into all the newspapers.

Then we took that check, and Bobby, to Minnesota to sign him under U.S. law. Bill Barnes and I flew in for PR purposes, to register with our fans that Hull was in the league. There's a picture somewhere of Barnsie, me, Bobby and young Brett Hull after the Minnesota signing.

It was *huge* for the league. We marketed it like crazy and we knew when Winnipeg came into our building we were virtually guaranteed to have a big crowd. We were originally going to put the first Winnipeg game in Boston Arena, but we were able to manipulate it so that we could play them in the Garden. We never sold the Garden out, but we came mighty close with Hull. He was an attraction. Just like Sanderson, Parent and McKenzie were attractions.

We weren't a team full of marquee names ourselves, but Jack Kelley was building a solid nucleus of players, all of whom came from winning traditions. The closer I got to Jack personally, the more I realized that he was the perfect hire for us because he was such a take-charge, hard-working guy.

The first confrontation we had was in June, before the first season started. We had set a budget of $650,000 for the whole team's salary, and Jack was relentless in trying to get more. His number was 750K. I remember saying to Coby, "You know what, John? We're never going to make it if we don't stand up to Jack and get our point across." With apprehension, I called Jack up and asked him to meet me at our offices at the Statler Hilton in Boston on a Saturday morning for the purpose of resolving the payroll issue.

Jack and I had a fabulous meeting, and it solidified even further what was to become a very positive working relationship. We split the difference, and the budget went to a compromise of 700 grand. He was happy . . . and I was really pleased. He now knew that there would be a line somewhere, which was a big moment for me, because Jack was more of an icon than I was. Actually, I certainly wasn't an icon at all.

Jack put together a terrific staff. His assistant GM and assistant coach was Ron Ryan, who had been coaching at U of Penn, had played for Jack at Colby College and who ended up being president of the Philadelphia Flyers. When Ron came out of Colby there seemed little doubt that he would have been the number one draft choice for the NHL — he was that good a player — but that wasn't the system when he played. They didn't draft back then.

Jack also hired Bob Crocker as an executive and scout, and Bob is still scouting in the NHL. His chief scout was Jack Ferreira, a former all-American goaltender at BU. Jack surrounded himself with people he'd worked with before and who were loyal to him. It worked well all the way around.

Jack really took charge of the hockey end of things, which was great because although I had no trouble with tickets and sales, I didn't really know that much about the on-ice stuff. We were doing quite well in sales, and had about 4,000 season tickets, more than twice what the Flyers had had in their first season, five years earlier. And we sold a bunch of smaller ticket packages as well.

We opened our first season at the Boston Garden on October 12, 1972, and drew 14,114 fans, nearly a sellout. We got off to a good start with a 4–3 win over Philadelphia, and we kept that start going, winning nine of our first 13 games. We got it up to 21–10–1 by mid-December and ended up with 94 points from 78 games, to finish first in the East Division and with the best record in the entire league. Winnipeg finished first in the West with 90 points. In our seven years in the WHA we were never a team that won a lot of league awards, but that first season Tom Webster finished second in the scoring race with 53 goals and Jack Kelley was named the first WHA coach of the year, which he richly deserved.

After our home opener we went down to Philadelphia for the Blazers' first home game, and that was the night the ice broke. The Blazers were playing in an old building, the Philadelphia

Convention Center, and when the Zamboni came out to prepare the ice for the game, it crashed right through. It was shell ice and extremely brittle. After the franchise had moved from Miami to Philadelphia, they'd signed Derek Sanderson of the Bruins to the largest contract ever given to a team athlete ($2.6 million for five years), and because he was the "face" of the franchise, I guess, they gave him the microphone to tell the fans that they were sorry, but the game would have to be postponed. Unfortunately the team had given away free commemorative pucks before the game and, this being Philadelphia, as soon as Sanderson finished talking, the crowd began pelting him with the pucks. I was standing with my old friend Joe Scott, the minority owner of the Flyers, and I was completely mortified.

The Blazers were kind of symbolic of the majority of WHA teams. They moved to Vancouver after the first year, their third city in two seasons, and two years after that moved to Calgary for two years before folding in 1977. There had been a lot of excitement around Philadelphia because of Sanderson, Johnny McKenzie and Bernie Parent, but they got off to a terrible start and the excitement soon fizzled. And after just eight games, the owners paid Sanderson a million dollars *not* to play for them, and he ended up back with the Bruins. Complete craziness. But very WHA.

There were a lot of arena problems in the WHA's first year. Actually, there were arena problems most WHA years. I was always really nervous about the Boston Arena. So the night of our first game there, against Alberta at the end of October, I got to the rink more than an hour early to check it out. I walked into the lobby and all the lights were out. It was like a blackout, and there were already fans milling around. The building manager, Chuck Toomey, came up to me and said, "Now, Howard, don't you worry about a thing, we've got everything under control. We'll get the lights going." And

I'm thinking, "Ay-yi-yi, we can't have this." So he said, "C'mon, I'll show you. It'll give you comfort."

We get to the electrical room and he opens the door and it doesn't give me any comfort at all. He's got three or four portable fans in there cooling down the fuses. That's the solution? I'm thinking, "Oh my God." But we got the game in. Every game there, and thank God there were only 19, I'd sit there and just stare at the clock, praying that the game would just end. We couldn't have played there another season, and luckily we had the Garden for the playoffs.

Even using the Arena for nearly half our games, we led the WHA in attendance at 6,981 per game, and the 8,874 we averaged in the Garden for playoffs was by far the highest post-season attendance. We beat Ottawa in the first round and Cleveland in the second, both times in five games, to qualify for the best-of-seven final against Winnipeg. Bobby Hull wouldn't have his two Swedish line mates for another couple of years, and we beat the Jets, again four games to one, to win the first WHA championship.

We took the fifth game 9–6 at home, with Pleau scoring three times and Webster twice, but right before the game I had this vague feeling that I'd never seen the league championship trophy, which was sponsored by Avco Financial Services. That's because there wasn't a trophy. It had not yet been manufactured. So Bill Barnes sent a PR guy out to a local sporting goods store and he comes back with this large trophy that cost 20 bucks. It was cheap but big, and it was shiny, so it looked good on 1973 television.

It really was a story of things falling into place nicely. It's not much of a stretch to say that we won everything that first year. We took on the toughest market in the league — Boston. With Smith in goal, Webster up front and Dorey, Selwood, Ley and Green on defence, we had a good team. We finished first in the division, won the Avco cup, led the league in attendance and Jack was coach of the year. It seemed as though everything we did that first year, we did right. It was great for us. We went from having a dream to the reality of winning the whole shooting match in the WHA's first year.

Right after we beat Winnipeg for the Avco cup on a Sunday afternoon, I went onto the ice with Bob Schmertz and on CBS national TV challenged the NHL to a championship game. The next day, NHL owners were laughing at us saying, "This is ridiculous. Their final game is 9–6, what kind of league is this?" But two days later, in game five of the six-game Stanley Cup final, Chicago beat Montreal 8–7. I mean, really. These guys, they were so easy to compete against then because they were so full of their own self-importance. It was easy to take them on because they were old and stodgy, and we were young and likeable — at least, I thought we were!

The "W-Howes-A" and the Whalers' Second Season

What has been long forgotten is that we had our very first merger talks with the NHL at the end of that first season. There was a rump group from each side: from the WHA there was a group led by Bob Schmertz, Nick Mileti of Cleveland and Benny Hatskin, and on the NHL side were Ed Snider, Bill Jennings from the Rangers and Peter O'Malley from Washington. A plan was formulated where all 12 WHA teams would pay $2 million each to enter the NHL. It was a hell of a plan, creative and ballsy, and it would have solved everything and prevented the escalation of the war that had already started and was only going to get worse. The Whalers would have had to pay an additional indemnity to the Bruins to play in New England, and the Chicago Cougars would have had to do the same thing in the Blackhawks' territory. But when the NHL militants found out — with Bill Wirtz and Clarence Campbell leading them— they went crazy and the whole plan blew up.

The Howes' situation didn't help thaw any of the ice between the WHA and the NHL. At the WHA draft in Toronto before our second season, Houston announced that they were taking Mark Howe, Gordie's younger son, with their first pick. This was a sensational event. Mark had scored five points in the final game of the Memorial Cup for the Toronto Marlboros only five days before that, and wouldn't turn 18 for another week or so. Therefore he wouldn't be eligible for the NHL draft for a couple of years. The WHA didn't have a formal age rule. We were a rebel league, remember? Even some of our own GMs were pissed, because they were hockey traditionalists. A few rounds later, the Aeros also took Mark's brother Marty, adding more fuel to the fire.

Originally, Bill Dineen of the Aeros didn't have it in his mind to sign Gordie Howe, who had been retired for two years after wrist problems and was working, unhappily, in the Red Wings' front office. But the Aeros ended up signing not only Mark and Marty, but also their hockey-legend father as well. NHL president Clarence Campbell had already called Gordie to warn him against having Mark sign in Houston. Obviously his warning didn't have any impact, because it was Gordie who phoned Dineen and asked if he "wanted another Howe."

This was a major marketing coup for the WHA. The first year it was Hull, the second year it was the Howe family. Of course, the NHL naysayers were ridiculing Gordie's age, but once the season got going and he led the league in scoring, that quieted down significantly.

From a marketing point of view, right away Bill Barnes and I knew we needed to take advantage of the signing. We had a lot of seats to fill in the Garden and I knew the Howes would help sell them. I met Gordie and Colleen Howe for the first time when Houston came to Boston in late November. We made a presentation to them at the old Boston Garden Club, gave them a gift and told them how honored we were to have Gordie in our building. We started a nice relationship with Gordie and Colleen that would blossom into something much fuller a few years later with the Whalers.

What Gordie did in his first year was extraordinary. He won the MVP trophy (named after Gary Davidson), finished third in scoring and led Houston to the league championship. Mark was rookie of the year. Together, the Howes increased Houston's home attendance by nearly 50 per cent. Gordie helped put people in buildings around the league too.

The WHA was proving to be a tougher sell in its second year, especially for us in Boston, where we were facing a lot of competition for the sports entertainment dollar and getting little help from Garden management, who kept sticking us with every little expense they could.

Going into the second WHA year, everybody, including me, misjudged the situation. The truth is that in the first year you get a free pass, in that it's a novelty. It's not unlike expansion. If you get an expansion franchise, your first year should certainly be profitable. People are so excited to have major-league sport, they're going to come out in droves regardless of the level of the product. The second year, reality will set in, you'll be judged by the production on the ice, and you'd better start having a good product to sell.

That holds true for new arenas as well. Of course, a state-of-the-art arena is needed for a team to have a chance to be economically viable. However, you must then have a competitive product fairly quickly because — bottom line — that is what sells tickets.

We knew we had to have a damn good product because we were in Boston, right in the heyday of the Bobby Orr–led Bruins.

In our second year we were able to play all our games in the Boston Garden, which proved to be a mixed blessing.

At the Arena in our first season we were averaging only 3,000 or 4,000 per game, but at the Garden it was 8,000 to 10,000. So in the second year, when the Garden people said they'd give us all 39 dates I said, "Thank God." I figured that average would carry right over.

I misjudged that.

The season opened in October, and we were doing 4,000 to 5,000 a night, and it quickly became clear that the bloom was off the rose. We were competing with an NHL team, an AHL team and an iconic NBA team. Including our own games, that consumes almost 160 dates in a seven-month period. Our relationship with the Bruins was always a bit of an adversarial one anyway, so right away we knew we were in trouble and we would have to act quickly.

An additional motivating factor to act quickly was that Bob Schmertz was starting to have a few financial difficulties. During our first year, Bob had also acquired the Boston Celtics. Basketball was his first love and the Celtics were a great acquisition for him, and frankly, it enhanced the credibility of the Whalers in the marketplace as well. Although I never had an avid interest in, or an understanding of, basketball, it was always a privilege when Bob came to Boston for a game, to sit with Bob and the national treasure, Red Auerbach.

Bob and I met and agreed that we should look for a new home for our hockey team and new ownership that could take Bob out as well. I obviously wanted to stay in as I intended to make this my life for the foreseeable future. I now had another big challenge in front of me.

And, as with the WHA, it was an article in the newspaper that led me to a new opportunity.

Goodbye to Boston

I saw the headline "Hartford Breaks Off Negotiations with Charlie Finley to Bring Basketball Team to City" and read that Finley owned the Oakland ABA team and was hoping to bring them to a new arena they were building in Hartford. But talks had fallen through.

So, once again, I reached for the phone and I called Bill Lillyman, who was manager of the Hartford Civic Center. Bill said, "Howard, we'd love to talk with you, come on down." Godfrey Wood, Bob Caporale and I were naive enough about the location of Hartford that we chartered a plane from Boston, when it is only a 90-minute drive. Off we went in a snowstorm, and we nearly crash-landed on the runway in Hartford. It was a rather inauspicious debut, and I told the pilot to go on back home. We were going to rent a car for the trip back because we were all terrified.

We met with Bill, and Don Conrad, the CFO of the Aetna insurance company, to discuss moving the Whalers to Hartford, as well as securing new local ownership. This meeting was like the first meeting we had with Bob Schmertz in New Bedford. We happened to be in the right place at the right time. It was clear to us that the city was desperate to have a prime tenant for the Civic Center, which was being built to revitalize downtown Hartford. And we just got lucky.

We were all starting families, so we wanted to find the nearest place in New England for the team. The people in Hartford hadn't solicited anyone else after Finley. So both sides were in the right place at the right time: it was a perfect match. We had found a new place to play and we agreed on a deal to sell 50 per cent of the team to a local ownership group made up of eight or nine Fortune 500 companies. We thereby had one of the strongest ownership groups in all of sport, not just the WHA.

Even though Hartford was just the fourth-largest city in New England, it had become one of the wealthiest cities per capita in the country because it was the "Insurance Capital of the World." The city was building a downtown arena with a mall attached, trying to become an entertainment and shopping destination, which was a very progressive concept in 1973. The agreement was that we would move the team to Hartford when the new rink was ready, and our group would keep 50 per cent of the team and the local business group would buy the other half. And they would pay off all the debt in Boston, which would be about $600,000 by the end of the year; we weren't doing well at the gate and Bob could no longer afford to put the money in. We also had to find a place to play until January 1975, when the Hartford Civic Center would open. So we arranged to go to the Springfield Civic Center, which had been built just the year before.

Today it would take a year to close a deal like that, but we did the deal in two months. We made the agreement in December and kept it out of the papers until late January, because we were still selling tickets to games in Boston and we didn't want people to know we were moving. We announced it ourselves at the end of February, but by then it had already broken in the press. Our fans were really mad at me because I was the face of the franchise. I always sat with the crowd because there were no such thing as skyboxes back then, but I had to stop going to games because the fans all wanted to kick my ass. I'm a big guy, but I couldn't beat all of

them up. They'd be waiting before the game, with their signs up —
"Keep Our Whalers Here" — that kind of thing. I don't remember all of them, but some of them got very personal. There was a
real hard-core group, which is what makes Boston fans great: they
are passionate.

The Bank of Boston had provided us with a line of credit. They
knew that the business group in Hartford was going to cover our
losses when the deal closed, so we were being given credit based
on that closure happening in the near future. And they knew that
if they didn't keep lending us money, we'd fold and they would get
nothing. But the account executive at the bank was really getting
impatient. We had a payroll every two weeks, and at one point late
in the season I called the banker up to make sure he was going to
back us on the next payroll. And he said, "Nope, I can't do it. I've
gone as far as I can with you. I just can't do it anymore."

I said, "Tell you what. I'm going to come down there and try to
convince you."

So I went and found an old key somewhere, went down to his
office and dramatically tossed the key onto his desk.

"What's that?" he asked.

"It's a key to the locker room," I replied. "We have a game
tonight. *You* go tell Ted Green, Jim Dorey and those guys that
you're not going to pay them. I'm not doing it, because it's *your*
team now."

He said, "I'll give you two more weeks, Howard."

As God is my witness.

By the way, that account executive was Chad Gifford, and he
went on to become chairman of the Bank of America. When I see
him these days, we still chuckle about that little scene.

Everyone in Boston was paid off 100 per cent, and I'm proud of
that, because I didn't want to stiff anybody, including the Boston
Garden.

We knew we had to shift our playoff games to the Big E in Springfield — a 6,000-seat arena that was nearly half a century old — because our Boston fans had disconnected from the team when they found out we were moving. So once we lost to Cleveland in our last regular-season game, we were done with the Garden. We still owed them rent, though, and while I was at home in Marion with a terrible flu, Cap called me up and said he'd received a call from the Garden's legal counselor, Charlie Mulcahy, and they were not going to let our equipment vans out of the building until we paid the rent we owed in full. So they had the Zamboni blocking our vans in.

I said to Cap, "To hell with them. They can keep the equipment. I'm going to torture them, because they've tortured us for two years."

We went back and forth all day. Who was going to blink first? The trainers were getting mad at me, the coaches were mad at me, but I said, "Just leave it alone." And sure enough, around 4:30 p.m., Weston Adams had to go home and his Corvette was on the wrong side of the Zamboni. So when the Zamboni moved to let Westie out, we immediately drove those vans the hell out of there.

We ended up paying them, in full, but we wanted to punish them a bit.

We finished up our second regular season in first place in the East Division by four points over the Toronto Toros, who had moved from Ottawa.

The Toros — which stood partly for the T.O. in Toronto and partly for the snorting bull that was their emblem — brought Johnny Bassett into my life. We were both young and adventuresome and would do some similar things in our careers: start hockey teams without much of a chance of succeeding, own a football team, get into the movie business and have a whole lot of fun.

87

We were close friends until John died of brain cancer in 1986, when he was only 47 years old. John came from a wonderful, high-profile Canadian family (his father had been part-owner of the Leafs), and he brought a great breath of fresh air into the WHA. Every moment I ever spent with John, I enjoyed. To this day, I still think of him often.

Start-Up Fever

The 1970s were the Revolutionary Years, the War Years, in professional sport. Football, basketball and then hockey all got new rival leagues, and toward the end of our first WHA season, another football league was in the works.

Gary Davidson left the WHA at the end of our inaugural season in order to start the World Football League. Originally, the WFL was supposed to start play in 1975, but the prospect of a rival league and an impending NFL players strike moved it forward a year. It might have been better to wait, as the WFL became the only one of the three Davidson leagues which did not result in at least some of its teams being taken into the pre-existing league.

I was one of what Gary called the "Founding Fathers" of the WFL. Bob Schmertz was another, and so were Ben Hatskin, Nick Mileti and Johnny Bassett, most of the WHA's "better" owners. Johnny had the Toronto franchise, called the Northmen, and had made a huge splash when he signed Paul Warfield, Larry Csonka and Jim Kiick, the stars of the Miami Dolphins' 1972 undefeated season. Those signings would eventually get Johnny and me out of a little hot water, but that's a WHA tale for a little later on. The Northmen never played in Toronto, because the Canadian government threatened legislative action to protect the CFL, and Johnny moved the team to Memphis.

My team, the Boston Bulls, never played in Boston either. I put some of my own money into it for the franchise start-up, part of which was for designing a logo. I can prove that the Chicago Bulls' snorting bull of today is a replica of our logo from the WFL.

I hired Babe Parilli, the famous old Patriot, as coach and Dusty Rhodes, the first female general manager, but I soon learned that I had way too much on my plate. I couldn't do the football and also handle the responsibilities of the hockey team moving to Hartford, so I made a deal with Davidson and Schmertz that Gary would help me sell the Boston football franchise and I would then relocate Babe and Dusty to Bob's franchise in New York City, the Stars, to help him get the team started there. Gary negotiated the sale of my former franchise to a Canadian gentleman named Bob Harris, who relocated the team to Portland, Oregon.

The New York Stars were playing at Downing Stadium on Randall's Island, a dismal place and the worst stadium in the league, and were going up against the Jets and Giants, so they didn't have much chance of succeeding despite getting a lot of publicity. I was already trying to get Schmertz out of the New England Whalers because of his financial setbacks, and soon he said, "Howard, *please* get me out of this too!"

A famous Broadway producer named David Merrick, who had won at least one Tony every single year since 1958, had called Bob when he heard the Stars were for sale. Bob said to me, "You handle Merrick. I just don't have the patience, the guy's high-maintenance." I did, and found he was a delightful guy to meet with. He made an offer for me to convey to Bob of $4 million. This would clear up the balance sheet for Bob, but would have given him no profit. Bob rejected it and said to look around for a better offer. After a while he called back and asked if I could go back to Merrick and see if I could revive the offer he had made. Merrick then said, "You tell that partner of yours I wouldn't pay a dollar for that team. He had his chance. It's over."

Then I reached out to Upton Bell, whose father, Bert, had been the commissioner of the NFL. Upton had been Patriots GM but was fired by the Sullivans. He loved football and was dying to get a team. Upton acquired the team for no cash down, and everything Bob was to receive was on the "if-come." If the money came, he would get some.

We signed this deal in Bob's beautiful Fifth Avenue apartment in NYC. I was relieved for Bob, as I now had been able to sell off his interest in Hartford and in the WFL. At the end of signing the documents Upton said, with a straight face, "Bob, this is so great, thanks for everything, *and* could you loan me 15 grand to open up an office?"

Despite that, Upton had enough money to get the team off Bob's back, out of New York and into Charlotte.

Almost everybody but Johnny in Memphis and Bill Putnam in Birmingham were announcing bogus attendance figures. The league had a very short life, which was probably longer than it deserved.

Hockey Comes to Hartford

With Boston in our past and Hartford in our future, our present was in Springfield, Massachusetts. With the Hartford Civic Center not scheduled to open until mid-January of 1975, the Big E in Springfield was where we would be for the 1974 playoffs and to start the 1974–75 WHA season.

The Big E was a relic of a building that was home to the AHL's Springfield Indians, owned by the famous and sometimes infamous Eddie Shore. It was a classic "cow palace," home to the state fair and also used for livestock exhibitions, rodeos and concerts. It was loaded with character, but that didn't help us in the 1974 playoffs. We were eliminated in the first round by Chicago, losing the seventh game 3–2 at "home."

We played a weird schedule in year three because, from mid-November until December 5, we had only one home game and 13 on the road. But we went 7–6 in those games, on the way to winning the East Division for the third time in the WHA's first three years.

The league had expanded to 14 teams, adding Phoenix and Indianapolis as expansion teams, and now had a Canadian division with Quebec, Toronto, Winnipeg, Vancouver and the Edmonton Oilers, who had dropped the "Alberta" from their name. And while we were planning our move from Boston to Springfield to Hartford, the Jersey Knights had already moved to San Diego as the Mariners, and the Los Angeles Sharks had moved to Detroit to become the Michigan Stags. It was a lot to keep up with. (The WHA would never get any larger than that. By January of 1975, Michigan was dead and we moved the Stags to Baltimore as a league-owned team called the Blades, just to finish the year. They were then folded at the end of the season.)

On January 11, 1975, the Whalers moved into the Hartford Civic Center, the arena part of which was called the Veterans Memorial Coliseum. It was a watershed moment for the city and for hockey too.

What was so incredible was that the city leaders had built an arena in a mall and made it into an entertainment center. One end of the arena ran along Trumbull Street and one of the long sides ran along Asylum Street. When we moved in, the arena had

10,500 seats for hockey, with no private boxes, which were still a luxury of the future. Since the arena footprint was small, the pitch of the seats had to be quite steep, so the sightlines were great. I remember at the beginning, though, we had to switch seats for some people who were a little anxious about the height.

Flanking the other two sides of the arena were two floors of mall spaces, with as many as nine restaurants, and upscale stores — Hartford is an insurance town, so there was money, a very high per-capita income — and a third floor of offices. The two outside streets which ran along the arena would restrict any building expansion for the future, but that was absolutely the last thing on our minds at the time. We were ecstatic to be in the new rink, and the city was glad to have us, and to have the downtown complex. You had the arena, you could shop, you could go to dinner. We were the first place that really had that. Now every arena and every stadium is replicating in some form what we did back in the early '70s — an entertainment destination center built around an arena.

It probably helped that we were doing pretty well (21–15–2) by the time we left Springfield to move to our new home, but the Whalers were welcomed with open arms from the start. Tom Webster, Larry Pleau and Wayne "Swoop" Carleton were scoring, and we still had the solid defence and Al Smith in goal. Hartford now had its own pro team, and the fans came out in droves.

We won our first game in Hartford 4–3 in overtime, over San Diego. I remember it was Gary Swain who scored the winning goal. After Minnesota beat us in our fourth home game, we went a month before losing again at home, and after the first 18 games at the Civic Center, we'd won 13 and tied 3. Obviously the Civic Center felt like home.

Our average attendance that year was only seventh in the league, at 7,845 per game, because we'd spent the first half of the season at the Big E, but the big crowds in Hartford were pushing it

up. In the playoffs, we averaged 10,174, and that probably would
have gone higher if we hadn't been put out in the first round. We
lost in six games to the Minnesota Fighting Saints, who had four
of the toughest players in the game in Gord Gallant, Jack Carlson,
Bill Butters and Ron Busniuk. Gallant had led the league in penalties the previous two years, but any of the others was capable of
that too. They were an intimidating, violent team. (Busniuk, Butters and Carlson all eventually ended up with the Whalers.)

The reason we did well in Hartford, even when we had some
weaker teams later on, was that the front office was solid. And the
market was solid too. It was the perfect blend of the corporate and
the political coming together in harmony. The key people in the
early years were Don Conrad from the Aetna; Nick Carbone, the
power broker on city council; and seven or eight business leaders from the insurance companies that owned the team who were
going to make damn sure that this team succeeded. The city had
built the arena, and the corporate sector had landed the team to
make Hartford a better place, building up the civic pride, and they
really threw themselves into it.

The half-dozen largest insurance companies in Hartford at the
time employed about 50,000 or 60,000 people, so you had a virtual
market within a market that we could call upon for sales. What we
did, led by Bill Barnes, was learn to implement the team sales into
their marketing culture. If you had a mid-week game against an
opponent that was somewhat of a dud, you'd get the word out that
there would be discounted tickets.

From my Flyers experience I had already learned a lot about
ticketing, marketing and listening to your customers. We applied
those lessons in Hartford. What I'm most proud of was that when
the Hartford team was sold in 1988, we had the third-highest gross
gate in the league, while playing in the smallest market and in an
arena with the smallest capacity.

In 1975–76, our first full season in the Civic Center, an average of 9,380 people came downtown on game night. That was second-highest in the WHA that year, just behind Quebec. The Nordiques were an exciting team with French flair, and Marc Tardif was setting the world on fire with 71 goals and 148 points. The league had clearly found a part of its identity in major scoring stars and rugged brawlers. Ulf Nilsson and Anders Hedberg had arrived the year before to play on the "Hot Line" with Bobby Hull, perhaps the greatest line in hockey history, and the European style was beginning to brand our league. Eleven players, including Hull and Gordie Howe, had 100 points or more, and six players broke the 50-goal plateau. But the WHA also had nine players with 200 or more minutes in penalties, and two, Curt Brackenbury and Kim Clackson, with more than 350 — nearly five minutes per game. Ron Busniuk, who came to us partway through that season after Minnesota folded, had 205 minutes, the first time a Whaler's name was associated with 200 or more minutes.

Things never stayed still in the WHA, and we started the 1975–76 season with 14 teams again, with the Denver Spurs and Cincinnati Stingers as expansion franchises, and with the Vancouver Blazers having moved to Calgary. But the Spurs were a bust in Denver, and the day after New Year's had to move to Ottawa, where they became the Civics. The Civics lasted a mere two weeks before they folded. And in late February the Minnesota Fighting Saints were disbanded. The players were disbursed to other teams, but it was nerve-wracking for the rest of the franchises, creating scheduling and legal nightmares and casting an air of instability over the league.

The WHA was still a 12-team league, but it was being driven by Canada: Edmonton, Winnipeg, Quebec and Calgary. One third of the league was north of the border, which was a much higher percentage than the NHL had (3 of 17) at the time.

I've always disagreed with those who say that Canadian teams aren't attractions in the bigger American cities. When Winnipeg had Hedberg, Nilsson and Hull, everybody knew about the Jets. Nobody had any trouble figuring out who Edmonton was once they had a great team, or the Nordiques when they excelled. We established and nurtured great rivalries in the WHA. In Hartford we sold out many a game against Indianapolis, Cincinnati and Birmingham, where you didn't have "natural" rivalries already existing. It was a competitive and well-balanced league.

We had a good post-season in 1975–76, averaging 10,100 fans per game after sweeping Cleveland in the first round, and then beating Indianapolis in seven games in the next round to advance to meet Houston in the semifinal. The Howes' Aeros had won the last two Avco cups and still had their mojo, edging us in the seventh game in Houston to go to the final. There they were swept by the Jets, who won the final two games at home by a total of 15–4. It was the first WHA title for the Jets, who would also win two of the next, and final, three Avco cups.

The fourth season of the WHA was over. We didn't know it then, but that was the middle year of our rebel league's life span. The more stable and better-financed franchises like Winnipeg, New England and Quebec were having success on the ice and at the gate, but most teams were losing big money, and franchises were moving or folding with alarming frequency.

Change was definitely in the air.

The First Go at Pittsburgh

We were selling the WHA as if it was going to keep going on, and we sold it well. Our fans loved it, and they kept showing up at 9,000 or 10,000 a night, even in 1975–76 and 1976–77, the New England Whalers' only two seasons below .500. Of course, it didn't hurt that we managed to make the third round of the playoffs in the spring of '76.

Two teams dropped out in the middle of that season and two more moved before the start of the 1976–77 season: Johnny Bassett transferred Toronto to Birmingham, where they became the Bulls, and Cleveland went to St. Paul to become the second incarnation of the Minnesota Fighting Saints. Yet, once again, Minnesota dropped out during the season, earning the nickname "the Folding Saints."

It's important to know about the mindset of my corporate partners at this time. The mandate from them, led by Don Conrad, had become, "We've got to get out of this league." It was clear that the league was shrinking every year. My partners were Fortune 500 companies and didn't want the uncertainty every spring about whether the league would be able to continue to operate. And at the time we were losing money. Not a lot, but we were losing.

By then, the Whalers had become leaders of the league, which benefited Hartford. The partners told me to try to make a merger happen or to find some other way to get out of the league. So we went down a couple of different paths: the merger path and the sub rosa path, which was to try to pick off an NHL franchise under distress, buy it, and jump leagues.

Which leads me to a story that not too many people know about.

Ed DeBartolo Sr. bought the Pittsburgh Penguins from Al Savill in February 1977. I soon reached out to Mr. DeBartolo about the possibility of acquiring the team from him. He referred me to his associate, Vincent Bartimo. Think Charles Bronson . . . and that's Bartimo. Cap and I met Bartimo at the Boston Airport, and to make a long story short, we did a deal to buy the Penguins. We were going to pay $4 million for the team.

I had the Aetna and the other partners all set, but on a Saturday morning Mr. DeBartolo called me, and I will never forget this call, as it plays a role in how I ended up owning part of the Penguins nearly 15 years later.

"Howard," he said, "we can't do the deal."

"Okay," I said. "But why?"

"My lawyers tell me, and I'm sure when you really dive into it your lawyers will tell you too, that we'll be sued for the next 20 years because the WHA will go out of business if New England leaves. My people and my league will never allow the sale. We just have to walk away from it. Now, I want your word that this will never get out."

I said it never would, and it never has. Until now.

I reported back to my partners, and they said we just had to continue trying to operate. The league was doing some cutting-edge things. For example, we had regular-season overtime. And because the league would be shrinking in size, we did play games that counted in our standings against European teams like the Czech All-Stars and the Soviet All-Stars. We were doing everything we could to make the league as interesting and exciting as possible. And Bill MacFarland had taken over as president, which was viewed very positively.

Letting Loose South of the Border

The one thing we all did in the WHA was have a hell of a lot of fun. We may have fought in the boardroom, but we all liked each other and when the meeting ended we would go arm in arm to a restaurant together and enjoy a nice evening out.

There were some hysterical moments at some of our league meetings. One of them was when the league was starting to get embroiled in lawsuits from disgruntled former owners.

At the annual meeting in La Costa, California, at the end of our fourth season, there was suddenly a loud knock at the conference-room door. In walked three or four armed sheriff's deputies carrying boxes of lawsuit material. This particular suit had come from Dr. Leonard Bloom, an early owner of the Los Angeles Sharks, who had also been part of the ABA and signed Wilt Chamberlain for his San Diego franchise. He'd sued the ABA too.

Johnny Bassett and I had become great friends by then. He came from a sports family — his father, John, had been a minority owner of the Toronto Maple Leafs and had cast the deciding vote to chase majority owner Harold Ballard into fraud charges. Johnny had played on Canada's Davis Cup team and was a film producer. Eventually, I would do my first film with him.

Once the initial shock of the incoming lawsuit had passed, Johnny and I just looked at each other and burst out laughing and decided it was time to leave the meeting and let loose. So we arranged to rent a car, then had too much to drink and said, "Let's head down to Tijuana," which was maybe an hour away, but with an international border in between.

On the way down, with Johnny driving, we got caught for speeding.

Johnny explained that he was a Canadian and unfamiliar with the road laws in the U.S. The cop let him off with a warning.

We kept on going, crossed the border into Mexico, and found a seedy-looking bar with dirt floors and started enjoying the tequila. We couldn't have been dressed more inappropriately for the setting. I was wearing white pants, a white shirt and my New

England Whalers blazer, and Johnny was dressed in his blue blazer. We looked totally out of place. At two in the morning, we decided to leave in order to make it to our next meeting in La Costa, which was at 9 a.m. I said I needed to hit the head before we left, but that I wasn't going to go in the bar's bathroom, because it was so dirty.

I was standing beside the car taking a leak on the dirt parking lot and all of a sudden I felt these arms grabbing me, and it's these two military policemen. They said, "You don't take a leak in our parking lot." I'm thinking, "Oh my God, here we are. 'Two WHA Owners Get Arrested'. . ." and I started mentally writing the next day's headlines. I said I was sorry, but they were still going to take me to jail.

We were hammered, but Johnny collects himself and he brings out this huge wad of cash and says, "We're going to settle this right now, boys." He takes the guy's hand and he slaps down a twenty in his palm. And another twenty. And *another* twenty until he gets up to 100. Then he folds the guy's hand up and says, "That's enough for taking a leak in a government parking lot in Tijuana. *Comprende?* Baldy, get in the car, we're going home." Those guys just stood there, and the looks on their faces said they couldn't believe these two preppy guys had just pulled what they had.

We fled the premises, crossed the border and immediately got arrested again. We were flying because we had to make the meeting, and 10 miles past the border a cop stopped us for speeding. And boy, he was a hard-ass. Johnny was driving, again, so he says to the guy, "Are you a football fan?" And the cop says, "Oh yeah!" So Johnny says, "Well, I'm the guy who signed Csonka, Kiick and Warfield." And it had just been on the cover of *Sports Illustrated*. The cop says, "No, you're not." Then he looks at Johnny, thinks about it a bit, and says, "Okay, I'm going to take your word for it." And we got off again.

We had about an hour to shower and shave and we made the meeting by 9 a.m.

When it's called to order, Johnny puts up his hand and says, "I'm going to tell everybody here the story . . . and then I'm going to pass the hat, because we just saved this league a lot of embarrassment! We're going to have a special league assessment right now because our illustrious partner here just took a hundred-dollar leak in Tijuana." The room broke up with raucous laughter and everybody kicked in.

As I said, those were the fun days.

And Howe! (And Howe, and Howe)

One day early in the fall of 1976, I received a call from George Bolin, who owned the Houston Aeros of the WHA.

Do you remember Rock Hudson in the movie *Giant*? If you do, well, that's George: blue jeans, big belt buckle, Stetson, cowboy boots.

"Howard," George said, "I can't take it anymore. Colleen Howe's driving me crazy. So I'm trading the Howes to you right now. They're all yours."

I started to say, "George, what . . ." But he just hung up the phone.

Gordie, Mark and Marty Howe were starting the fourth year of the four-year deal they had in Houston. People knew they were discontented there, and Colleen, who acted as the agent for her sons and husband, was pushing for the Aeros to do the right thing by her family — either sign them for what they were worth, or trade them. We quickly learned that a trade was not possible. Gordie had never been traded in his career and didn't want to start now.

Plus the Howes were honorable people and wanted to abide by their four-year commitment to Houston.

Colleen could be absolutely relentless, and George just didn't understand her.

She was years ahead of her time. She was a staunch advocate for Gordie and the boys, and they could not have had a better agent than her. She was the first female to do this kind of job, and the fact that she was also the wife and mother didn't make it easier. Added to that, clearly George was a male chauvinist and had a hard time dealing with Colleen running point on the negotiations. He'd even hired a psychiatrist to pose as an accountant during negotiations because he was so puzzled by Colleen.

We had never had a pre-established star with the Whalers, and I had always mentioned to George that if he was thinking of trading Gordie, I'd be interested. After he called me, Ronnie Ryan, who was our GM then, said, "He can't be serious. Let's just see what happens."

Then my phone rang again, and it was Colleen. She had a really good sense of humor about it all, and she asked, "Did you happen to get a phone call from George Bolin?"

"Yes I did, Colleen, and I want you to know that I had nothing to do with this other than to take the call."

She said, "We can't wait to negotiate with you, when it's time to negotiate. But we're going to make them pay the Howes for this coming year. We're not going anywhere, and I just wanted you to know that."

We then shared a good laugh over Bolin.

I was very amenable to that plan. We knew that Boston was going to react strongly, because Mark was drafted by Boston and we knew they wanted him in the worst way. Detroit still owned Gordie's NHL rights (and we later made a gentleman's agreement with them not to claim him back when we joined the NHL) and Montreal owned Marty's rights. Everybody assumed that Mark Howe would be going to the Bruins after the Houston deal was up, and if he went there they would have created a chance for Marty there too. We really wanted them in Hartford but thought we had very little chance. The Howes knew as much as I did about the potential merger with the NHL that we were working on that season. They knew that if they were in Houston and Houston didn't get into the NHL in the merger, they'd probably go to Boston because they would have no choice.

My pitch was that we wanted all four of them in Hartford.

"Colleen, I want you in the office with me. We're going to market the family. This is just not one young man signing to play hockey. We want Gordie involved, we want Marty, we want you in the office. We want the family."

At the time we weren't doing as well on the ice as we had been, so we needed a jolt and something to add enthusiasm not only to the fan base but, overall, to the mind-set of my partners as well. Signing the Howes would be a huge coup all the way around.

The negotiations took time and weren't easy.

I think if you asked Mark or Marty, they'd say we won it because we pitched for the family. I genuinely liked Colleen. She knew it, and I think Gordie knew it. I respected the hell out of the fact that she was years ahead of her time. She could drive you nuts at times, but I loved her. She worked hard for her children and for her family. She was a good person and she had a terrific sense of humor, which helped.

I remember one time they came into Hartford and my son, Howard Jr., was about five, and he had these new cowboy boots. We were driving to the airport and Colleen said, "Those are nice boots, did your dad get them for you?" "Yeah," he said. "These are my shit-kickers." She got the biggest kick out of it.

That spring we lost in the first round of the playoffs and Houston was eliminated in the second round, so by mid-May the Howes were finished with their contracts and had gone to a friend's farm back near Detroit. And negotiations began, not only with us but with Boston as well.

After some long back-and-forth negotiations, I finally said to Colleen, "We are going to come to Detroit and stay with it until we get it done."

I sent Jack Kelley and Davie Andrews to Detroit on a Wednesday and told them to call me when it was getting close. Poor Jack, he was old-school, and he didn't have a whole lot of patience for these kinds of protracted negotiations.

After two days of their discussions in Detroit, Jack and Davie called me and said, "You come in. Now is the time to either get this done, or end it." I could tell they were right out of gas on it.

I went to Detroit immediately and drove out to the farm, and there was Colleen in the middle of a field with some llamas. There was also a goat. And as I was climbing over the fence to go see her, I got attacked by the goat and it bit me on the side of the leg. (At our first press conference she gave me a figurine of a goat to commemorate the event.)

After a wonderful dinner all together, we went back to the hotel to try to close the deal. At around midnight Gordie could sense that I was running out of gas too. He stood up and said to Colleen, "Let's go in the other room and talk it over."

Jack and Davie and I sat there, and within half an hour the door opened and Colleen said, "Congratulations, you've got yourself some Howe hockey players."

We were elated as well as exhausted, particularly Jack and Davie, who had a two-day jump on me.

I knew it would take a while to get them on a formal contract. The Howes were not quick in this area, and in fact when we got into the NHL, all three Howes played on WHA contracts for a while — probably the only players ever to play in the NHL without NHL contracts. But I knew the most important thing for me to do was get the deal announced quickly because I didn't want anyone changing their minds. I knew the Bruins would make a last-ditch effort to sweep in so I said, "Colleen, we have to announce this at the beginning of next week." And she went right along with it.

Unbeknownst to me, they apparently didn't call the Bruins at all to tell them they had signed with the Whalers, or if they did they just left a message. That didn't help my relationship with the Bruins during merger talks with the NHL.

The deal was for 10 years — 350 grand a year for Mark, for Marty and for us to be able to market the family. When Gordie decided to play, we paid him an extra 100K per year. At first we weren't 100 per cent certain Gordie would play, because he was 49 and was making his mind up every season during training camp — but, that said, we were 99 per cent sure he would play!

This was a huge moment for us. We already had 4,000 or 5,000 season tickets and had never played before for less than a 75 per cent paid house, and now we had the Howes. It was good for season tickets and just general fan interest. We had a great press conference on the Monday, and it was the biggest announcement that the Whalers ever made.

Merge Ahead

At some point in the early winter of 1977, Don Conrad reached out through a mutual friend to Arthur Wirtz, owner of the Blackhawks and Bill's father, with the hope of opening some dialogue regarding the NHL and WHA merging.

So a dinner was organized at Arthur Wirtz's home in Chicago, with Arthur, Bill, Don Conrad and me. Clearly, Mr. Wirtz Sr. was fed up with losing money. As hard as it may be to believe today, the Blackhawks, Red Wings and even the Bruins were only drawing 4,000 to 5,000 people to some games. The sport was suffering and something had to be done.

And while the WHA was constantly worried about teams moving and folding, the NHL was not immune to instability at that point either. Before the 1976–77 season, the NHL, which hadn't had a franchise relocate in 42 years, had two site changes: the Kansas City Scouts moved to Denver and the California Golden Seals moved to Cleveland. And a rumored expansion to Denver and Seattle was killed.

Up until that point, Bill Wirtz had been a hawk in regard to the WHA, but Arthur had clearly given him a mandate to see what he could do with the WHA guys. That's when a committee from each league was formed.

The WHA committee had Bill DeWitt, Nelson Skalbania and me. Bill was the owner of the Cincinnati Stingers and really wanted to get into the NHL. He is a great guy and now owns the St. Louis Cardinals of Major League Baseball. Bill would have been a great owner for the NHL too. For the NHL, the committee included Bill Wirtz, Gil Stein, Peter O'Malley, Sam Pollock and John Ziegler.

We met in Montreal, because that's where the NHL held their annual meetings in conjunction with the draft. The discussions we had after the first WHA season had been kept quiet, but people were well aware of the 1977 meetings. We tried to keep them secret but the media got wind of it right away, and everywhere Bill and I went we were followed. We'd pick up the Montreal papers the next day and they knew not only who we'd had dinner with, but also what we had to eat.

Also, the lines were hardening. Harold Ballard referred to me in the paper as some "mackerel-snapper from Providence." So, foolishly, instead of just shutting up, I said, "At least we don't have a league of people who have gone to prison." That made the headlines in Canada. I referred to Clarence Campbell too, I'm afraid. It was pretty heavy, but it was true. So then guys like Ziegler got mad at me, and I was wondering why they didn't get mad at their own people.

I saw Clarence Campbell, the NHL president, only once at any of those meetings, and it was quite a sighting. We were in his hotel suite, and he always travelled with his secretary, so there were two bedrooms off the suite. I'll never forget this. It was me, Nelson and Bill, talking with Pollock, Wirtz and Ziegler, and the door opens and it was Clarence Campbell . . . completely naked. He walks casually through our room to the other bedroom and says, on the way, "Good evening, gentlemen!"

I swear to God.

Out of those meetings came a plan that, to this day, I think was brilliant. Six WHA teams were going to be admitted to the NHL, and it would be called an expansion in order to get around antitrust issues. But of course it was a merger.

Edmonton, Quebec, Winnipeg, Houston, Cincinnati and New England from the WHA would form our own division, and we would phase in with the existing NHL teams over five years.

We all had to fill out application forms and file 18 copies with the league, one for every one of its teams. One Saturday morning I got a call from Mr. Campbell and he said, "We've got a problem." I'm thinking to myself, "We've got more than one." But apparently the Quebec Nordiques had filled out their application completely in French. I called Marcel Aubut, the Nordiques lawyer, and said, "You're just trying to stick it up their ass!" Which he was. We did get all the i's dotted and t's crossed, but then in August, the militants — Ballard, Paul Mooney from Boston and Molson Brewery, the Canadiens owner — got their steam up and we were voted out of the NHL again. They pulled the plug and were able to undo all that we had done.

So we got in in June and were out in August. Nice.

It was after that decision that I took over as WHA president and we moved the league headquarters to Hartford. Everybody knew that the handwriting was on the wall for the WHA. Our ownership was the strongest in the league, without question, so the other teams felt that I was the guy to handle the NHL merger. Primarily, I was there to make sure that a merger got done, because without it, at some point we were all going to be toast. We were like Lily Tomlin in *The Incredible Shrinking Woman* — eventually we were all going down that little drain.

It was during these merger discussions that we knew for sure we had to shrink the league. So we changed the way we handled franchise problems. When a team got into dire economic straits and had to surrender, not only would we not bail the owner out, we'd swoop in there, pay him two or three or four hundred grand and get fully signed releases. We wanted total transparency so nobody could say they were forced out of business and come after us legally. And there was nothing that the players' union could do.

That was our approach that spring and summer, when San Diego, Calgary and Phoenix dropped out. We didn't bail them out, move them or seek expansion replacements. And those of us who knew we might be going on to the NHL one day improved our teams with players from the folded teams, as we did in New England with Dave Keon and John McKenzie from Minnesota. But some teams weren't going to be able to go on; they just weren't.

So we opened the 1977–78 season with eight teams in only one division, and added some spice by playing all-star teams from the Soviet Union and Czechoslovakia when they toured North

America, and we counted the results in our standings.

I wanted to be home for my family as much as possible, so I made a deal with the league that I would be president and wouldn't take any salary, as long as I could charter a plane for the meetings far away so I could get right back to Hartford to take care of the family. Ron Ryan was the day-to-day head of operations for the league. My partners in Hartford were delighted that I was willing to do this, as they knew that without a healthy league, there would be no Whalers.

After the NHL had voted us out in August 1977, we immediately had a WHA meeting in Toronto, and we all looked at each other and said, "Look, we've got to come up with a strategy that will kick these guys in the balls." We wanted to attack them where they were most vulnerable in order to bring them back to the table and effect a merger.

So part one of the plan was to sign underage juniors. I had already been fined $100,000 by the league (which I never paid) a couple of years earlier when we signed Gordie Roberts at the age of 17, when both we and the NHL had rules which said nobody under 20 could play in our leagues.

And part two of the plan was to drive the prices of the NHL's players as high as we could, and still not quite sign them ourselves. I remember sitting with Rod Gilbert in Don Conrad's office and we offered him 175 grand a year for five years because it was time to give the Rangers a little message. The whole time I was saying to myself, "I hope to God this guy doesn't take this contract." And he didn't. We targeted players from the NHL clubs that we knew had money, so they could afford to match our offers when we drove the price up. This also had a ripple effect with the other players that they were trying to sign.

What was most effective, however, was signing the 18- and 19-year-old junior players. That really got them.

Ken Linseman was already challenging the NHL's draft-age rules in Canadian courts when Johnny Bassett signed him as a 19-year-old junior in 1977. We knew *exactly* what we were doing on the Linseman thing. It was all orchestrated.

Art Kaminsky represented Kenny and we knew he'd challenge our age requirements. We also knew it would be thrown out right away because Kenny was over 18 and he had a right to sign a contract. So we went into a Hartford court and Kenny and his father got an injunction against the WHA, so Kenny was allowed to play in Birmingham. Perfect. The ruling soon changed the way the NHL handled their junior draft too, but for us it was just what we needed at the time.

We didn't want to tick off the Canadian amateur hockey system, so I had to publicly fine Johnny for going against the league rules. Like my fine with Roberts, it was $100,000. And like my fine with Roberts, Johnny never paid it. I even went down to Birmingham to fine him, and from the outside it looked like we were battling, but really we were having the usual great time together.

In typical Johnny fashion, he was portraying himself in the media as the victim in the case. "Look what I'm doing for Birmingham, and look what the league is doing to me." So during the game Bulls fans are pounding on the door of the private box trying to get at me because I'd fined their beloved owner.

Johnny was nervy and, like every WHA owner, he ran into lots of interesting situations regarding player personnel. In the league's second year, Ken Dryden had taken a year off to go back to school because he was unhappy with the Montreal Canadiens' contract offer. Johnny had him doing color commentary for the Toros, his Toronto franchise, and thought he had him ready to play for the team the next year. But when the Toros went down to play against the New York Golden Blades at the Cherry Hill Arena in Jersey, my first rink in the game, it took Ken about half an hour just to squeeze into the ridiculous press gondola. "There's no way I'm playing in this league," he said. "No way." And Johnny would always laugh about it: "That goddamn game cost me my goaltender."

And the year after he signed Linseman, Johnny kept playing his role as a pain in the ass to the NHL by signing the six underage "Baby Bulls" — Gaston Gingras, Pat Riggin, Rob Ramage, Craig Hartsburg, Michel Goulet and Rick Vaive — which really helped get an agreement with the NHL. Today, people forget that great players came through the WHA and that's what got the NHL to stay at the table to the point where we got a deal done.

The Roof Collapse

I was able to spend so much time on league-related business in 1977 because we had such a good and reliable staff with the Whalers. Davie Andrews was running the business operations, Bill Barnes was a terrific marketer, and my secretary, Camille Beck, was absolutely key to the organization. Ron Ryan was our general manager and Harry Neale behind the bench really had the team going. Al Smith was on his way to becoming the first-team All-Star goalie, and the Howes were playing great. We would eventually make it to the league finals against Winnipeg — Hull vs. Howe for the championship — which, sadly, the Jets won in four straight.

By late November we were 15–1–1, and at the break for the All-Star Game in Quebec, we were still 25–11–3. It had become WHA standard that the night before the All-Star Game there would be a big banquet. I'd gone up there with Brewster Perkins, my old friend and classmate from Salisbury School, and we took part in all the festivities.

At 6 a.m. the next day, the phone in my room woke me out of a deep sleep, and it was a radio reporter from Hartford. "The roof on the Hartford Civic Center has collapsed," he said, and he wanted my reaction.

But I figured it was too early in the morning and asked him to call back later.

I just figured, "So the roof blew off. The roof blew off in Philly too, so probably some tar paper came off in Hartford and we'll just fix it. No big deal."

Then the phone started ringing again and again, all reporters, and then Davie Andrews called and said, "Howard, this is a real mess here. This is bad."

I knew then that this was not the same as the Spectrum roof problem 10 years earlier. This time there was serious structural damage. We found out later that there was a faulty drainage system on the roof, and the extra weight of the frozen snow and ice from a 10-day storm caused the collapse.

Luckily, it happened at 4 a.m. The night before, 7,000 people had been in the building for a UConn basketball game. There were reports that a falling bolt had almost hit a basketball fan, so maybe that should have been a warning. The closest anybody got to being hurt, though, was a homeless person whose sleep was interrupted by the noise of the collapse. He got a few minutes of national fame describing the horrific sound.

I asked Davie to get everyone together and try to work it out with Springfield for a temporary place to play. It was a critical time in our relationship with the NHL, and everybody in the WHA knew that the continued health of the Whalers was critical if the league was going to have any chance with the NHL. In our Quebec hotel, my league partners were already begging us to find a way to continue. The tension was incredible.

I then called Camille and had her arrange for a jet to come into Quebec and pick up Brewster and me. But a blizzard started pelting Quebec City, and I don't like white-knuckle flights, which this one would be, if we could even get off the ground. I'd flown before with the pilot who was coming to get me, and he's a great guy, but I was almost hoping that he would decide not to come in. But he did: he landed, collected us and took back off, the last plane allowed out of the airport for the next 24 hours. But it's not as bad flying out of a blizzard as it is into one, and soon we hit blue sky.

When we got near Hartford, the pilot said, "Howard, do you want to fly over the building?" I said, "Yeah," still hoping it was not that big a deal.

Wrong. It looked like a scene out of a Godzilla movie, with the left foot of Godzilla stomping on the roof of the Civic Center. It was just steel beams jutting up into the air.

"Holy shit," I said. "What a mess. We are so screwed."

The story had already gone national and dozens of reporters were waiting at the landing strip, but we emphasized that this was an emergency and told them we would have a formal press conference later.

It was our front office's finest hour. Bill and Dave had already nailed down the new Springfield Civic Center, and by late that evening we had a whole schedule worked out for the half-season left to play.

We had a partnership meeting that night and the partners, led by Don Conrad, were extraordinary in their commitment to the franchise and to the city. I suggested that our options were either to give up and fold, or to fund losses while the Civic Center was rebuilt, however long that would take.

Nobody missed a beat. They said, "This is a crippling blow to the city. But we sure aren't losing a building and the team. We're keeping the team here. So, Howard, you come to us with a plan."

We came back within 48 hours and, noting that there were only 7,800 seats in Springfield, suggested that all the partnership corporations could buy enough season tickets and sponsorships to ensure there were no losses until we got back to Hartford. And that's what happened. They were 100 per cent behind me, and this should give some clear insight to anybody who has ever wondered why I stayed so loyal to those partners and to the City of Hartford.

Within four days, we were in Springfield. Bill Barnes — who, as I have previously said, was a marketing genius — lived up to that reputation by creating the 91 Club, in reference to the highway Whalers fans took from Hartford to Springfield. The club created the perception of Whaler fans being extra-loyal ones, making the drive to see their team. At the first game in Springfield, the late, great Governor Ella Grasso, who was a devoted Whalers fan and a friend of mine, cut the ribbon to inaugurate what would be a two-year stay in Springfield. By the time the Civic Center was rebuilt, the Whalers would be halfway through our first season in the NHL, so we had played our last WHA game in Hartford (a 5–4 overtime loss to Houston).

Until we started writing this book, I hadn't realized how little time we'd spent in Hartford as a WHA team. We didn't get into the Civic Center until January of our third year, and the roof forced us out in January of our sixth year. And Springfield saved our asses a couple of times — before we moved into Hartford, and when the roof collapsed.

My partners were at my side during the press conference when I said, "Even if it means flooding my own backyard on Prospect Avenue, this franchise is going to continue to operate and will not miss a beat." The quote made just about every media outlet in North America.

For me, it was one of the proudest moments for our franchise, the staff, the partners and the city.

For the Whalers, in a way, the hockey gods had shone on us. We had only 10,500 seats in the Civic Center and the most we could have economically gone up to with a renovation was 12,500. But the NHL had a 14,500-minimum capacity rule at the time. We didn't know if they would stick to that with us, but we were worried. When we had to rebuild, we could get the capacity up to 15,500, so without the roof collapse we may never have qualified to get into the NHL.

The Whalers and ESPN

The first time we came to Springfield, in 1974, we hired a charismatic fellow named Bill Rasmussen, the sports director of WWLP TV, as the commentator on our game broadcasts. He became Whalers' director of communications and sold ads for us too. Sometime during the winter of 1978, we decided to go in a different direction with our advertising sales and were going to employ young people on a commission-only basis.

So Bill and I both agreed it was necessary to part company. He gave me a big hug, said he understood completely and that he appreciated the way I'd handled it, we'd keep in touch, yada yada yada. I don't like to burn bridges, and told him if there was anything I could ever to do help in the future, all he had to do was ask.

Cut to three or four months later, and Rasmussen came to visit me in the office, and when I asked him how he was doing, he said, "Great, I bought a little satellite time and signed up UConn, and

I'm starting an all-sports network out of Bristol, Connecticut."

He'd become the founder of ESPN!

Like all people, I was skeptical of his venture because I didn't think he'd get enough programming. However, being a dreamer myself, I supported him and said, "Billy, all I want you to do is promise me that the first pro hockey game that you put on ESPN will be the Whalers."

"You've got a deal," he said.

And he was good to his word. The first NHL game on ESPN was the Washington Capitals vs. the Hartford Whalers, and I think that conversation probably had a lot to do with that being the game.

The Final Six . . . and the Deal

We were going after junior players as part of our strategy to leverage the NHL, and there was no greater junior player ever than Wayne Gretzky. One day in the spring of 1978, Jack Kelley said to me, "Howard, I got a call from Gus Badali, Wayne Gretzky's agent, and he feels that we could sign Gretzky."

At the time, Wayne was a 17-year-old junior playing in Northern Ontario for the Soo Greyhounds and averaging about three points a game. Contacting us was smart for Gus, because we were the solid team in the WHA. And of course the league was signing juniors. Jack went up to Toronto and called to tell me that we actually could sign Gretzky.

But I'm thinking, "Now what do I do?" because I had only one objective, which was to get us into the NHL.

My thinking at the time was that, all things being equal, Hartford was not on the top of anyone's expansion list. The only way that Hartford was going to get into the NHL was by becoming a solution to a problem, not by creating new ones. So I felt, rightly or wrongly, that if we signed Gretzky, then we'd be on the NHL's shit list. Big time. And by then, we were the only American team that had a chance to get into the NHL, if they took any WHA teams in at all, not because of the city but because of the ownership. The NHL had a disease that wouldn't go away called the WHA. And the NHL knew we were the glue that was holding the WHA together, and so they had to get rid of us in order to get rid of the WHA. We were a solution to a problem.

So I said, "Jack, we can't do it, it will really hurt our chances of getting into the NHL." And he was pissed at me. We could have had Gordie Howe and Wayne Gretzky on the same line.

Although I didn't want to see him sign in New England, getting Gretzky into the WHA did fit the strategy of taking the cream of the junior crop. Therefore, I called up Nelson Skalbania in Indianapolis.

I called up Nelson because I knew he would understand that it was a huge opportunity and would help facilitate our strategy. And he knew his team wasn't getting into the NHL anyway. Why? Because Indianapolis was a small market not on the NHL radar, and we were pretty well convinced that the NHL wanted only four franchises: Quebec, Winnipeg, Edmonton and New England.

So Nelson flew in and signed Gretzky. Wayne played only eight games for Indianapolis before Nelson sold him and 50 per cent of the Edmonton Oilers to Peter Pocklington, who already owned the other half of the Oilers. Most leagues had a rule against owning more than one team, but we didn't.

Clearly, Indy wasn't working out for Nelson, so on December 15, he folded the Racers and we stuck to the process of shrinking the league rather than propping up the franchise. We bought him out, the way we bought out the others before him, as part of the cleanup that would be required to get into the NHL. The NHL wasn't going to do anything unless it was squeaky clean.

That meant we would finish the 1978–79 season with just six teams. The NHL had had its Original Six, and the WHA would have its Final Six.

By then, there was a lot of communication between the two leagues — we'd been playing pre-season games against each other for a while — and we had narrowed it down to which four WHA teams, if any, would be absorbed into the NHL: the Winnipeg Jets, with Barry Shenkarow and Michael Gobuty, who had bought the team from Benny Hatskin before the start of the season; Edmonton, with Peter Pocklington; Quebec, with ownership represented by their lawyer, Marcel Aubut; and us.

In the spring of 1978, Bob Caporale, Don Conrad and I went to the NHL's annual meeting in Detroit, where the league had just had a vote about formally trying to work something out with the WHA. John Ziegler and Bill Wirtz met with me, Don and the other three WHA team reps and informed us that the vote had failed. At the same time, they made it plain that it was very close and now was not the time to do anything foolish or rash. John Ziegler made it very clear: "Howard, hold your house together. You and I will stay in touch, let a couple of months go by, and we'll go right back at it at the end of the summer."

The feeling coming out of Detroit was that we were over the emotions and we could sit down like businessmen and make a deal. But we knew it wouldn't be easy, as the NHL still had a few militants, such as Harold Ballard. As we went into the late summer, Ziegler and I were on the phone frequently. He and Bill Wirtz told us not to give up and they urged us to work with David Stern, who was a lawyer from the enormously powerful Proskauer Rose law firm, which had major connections in sport. We were now getting into the realities of the legal ramifications of doing a merger between the two leagues, so we had to construct an environment that avoided anti-trust litigation from any and all parties. That is why when you read about any announcements from that period, it was always referred to as an expansion and not a merger. The strategy was that the WHA would fold and then four of the former franchises would be taken into the NHL as expansion teams. David Stern was the WHA lawyer for a short time before he went on to become general counsel for the NBA and, shortly thereafter, the NBA commissioner.

Dealing with our own side was extremely difficult too. It was a very delicate balance. Gobuty and Shenkarow in Winnipeg were great. Pocklington in Edmonton was great. Aubut in Quebec was a great partner, but he was way more hung up on keeping certain players, like Robbie Ftorek, than he should have been. We made the point to him that players had a short shelf life, but that this expansion would be forever. And if this deal broke up because of players, then New England was out and Quebec would end up with nothing.

But make a deal we did — or so we thought. Each WHA team would pay $4.25 million to get into the NHL. Each of us would be allowed up to four "priority selections" in the "expansion" draft, meaning we could each protect up to two skaters and two goalies. The NHL teams got to choose back WHA players whose rights they held — and the ones they didn't want, we could keep.

John Ziegler and I both felt confident that he could bring this framework to the NHL at its mid-winter meeting in the Florida Keys and, in our various cities, we all waited on pins and needles, hoping to get the good news from John. Don Conrad even had the Aetna jet ready to fly down to Florida if necessary.

Thursday morning at 8 a.m. the phone rang and it was John Ziegler. I thought it was going to be to tell me to get on the plane, although I knew that 8 a.m. phone calls are rarely good news.

"We couldn't get it done," he said. "We lost by two votes. Vancouver and Montreal shifted gears on me."

I could hear in John's voice the pure disappointment and frustration. Just imagine the common sense, or lack of it, of Montreal and Vancouver and the few others, including Toronto, who voted no. They were going to receive $17 million in cash, most of their players back, and economic stability. Yet six franchises voted against it. Even "stupid" is not sufficient enough to describe those six teams.

I immediately set up a call with our group and informed them of the news. We all agreed we had to give off the immediate impression of proactivity and solidarity. Which we did. In Hartford we held a press conference to do so, as did the other WHA teams.

What none of us predicted, though, was the backlash in Canada toward Vancouver and Montreal. Imagine, you had three Canadian teams that were getting into the NHL and you had three other Canadian teams killing that opportunity.

At the Molson office in Winnipeg, there was a drive-by shooting. Nobody got killed but the shots came through the office window. There was a national hue and cry and a massive negative reaction against Molson, which owned the Canadiens. And in Vancouver there was a huge outpouring against the Griffiths family, who owned the Canucks.

Now it's Friday and I wake up with a strange sensation, a premonition that maybe, just maybe, it is not over yet. Incredibly, my phone rings and it's John Ziegler. He says, "Howard, do you think you can get your guys back together? Molson has called up and they're going to change their vote, and so is Vancouver."

I said, "John, I will do my best," trying to sound a little uncertain, then I called a WHA meeting for early in the week in Toronto.

Shortly after John hung up, Morgan McCammon, the chairman of the board of Molson, also called. In his deep voice he said,

"We made a mistake and I'm really counting on you to keep your guys together. I'd really like to fly you up to Toronto, have dinner with you and persuade you that we can change this whole thing around."

I flew into Toronto the night prior to the Tuesday meeting and had drinks with Morgan McCammon. It was clear that he was on the hot seat and was counting on me to keep this together. And for the first time I was completely confident that we were finally going to pull this merger/expansion off.

Who is kidding whom? We might have been able to go on for another year with the WHA, but it would have been really, really hard. Now it looked like we wouldn't have to.

As part of the merger plan we had to clean up the last two WHA teams — Birmingham and Cincinnati. We had agreed to pay Johnny Bassett $2.4 million because Birmingham wasn't going to get into the NHL, and we had to negotiate with Bill DeWitt for his exit fee. The NHL didn't want Cincinnati, and that really hurt Bill. And he would have been great for the NHL, so it was their loss. Because he felt hurt, Bill was difficult about his final settlement number, which ended up being $4.25 million.

The NHL had their vote, and we got in.

We made the announcement in February, then we had to clean everything up, pay off all the bills, pay off Ron Roberts and the players' association and finish our final season. For posterity's sake: at the final WHA All-Star Game that year, Gretzky did get to play on a line with Gordie and Mark Howe; Winnipeg won the final Avco cup over Edmonton; and Bill DeWitt's final game with the WHA came against the Whalers in Springfield, where we eliminated Cincinnati in the first round of the playoffs. The next time we would play a hockey game (still in Springfield), it would be as an NHL team.

So, after seven years, the WHA was gone.

I'll argue until the end that the league changed hockey forever. The reserve clause was gone and salaries had soared, so every player now has Gary Davidson to thank for that. We brought a wide-open, exciting European style into the game. We helped Canada double its number of major league teams. We introduced a number of new markets to hockey, including some in the Sunbelt. And, thanks to the efforts of Marcel Aubut, we also introduced regular-season sudden-death overtime, an element that the NHL adapted into their games as well. Players such as Wayne Gretzky, Mark Messier, Mike Liut, the Stastnys, Ulf Nilsson, Anders Hedberg and many others came into the NHL via the WHA.

The City of Hartford, thanks to the Whalers, was to be the only American city to join the NHL as a result of the war between the two leagues. Hartford beat out cities such as San Diego, Phoenix, Denver, Indy, Cincinnati and a few others to be part of the NHL.

And when the four teams were introduced by the NHL as new "expansion" members, I looked around and realized that of all the people there, the only one who had also been at that first meeting to officially create the WHA was me.

The WHA chapter of my life was now complete. Miraculously, a league that started with nothing but smoke and mirrors in 1970 was able to effectuate a merger in 1979 and dramatically change the sport of hockey. I am often asked if the WHA was a success or a failure. The best answer I can give you is that it was a "very successful failure." Although the league itself was short-lived, it opened up the sport of hockey to many new markets in North America and introduced some fun concepts that were eventually adopted by the NHL. The smartest thing the NHL could have done was to have agreed to the merger at the end of our first year. Unfortunately, the Original Six were so used to the monopoly that it was difficult for them to swallow their pride and think like businessmen.

The pioneers of the WHA were people such as Gary Davidson, Dennis Murphy, Ben Hatskin, Bill Hunter, Johnny Bassett,
Bill DeWitt, Marcel Aubut, Mike Gobuty and Peter Pocklington.
To a man, all had great spirit and great love of the sport. Our own
internal group in Hartford — Bob Schmertz, John Coburn, Godfrey Wood, Bill Barnes, Jack Kelley, Ron Ryan, Dave Andrews,
Don Conrad, Bob Caporale and I — all had a passion and commitment to build a franchise in a city that was in desperate need of
a team to rejuvenate the downtown of the state's capital city. And
we were now in the NHL.

As I look back on the WHA Whaler years, I think about some
of the extraordinary events that to this day still have great meaning. We were one of the first WHA or NHL teams to have our own
store that sold team merchandise to the public. It was iconic in
that the entryway was actually designed to look like the mouth
of a whale, in honor of our mascot, Pucky, a friendly whale.
Pucky was created during the WHA years and was a fan favorite.
Our theme song, "Brass Bonanza," is still played today at special
events such as Red Sox games, college games and even at the Sochi
Olympics. PRISM was one of the original all-sports networks. It
became SportsChannel of New England and is known today as
Comcast New England.

We launched some great careers. Bob Neumeier, our broadcaster, went on to become one of Boston's top sportscasters and
is frequently seen on NBC national broadcasts. Bill Rasmussen
founded ESPN. Harry Neale went on to coach in the NHL and
then became a favorite on national Canadian television broadcasts. Many of our players went on to coach in the NHL or to
become successful front-office executives.

The previous eight years had been a roller coaster for me. I
couldn't help but hope that I could now, at the ripe old age of 37,
relax a little and enjoy the fruits of my labor. Little did I know that

Jersey Devils Team Photo 1966. That's me in the front row, fourth from the left. Courtesy Howard Baldwin

Vic Stasiuk, Marcel Pelletier, and Jerry Rafter celebrating a first round playoff victory. Courtesy Howard Baldwin

PHILADELPHIA FLYERS

Chairman	Edward M. Snider
President	William R. Putnam
Vice-President	Joseph C. Scott
Vice President, General Manager	N.R. "Bud" Poile
Treasurer	Kenneth P. Blackburn
Coach	Kelth Allen
Assistant to President	Kenneth Blackburn
Public Relations	Louis Scheinfeld
Director of Press Relations	Joe Kadlec
Ticket Manager	Howard Baldwin
Club Physician	Stanley Spoont, M.D.
Trainer	Dick Bielous
Assistant Trainer	Frank Lewis
Chief Scout	Alex Davidson
Coordinator of Player Personnel	Marcel Pelletier
Executive Office	The Spectrum Pattison Place Philadelphia, Pa. 19148
Telephone	(215) 465–4500
Home Ice	The Spectrum
Seating Capacity	14,700
Location of Press Box	Mid ice, north side, concourse level
Dimensions of Rink	200 feet by 85 feet
Ends of Rink	Herculite tempered plate glass extends above boards all around rink
Nickname	Flyers
Club Colors	Orange and White
Uniforms	Home: Base color orange, trimmed in white and black Away: Base color white, trimmed in orange and black.
Clubs train at	Le Colisee, Quebec City, Quebec, Canada
Play-by-play Broadcaster	Stu Nahan

How times have changed! Believe it or not this was the entirety of the Flyers' front office staff for the 1967–68 season. Today the list would be about five pages long — around 180 people. 1967–1968 NHL Guide

Bob Strickland, who replaced me as ticket manager, Chairman/Owner of the Flyers Ed Snider, and I say our goodbyes as I head to Boston in pursuit of my dream! Courtesy Howard Baldwin

The first WHA draft in Orange County. Left to right: Ron Ryan on the phone with Jack Kelley (who was in Boston), me, John Coburn, and Godfrey Wood. Geniuses at work — following Jack Kelley's instructions! Courtesy Howard Baldwin

Larry Pleau was the first Whaler ever signed— Jack Kelley and I witnessed the contract. Courtesy Howard Baldwin

Team Captain Ted Green on opening night at the Boston Garden. Courtesy Howard Baldwin

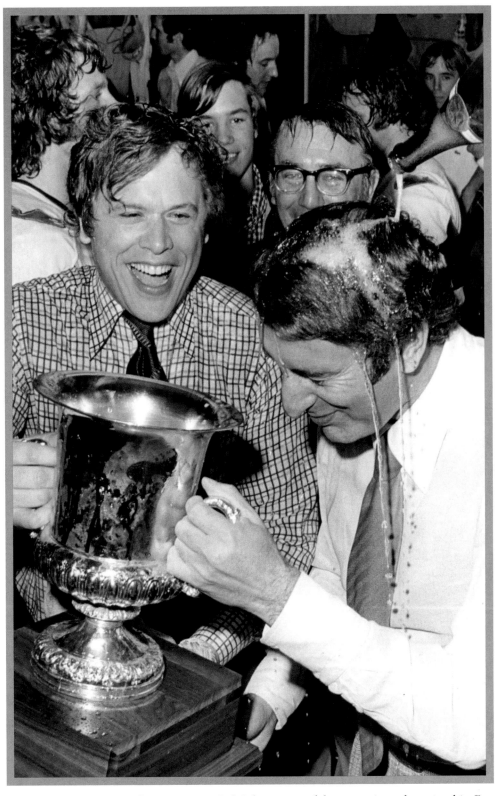

Jack Kelley and I pouring champagne over Bob Schmertz to celebrate our Avco championship. Fun note: see a young David E. Kelley behind his dad in the background. Courtesy Howard Baldwin

The WHA official signing of Bobby Hull. We had the foresight to bring a Whalers poster to the press conference for our own marketing purposes. Left to right: Bill Barnes, Bobby Hull, Brett Hull, Gary Davidson, and myself. Courtesy Howard Baldwin

Opening night of the Hartford Civic Center — a sell out! Left to right: Bill Rasmussen, Dennis Murphy, Mayor George Athanson, Donald Conrad, Jack Kelley, and yours truly. Courtesy Howard Baldwin

Johnny Bassett, a dear friend whom I miss to this very moment. Courtesy Howard Baldwin

The Howes come to Hartford. Left to right: Marty, Gordie, Colleen, GM Jack Kelley, and Mark.
Hartford Courant

A bird's-eye view of the Hartford Civic Center roof collapse — Godzilla couldn't have done a better job! Arman G. Hatsian, *Hartford Courant*

A joyous Rebecca and Howard Jr. with Whaler Alan Hangsleben at a team function. Alan was Rebecca's favorite player. Courtesy Howard Baldwin

Scott with hockey legend Bobby Orr prior to a Bruins game in Hartford. Courtesy Howard Baldwin

My only picture with Clarence Campbell. Bill Dewitt, pictured with me on the left, currently owns the St. Louis Cardinals. Dan Dowling cartoon, courtesy Howard Baldwin

The formal announcement of the merger (expansion) of the NHL and WHA featuring myself and John Ziegler. Courtesy Howard Baldwin

Ron Francis, #10, in his early years with the Hartford Whalers. My definition of a treasury bond. Getty Images

Karen and me with Ron Francis at the Whalers Annual Waltz in honor of the UConn Children's Cancer Fund. Courtesy Howard Baldwin

Welcoming #99, the great Wayne Gretzky, to Hartford for All Star '86. Courtesy Howard Baldwin

This *Hartford Courant* cartoon speaks for itself. The numbers are: 9 — Gordie Howe, 14 — Dave Keon, 2 — Rick Ley, 19 — John McKenzie, and my uniform — a suit! Bob Engelhart, *Hartford Courant*

A proud son with his dad at my induction into the Whalers Hall of Fame. I was inducted at the same time as Dave Keon. Courtesy Howard Baldwin

Gil Stein, Bryan Trottier, Mario Lemieux, me, and Tom Ruta celebrating the Wales Conference championship in the very same Boston Garden locker room where we celebrated the Avco championship in the WHA. Diane Sobolewski

Howard Jr., Karen, and me — a proud family moment with the Cup during the locker-room celebration! Courtesy Howard Baldwin

Hockey, American Style:
Russian Penguins mania takes Moscow.

Full house! Courtesy Howard Baldwin

Selling the brand! Years ahead of other NHL teams. Courtesy Howard Baldwin

Steve Warshaw treating our Russian friends to a pregame meal. Courtesy Howard Baldwin

Left to right: Morris Belzberg, me, Tom Ruta, with Lord Stanley's Cup in front. Courtesy Howard Baldwin

My mother Rose with me and Jamie Foxx at the Golden Globes. Courtesy Howard Baldwin

Karen, Oscar, and me at the luncheon honoring all Academy Award nominees the year we were nominated for *Ray*. © A.M.P.A.S.

that was not in the cards. In fact, the pressure dial was just about to be turned up a notch, not only in my professional life but in my personal life as well. During my first year with the Flyers, I married Anne Reddy and assumed the responsibility of being a father to her two-year-old son, Scott, whom I legally adopted. In 1969 my first child, Rebecca, was born. In 1971, Howard Jr. was born — the same year as the New England Whalers were "born." The pressures of three children and launching a highly complicated business put tremendous pressure on the marriage. Sadly, right at the time the Whalers entered the NHL, Anne and I separated and were divorced.

PART THREE

The NHL:
The Prosperous '80s

Into the NHL at Last

Once we did the merger — or the expansion, as the lawyers will call it — there was no more WHA, and therefore no more interleague competition for players. So, in the 1980s, the pendulum would swing back to ownership's side.

We had peace in the valley. I would describe the '80s as the Prosperous Years.

It had been expensive to join the NHL. The expansion fee was $4.25 million for each of the four WHA teams, plus there was another $1.75 million needed for each of the four surviving teams to "clean up" the WHA.

Before the merger, my Hartford corporate partners expressed to me that, in anticipation of the merger, they would prefer to have me as the only individual to own part of the Whalers.

They gave me a reasonable bank of money to buy out the other individual owners. So I reached out to each partner to acquire their interest, and they were all pleased to receive a fair return for their contributions.

I never really owned a large piece of the team. I had varying amounts over the years, starting at 12 per cent when we made the original deal with Bob Schmertz. Then, as money had to be put in for the NHL acceptance, my percentage was obviously diluted. Yet even though I had only a small percentage, I was the only individual owner and therefore was the face of the franchise. The way the partnership was structured, I had control of all operations, as long as I adhered to an agreed-upon budget that was approved annually.

As had been the case with the WHA, we entered the NHL playing in an arena that was not going to be our permanent home. The two-year rebuilding of the Hartford Civic Center would keep us at the Springfield Civic Center until early February of 1980. At the same time, we had a name change. We were no longer the New England Whalers — we were the Hartford Whalers.

The corporations that owned the team, being Hartford businesses, were motivated to promote the city, and their investment had been made as a civic responsibility to the City of Hartford and the State of Connecticut.

When all the smoke had cleared from the expansion draft, we weren't stripped of as many players as the other three WHA teams were. We'd made a gentleman's agreement with Detroit that the Red Wings wouldn't reclaim Gordie Howe and, overall, we really only lost Brad Selwood, George Lyle and Warren Miller to the NHL, and we ended up getting both Lyle and Miller back within a couple of years.

Our first year in the NHL, we did well. We were placed in the Norris Division with Montreal, Pittsburgh, L.A. and Detroit, and we finished fourth, 10 points ahead of the Red Wings, with 73 points in 80 games, the most of any of the four WHA teams. Both Hartford and Edmonton made the playoffs, which can't be said about too many NHL "expansion" teams.

Mike Rogers, who'd spent the last five WHA years with us, finished fifth in scoring with 105 points and would go on to do something that nobody else but Wayne Gretzky, Mario Lemieux and

Peter Stastny would do — score 100 points in each of his first three NHL seasons. And he scored significantly more goals in each of those three NHL years than he did in any of his five WHA years. Meanwhile, there were four WHA grads in the top 11 scorers and Wayne Gretzky won the Hart and Lady Byng Trophies. So maybe our rebel league wasn't as easy a place as many hockey people, especially in the NHL, had assumed.

For us, Blaine Stoughton also ended up with 100 points and Mark Howe had 80. Dave Keon put up 62 points and Gordie, who was 51 and in what would be his final season, still came through with 15 goals and 41 points. We hadn't been sure Gordie would even play because he'd had dizzy spells near the end of the last WHA season and underwent a bunch of medical tests before he was declared healthy enough. But he was terrific.

We were a good team that year but we were also ridiculed by certain NHL teams, such as Toronto, because we had 51-year-old Gordie Howe and 40-year-old Davey Keon, and then late in the year we signed 41-year-old Bobby Hull.

Sometimes our coach, Don Blackburn, who had a good sense of humor, would throw all three out there on the same line. Harold Ballard thought we were jerks and made great fun of us and the WHA: "Gordie Howe and this league that has all these relics." That kind of thing.

There was also bad blood between Ballard and Keon. Keon was a beloved Leaf captain in the early '70s. I don't know what went on with him in Toronto, but with us you could not have asked for more. I loved Dave Keon, a first-class quality guy. Harry Neale couldn't say enough about him. Harry was a great guy and I trusted his judgment.

So we went into Toronto's Maple Leaf Gardens on Halloween and beat the Leafs 4–2. Gordie got the game-winner and Keon got two goals. I had seats with Jack Kelley down in the corner of the stands, and Harold was located up the wall in the corner in something like a bunker, like the Germans used to have in the war. He and his older buddy King Clancy were sitting in there and they looked like a couple of bobblehead dolls. When we won that game, the fans in that section turned around and they really gave it to Harold. I got a lot of satisfaction from that game. Jack and I left the arena on cloud nine, not only for us but for Gordie and Keon as well.

In the middle of that season, Jack Kelley traded Alan Hangsleben to the Washington Capitals for Tom Rowe. Hangsleben had been with the Whalers since 1975 and my daughter really liked him. Rebecca was 13 at the time, and she was mad! She wouldn't even talk to me after the trade. One day after she finally started to warm up to me again, we were watching practice and there's poor Tommy Rowe standing there. And she said to him, as only Becka could, "My dad traded my favorite hockey player for you." I cringed in embarrassment, but Tommy was a great sport about it.

My three kids literally grew up with the Whalers. They loved the players and the players loved them. I would pull the kids out of school — too much, I admit — to take them on hockey trips. I remember we went to Winnipeg for a big playoff game when Rebecca was eight. She got tired partway through the game, so I took her down to the dressing room and she went to sleep on the trainer's table. We won the game and the players stormed into the locker room and were really whooping it up. But as soon as they realized Becka was sleeping, you could have heard a pin drop. They just shut right up. I came down all excited and nobody in the room is saying a word. I'm wondering, "Did somebody die here?" Then I looked in the training room and there was my daughter, sound asleep.

We played our first 22 NHL home games in Springfield, then opened the rebuilt Hartford Civic Center on February 6, 1980, two years and 19 days after the roof collapsed. The place was sold out. We beat the L.A. Kings 7–3. The night before, at the NHL All-Star Game in Detroit, Gordie Howe was our only representative. It was his final NHL All-Star Game and it was Wayne Gretzky's first. The crowd at The Joe gave Gordie two standing ovations and he had to skate to the bench to make them sit back down.

Three weeks after that, we got Bobby Hull from Winnipeg in a trade for future considerations. He'd come out of retirement to play for the Jets just 20 games or so earlier. We'd had a shot at signing Bobby before the season, but when Jack and I met with him in Boston to see how he felt about playing for us, he was very negative toward Rick Ley, and Rick was our captain. In fact, Rick's sweater now hangs from the rafters in Hartford. I'll never forget Bobby's comment: "Rick Ley? I wouldn't piss in his ear if his brain was on fire!" I'm thinking, "I don't think this will work." I usually just start to laugh at things like that, but Jack was horrified, so we didn't sign him then.

But when we did get Hull, it went great. He got seven points in the nine regular-season games he played. We lost in three straight to Montreal in the preliminary round of the playoffs, and when Bobby and Gordie skated off the ice at the Hartford Civic Center, it was the last game for both of them.

Off the ice and in the boardroom, there was a bit of what-goes-around-comes-around to our inaugural NHL season.

One of the very first NHL issues I had to vote on as Whalers governor was the sale of the Los Angeles Kings from Jack Kent Cooke to Jerry Buss. That made me pause for a moment, because it was Mr. Cooke who first offered me an interview way back in 1965, when I had to turn him down because I was on crutches. And now I was voting on his successor. It was a complicated transaction, but Jerry bought the whole shooting match: the Forum, the Kings, the Lakers and Mr. Cooke's huge ranch in California too. Jerry turned out to be a good owner, and people don't give him enough credit for creating things like club seats, which every arena in the world now has. He took that lower level of the L.A. Forum and said, "You're not getting a seat between the goal lines there unless you buy everything." Meaning NHL, NBA, concerts, everything. And it was big money back then, something like $15,000. He was a very smart guy. And he loved the girls. Before the boxes were put in he had those seats in the end zone that I called a Fornicatorum.

And, of course, there was the Halloween-night visit to Toronto. The first year I was in the NHL was really fun because we'd go to all these buildings that we had heard and read so much about, and Maple Leaf Gardens was one of them. At the start of the WHA, we hurt the Leafs more than anybody else when we took Jim Dorey, Ricky Ley and Brad Selwood off their defence, and Ballard always had issues with me because of that. We targeted teams that were incompetent, and Harold was set in his ways and living in a cave, metaphorically speaking, so the Leafs were easy for the WHA to compete against.

And we were competing well in the NHL. With the new building and a playoff team, you'd have to say that our first year in the league was a good one.

Then it all went downhill.

The Whalers' Dark Ages

After we made the playoffs in our first season in the NHL, we then had five years of on-ice futility. The seasons from 1980 to 1985 were what I call the Dark Ages.

We played one more year in the Norris Division and then moved into the Adams Division with Montreal, Quebec, Boston and Buffalo. It was a really tough division but it didn't matter who we were playing, we were just losing. We finished last the first four years we were in the division, and in 1982–83 we won only 19 games.

Two days after Christmas in our second NHL season, Mark Howe had a horrifying accident when he slid into the net and virtually impaled himself on the pointed piece of metal that balanced the back of the net. He had a deep cut on his thigh, lost 35 pounds and nearly lost not only his career but his life.

During the Whalers' first couple of years in the NHL, Anne and I had separated and were going through the pain of that separation as we started a divorce process. This caused additional pressure on me that I was never expecting and, as a result, I was impulsive and made decisions for the hockey club that were not well thought-out, instead of methodically talking to people and thinking things through.

One of the decisions I most regret was the parting of ways with Jack Kelley as our GM. Sadly, there were people working for Jack who weren't as loyal to him as he was to them. And I listened to the wrong people. I went along with changes that ended up being detrimental to our growth process on the ice. Subsequently, Jack and I worked together again in Pittsburgh, and we remain close to this day.

Jack and I have so much history together. One of the stories that is rarely told in Whalers history is that Jack left the team in 1976 to return to coach Colby College. I was really disappointed and didn't want him to go. Ron Ryan became the GM and Don Blackburn the coach, but I brought Jack back to Hartford in 1978 as the GM. I admire Jack's whole family. Karen and I have worked on two film projects with Jack's son David, and Jack's other son Mark has won two Stanley Cups as a well-regarded scout for the Chicago Blackhawks.

Overall, there were just too many changes in the Whalers hockey department. Larry Pleau, who had taken over as coach and GM when we fired Don Blackburn, was only 34 years old. We had three different coaches in 1982–83 alone. And Larry then traded away some of our biggest stars to try to get some depth and get a little younger — Mark Howe and Mike Rogers, who were the first Whalers voted into the NHL All-Star Game. Those were two trades that didn't work out well for us.

As bad as we were on the ice for the first five years of the '80s, those were the years that defined Hartford as a great hockey market. I say that because even though we were struggling on the ice, we never dropped below 72 per cent paid attendance.

The definition of a solid market is one which supports its team during losing streaks as well as it does during winning streaks. It's easy to support a winner, but it's not so easy to support a team that is consistently losing games.

"The Cat" Emile Francis used to say this all the time: Hartford was the Green Bay of hockey.

We did all the things a team should do off the ice, immersing ourselves in the culture of the community. The players did more events than any other team, and we won league awards for that. The players were beloved in our market. It's very hard to root against a team whose players would come to your local school and read to your kids in the classroom or spend their free time encouraging sick kids in the local hospital. Hartford is different than other places because the Whalers were the only show in town — we were the only professional team the city had ever had. We became a fixture in the marketplace, and despite all the losing, we still would never draw a crowd of less than 7,000 or 8,000.

I was fortunate to have had the experience I'd picked up in Philadelphia. We had just over 15,000 seats in Hartford, which was the smallest capacity in the league, but the key is not so much the number of seats as the gross dollars you generate from them. It is critical that you scale the house in such a way that you generate a gross gate that allows you to compete with teams in bigger markets. At the same time, you have to be very cognizant of having a low price for those fans who are more economically challenged.

Quite frankly, when you get into the upper price tiers, the cost itself isn't that big a deal. Back then it would have been $15 to $20 for the top seat. Today, the difference between a corporation paying $100 or $150 isn't that big a consideration. So we worked hard at trying to price it in such a way that we touched all the bases. What we ended up doing in Hartford was making the lower level seats all one price.

We worked at it constantly, and one of the things I'm most proud of is that when I left in 1988, we had the third-highest gross gate in the league in the smallest building, in the smallest market. Hartford had become a cult team. And even though the team no longer plays in Hartford, sales of the old Hartford Whalers merchandise still rank among the top in the NHL.

Francis and Francis and Co.:
The Renaissance Begins

They always say that a winning streak begins while the team's still losing, and that can be true of a franchise's fortunes too. Our two biggest moves — drafting Ron Francis and hiring Emile Francis — came while we were in the midst of five seasons out of the playoffs.

Ronnie wasn't going to be our first choice in the draft of 1981. We thought we were going to get Bobby Carpenter. He was the best American player at the time, he had been on the cover of *Sports Illustrated* and he was a local boy from New England. But right at the draft, Max McNab leaped over us with a trade into the third slot and Washington selected Carpenter.

So Larry Pleau, who was GM, then picked Ron Francis from the Soo Greyhounds. I really think it was a credit to Billy Dineen's advice that we made that choice and to Larry for having the courage to support it. I love going back in time and looking at the drafts because you see what an extraordinarily imprecise business it is. This draft was memorable in that it had two Hall of Famers in the top four: Dale Hawerchuk to Winnipeg first overall, then Ronnie at number four. And Bobby Carpenter became the first American to go from high school hockey directly to the NHL, and he eventually made the U.S. Hockey Hall of Fame.

Pleau had a philosophy that a player had to serve time in the minors. So when we started the 1981–82 season, Francis was back with his junior hockey team and we started off October and November losing many more games than we were winning. It was not good.

In early December Ron was called up for a game because of Whaler injuries and he scored a couple of points. Everyone in the building could see that he was something special, and it was like a dark cloud had lifted when he got on the ice.

We won the game and it seemed clear to me that this was a turning point for the franchise. For the first time that year, we got some positive local press. But I arrived in the office the next morning and Larry informed me that he was going to send Ron back to junior hockey.

I was totally dumbfounded and said, "Larry, we finally get something to hang our hats on and you're going to send him down? That is ridiculous, we need to keep him here!"

Larry stubbornly said, "Well, I'm the GM."

My reply: "Well, you're the GM, but that can change too. We have tickets to sell and sponsorships to sell, and just when we finally get a young player that people can hang their hats on, you are going to send him back? That makes no sense."

I believe that Larry felt that Ron was so young at 18, that it was too much too soon. And he was trying to stand up for what he was doing as GM.

Bottom line: Ron Francis ended up staying — for a decade. To this day, he is the most beloved Whaler of them all.

It was risky for me to take that stand, because when you become part of the GM's decision-making, then you become part of the crime. And it is hard to tell a GM he is fired when you are responsible for many of the decisions he has been making.

That said, Ron ended up with 68 points in just 59 games that year, so he was by no means out of place in the NHL.

The next year, we drafted Ulfie Samuelsson, Ray Ferraro and Kevin Dineen, all in the third round or later. That's what made the franchise. Those guys all came together at the same time. Those kind of back-to-back drafts are what made all the good teams of that era, the Oilers and Islanders particularly.

If you said to me, "Of all the players who played for you, who were your favorites?" Ronnie would have to be at the top of the food chain. The closest comparison I can make is Derek Jeter. Totally professional, never going to say the wrong thing. They have the highest level of professionalism . . . and they're good. Ronnie's a great guy and was like a treasury bond. Every year you knew you were going to get 80 to 100 points from Ronnie Francis. And quietly, at the end of 20 years, he accumulated enough to be fourth in all-time scoring. Of course, I loved Gordie too, but in a different way. It was such an honor just to have him on our team.

When you're building a team, how could you do better than to have a Ron Francis as your leader on and off the ice? He was captain of the Whalers franchise twice, and was captain of Pittsburgh twice, the only NHL player ever to do that. I don't think Ron ever got enough recognition until he joined the Penguins. As soon as he came to the Penguins, they won two Stanley Cups.

In the spring of 1983, as we were about to miss the playoffs for the third straight year, my partners and I sat down and decided we'd have to get a real strong person in to run the hockey organization.

So we hired Emile "the Cat" Francis as general manager, to take over from Larry Pleau. The Cat had just spent eight years as GM in St. Louis, helped them find a new owner and went behind the bench twice to coach. Elected into the Hockey Hall of Fame only the year before, the Cat was a guy who knew how to take control and run things.

The Cat had been a professional goaltender, mostly in the AHL and the Western Hockey League, but he also played for the Blackhawks and Rangers in the late '40s and early '50s. He got his nickname because he was small and fast in the net. Even as a player he was known as a leader, and it had been his idea to change the goalie's catching glove to resemble a baseball first baseman's mitt — easier for catching the puck, and not so hard on the goalie's arm.

The Cat coached the New York Rangers to the Stanley Cup final in 1972 and spent 16 years in that organization, including 11 as the general manager. Then he became coach, general manager and vice-president of the St. Louis Blues, and they set a franchise record of 107 points just two years before we hired him.

When the Cat was formally introduced, Larry wanted to resign. So I called him up and asked him to meet me for a private breakfast meeting. I said, "Larry, you can't quit. You are a young man. Blame me for putting you in a position you weren't ready for. You've got to suck it up. Go to Binghamton to coach, or do whatever the Cat wants you to do. You're learning from a guy who's had a thousand years of experience, and you'll come back. Don't quit."

I'm proud that Larry didn't quit. He went to Binghamton and coached for four years. He then made it back to coach the Whalers and was still in Hartford when I left in 1988. Larry has gone on to have a great career. He worked for the Rangers and then became GM of St. Louis. He swallowed his pride and became a top-notch hockey guy.

So, with Emile Francis and Ron Francis both joining the organization, things were getting better.

A Taste of Hollywood

Not long after this, Bill Minot sent me a movie script called *Flight of the Navigator*. Bill was one of my best friends, another guy that I knew well growing up in the summers in Massachusetts.

Bill had been a very successful investment banker but decided to leave the business and go out to Hollywood to work in marketing. He was one of the pioneers in product placement. It was a simple, yet new, concept. You're making a movie that's going to be seen by millions of people, and if there's a scene where a guy's drinking a beer, you go to Coors and ask if they'll pay to have the actor drink their product. If they won't . . . the guy's drinking Schlitz.

Bill had a Whaler connection from more than a decade earlier. It was just before Christmas in our first year in the WHA and we needed a Santa Claus for the home game over the holidays. Bill is a big boy — think John Candy — yet a gifted athlete despite his size. Bill never played hockey, but he felt he could handle skating around that rink with ease. After the first period, he was meant to skate around the ice surface in his Santa suit with a sack full of candy and throw the goodies into the crowd.

There was no separate place for him to change, so he had to do it with the players in their dressing room. Teddy Green and the guys all got a huge kick out of Minot's humor and spirit. He was the funniest person I knew, very smart and very quick-witted.

When Bill came out in the Santa suit, I was sitting right in the seats by the vomitory. Bill looked nervous, and his knees were wobbling. I asked him if he was all right, and he replied, as he eyed the crowd of 12,000 fans, "How did I ever get into this?" Then he gets out there, and realizes it's *hard* to skate, especially in a Santa suit with a sack of candy over your back. But he did it, to the joy of all the fans and the players who actually made the effort to come out and watch him.

Like everyone else in Hollywood, Bill really wanted to be a producer, and had once said to me that if he ever came across a script which he felt was good, would I help finance the development of it? I said sure I would.

Bill then sent me *Flight of the Navigator*, to this day one of the best scripts I've ever read. It was a clever science fiction piece about a young boy who is abducted by aliens and becomes a pilot for their spacecraft.

Bill needed $50K for the option on the script and a rewrite. I made the investment and we doubled our money. We got a presentation credit for the movie, but if I knew then what I know now, I would have asked for a producing credit.

So now I had a taste of the movie business, yet I was still fully immersed in the hockey business. The careers I've chosen to pursue are difficult. That doesn't mean that other careers aren't difficult as well, but my business-life choices are incredibly visible, and since they seem like "fun," everyone thinks they are easy and they "could do that too." Everybody thinks they can put a sports team together, and everybody thinks they can do a movie. The problem is that everybody *wants* to do it, so both of these businesses become very competitive.

There would be significant crossovers between my hockey life and movie life. For instance, after my taste of film with Minot, I then acquired two additional film projects with my friend John Bassett. Later on, it was via hockey that I met Phil Anschutz, who owned the L.A. Kings and several MLS soccer teams. Phil, Karen and I became partners in a company called Crusader Entertainment. When we were cleaning up a multitude of legal issues as part of the NHL merger, our lawyer in California, Stuart Benjamin, and I developed a great friendship and partnered a few film deals of our own together. We did *Billy Galvin*, we were part of the development of *Hoosiers*, and later on we'd do more films together.

And *Billy Galvin* was very helpful in bringing Karen Mulvihill into my life.

Karen

Karen Mulvihill came into my life in the summer of 1985, when she was working for the NHL as a local marketer for the next year's All-Star Game. Two years earlier, I'd bid to bring the 1986 NHL All-Star Game to Hartford, and we landed the game for February 4, 1986, a Tuesday. (It wasn't on the weekends back then, because weekends were too valuable to lose from the regular-season schedule.)

Hartford had hosted the WHA All-Star Game in 1977, but the NHL game was a much bigger event and planning had to start about 10 months in advance. Technically, it was an NHL event hosted by the league as well as the local team. Therefore the NHL hired some local staff to work on the project, and Karen was hired to work out of our offices as the assistant to the NHL coordinator, George Ducharme. Today, it is dramatically different — the NHL has a full-time staff to organize their events.

Karen's Mom and Dad, Mary Jane Mulvihill and Jim Mulvihill, grew up in Connecticut. Jim was head of the UConn Health Center, a huge local hospital, and the Children's Cancer Fund at the hospital was the Whalers' designated charity. So we also made it the charity for the All-Star Game.

Karen was young, 21, and I was 42 at the time. Twice her age. But as my good friend Bill Minot would joke, I was immature and she was mature, so it evened things out.

It was really kind of strange the way we started dating.

Jim Mulvihill said to me, "Karen's so glad to be working at the Whalers, but did you know that she loves the theater and would probably enjoy learning more about what you're doing in the movies," or something to that effect.

That gave me my opening to get to know Karen. When I first met her at the Whalers office, I just had this feeling that she would become a permanent part of my life, so I saw my opening and took it. I offered to bring her up to Boston, where we happened to be filming *Billy Galvin*.

I told Jim, "If Karen would like, I have to go up there a few times and she could go up with me and spend a day on the set." So that's what happened, and one thing led to another and we became a couple. And the rest, as they say, is history.

Karen's family are really devout Catholics, and here their older daughter is going out with a guy who's twice her age and divorced with three children. Scotty was 19, Becka would have been 16, and Howdy Jr. would have been 13. So it was an adjustment for all of us.

Karen and I knew instinctively that we were meant for each other. So even though it might have been awkward at times, we were adamant that we wouldn't hide the relationship. We needed to get people as comfortable with it as we were.

We have many bonds, but the strongest is our friendship with each other. We genuinely enjoy being together. We met via the office, so it is natural for us to work together.

After the All-Star Game was done, we got engaged and started to go to L.A. more and more frequently. Karen was able to get a manager and an agent out there, and over time she has had 10 or 11 roles in movies and TV. In some of the movies she had the second female lead. In *Sudden Death* — a movie that Karen wrote the treatment for and we shot in Pittsburgh — she opens the movie as an ESPN producer directing the telecast.

I marvel at the ease with which Karen was able to do the acting roles. It's not easy. When you watch a movie as a fan, all you see is what is put on the screen, but when the film is being made there are hundreds of people around behind the camera. Karen had some terrific training — she was in classes with Brad Pitt, Johnny Depp and some other young actors who became stars. It's important to realize, though, that not everyone can just walk in and sign up for that kind of training. You have to audition and show talent; it is very competitive. Then Karen worked with the Groundlings, a famous improv group.

We were married on October 17th, 1987, in a true family wedding. Karen's sister Kristen was her maid of honor, her brother Jason was the ring bearer and my son, Howard Jr., was my best man. My other son, Scott, was an usher. That hockey season, we spent more time in Los Angeles, as Karen was acting and I was producing films.

We bought a house in the Hollywood Hills, on Blue Jay Way. We bought it from Frank Valli of the Four Seasons, and it was also the house that the Beatles rented when they did their song

"Blue Jay Way." It was a great house with a drop-dead view. We were going back and forth from the west to the east. I was still the president and managing general partner of the Whalers, but I was really starting to put my foot into the film business, and I knew I was getting a bit bored back in Hartford.

Moving On

It was the 1985–86 Whalers team that turned around our string of missing the playoffs. That was a great team, with Dave Tippett, Kevin Dineen, Joel Quenneville, Johnny Anderson, Ronnie Francis, Sylvain Turgeon, the tandem of Mike Liut and Stevie Weeks in net and a really good, solid coach in Jack Evans. That was an exceptional group of guys on and off the ice. Emile Francis had hired Jack when he came to Hartford. Jack was a quiet, soft-spoken fellow, but when he played he was a classic NHL tough guy.

On the Sunday two days before the All-Star Game, we played at home against Washington, and NHL people had started flocking into town that day, so we had a lot of them at the game. We went ahead 4–1 but wound up losing 5–4 when Washington scored four goals toward the end of the third period. It was our fourth loss in a row, and it was a devastating one. Of course, many of the early arrivals for the All-Star Game witnessed it, and I'm thinking, "There is no hockey god."

Thankfully, the All-Star Game was a great success. And shortly thereafter we started a 14–7–2 run to the end of the season that put us into fourth place, just three points out of second, and into the playoffs. It was during this streak, when I was in the locker room congratulating the players after a win, that John Anderson noticed my Gucci loafers and asked where he could get a pair. I foolishly said that if the team made the playoffs, I would buy every one of the guys a pair — not really thinking that that was something I would have to "make good on." Suffice it to say I was out several grand — but the guys had new shoes for the playoffs.

Quebec, Edmonton and Winnipeg also got in. It was the last time for the next 13 years that all the WHA franchises would make the NHL playoffs.

We beat Quebec in three straight games in the preliminary round, which turned out to be, amazingly, the only NHL playoff series ever won by the Whalers. In the next round we played the Canadiens, who had decided to use the rookie Patrick Roy in goal. Wise choice, but we beat them 1–0 in game six in Hartford to force a seventh and deciding game in Montreal two nights later. At this point, hockey support in Hartford was at a fever pitch. The whole city and state were passionately behind our team. Unfortunately, in a great seventh game, Claude Lemieux scored for Montreal in the sixth minute of overtime to eliminate us 2–1, and the Canadiens went on to win a surprise Stanley Cup.

We finished first in the Adams Division the next year but lost to Quebec in the first round, part of a seven-year run in which the Whalers made the playoffs every spring.

But I wasn't in Hartford for the last four of those.

As I mentioned, the '80s were hockey's Renaissance Years. We had solved the war between the two leagues and many teams were now profitable. The corporate partners felt that now that the team was making money, it was time to sell. For them, their investment had been a civic gesture to revitalize the city. Now that had finally happened, and they felt their "job" was done. Downtown Hartford was booming. It was great fun to see it and to be an integral part of it.

I was instructed to find a buyer, or buyers, and to generate the maximum possible return for the partners.

As I've previously articulated, Don Conrad, the CFO of the Aetna, was instrumental in the Whalers coming to and staying in Hartford, and in helping me effectuate the merger. Therefore Don felt some sort of entitlement to an inside track on the acquisition of the team when it came time to sell it. This, coupled with the fact that he wanted to leave the Aetna, put me in a very difficult position.

Don actually came to me to see if I wanted to be part of his bid. But if I did, he would assume my role as managing general partner, and I would have a secondary role. Since I was the person who gave birth to the franchise (granted, with the help of others), it would have been difficult for me — and frankly not too good for Don — to agree to his plan. I also felt that my first responsibility was to all the partners, including the Aetna, which owned 35 per cent of the team. It was my job to represent them all and to do my very best to see that they received a fair return for all of the money they had invested into the team over time.

I made it clear to Don that I was in a tough situation, and that while he had done a lot for me and the franchise, it was my duty to represent all the partners.

Don then found a money partner in a local real estate investor named Richard Gordon. They came in with an offer of $19 million, which I took to my executive committee, but with the recommendation that they not accept it because I felt it was too low. It was not a fair price. The partners told me that I had their support and to keep working to get us an offer that reflected fair market value and the investment they'd made.

That was the point where Don and I had a serious rift, because I would not support his bid. I was then able to find another bidder to compete with him, generating what ended up being a very fair price of $33 million. That was the largest purchase price, ever, for an NHL team at that point in time. And in the end the buyer was Don Conrad and his new partner, Richard Gordon (although shortly thereafter, Gordon and Conrad had a partner dispute and Gordon bought Conrad out).

My Whaler experience was now at an end. We had taken the dream of a new team in a new league that we acquired for $25,000, and we had sold it for $33 million as a profitable NHL franchise. We had been instrumental in the resurgence and revitalization of a city and community that desperately needed something. We made an impact on and off the ice, and to this day the Hartford Whaler brand lives on.

My children grew up there, and Karen and I met there, so I was sad to leave but at the same time I was ready to leave. I was prepared for new challenges and new adventures.

I feel great pride when I look back on the Whaler experience. I would be the first to acknowledge that there were certain decisions I made that were impulsive, yet overall I was pleased with the job I had done. When the sale was officially approved by the NHL in the summer of 1988 and the power was transferred from my hands and the hands of the corporate partners to the Gordon/Conrad interests, I felt they were taking over a team that was poised for great success in the '90s.

John Ziegler would frequently use the expression, "If it ain't broke, don't fix it," but sadly, the new ownership of the Whalers did not heed that concept. Within a very few years they undid everything we had worked so hard to achieve in the '70s and '80s. On the hockey end, they fired Emile Francis and traded Ron Francis, Ulf Samuelsson, Dave Tippett and others. On the business end of the franchise, they eliminated Bill Barnes, Phil Langan and Mark Willand and almost the entire ticketing staff. They even eliminated the Whaler Store, which had become a gathering point not unlike a community's general store. They turned the store over to an outside firm, thereby getting rid of Mike Reddy and Joan Hayes, who had been with the organization since day one. "Brass Bonanza," the song played after every Whaler goal, was eliminated.

The new group completely missed the point of what the Whalers stood for. The team started to lose its heart and soul, and therefore the solid fan base built up over the decades began to erode. Ironically, when the team was in corporate hands it was not run like a corporate team, but when the team transferred ownership to two individuals, it became more like a corporate team. A few people, who should have known better, did not advise Gordon well, and all the good which was done in the '70s and '80s was undone in a short period of time. The franchise would then be allowed to move to Carolina, which was a great crime.

Richard Gordon was the one who ended up selling the franchise to Pete Karmanos, who then moved the franchise to North Carolina in 1997. I don't think it was Karmanos's original intention to move the team, but I also don't think that Hartford was where he wanted to be. He had intense negotiations with the City and with the State of Connecticut, and both sides stubbornly dug in their heels. So when Carolina made Karmanos a better offer, he moved the team there. Over the years, I have grown to really respect Pete Karmanos. He has given a tremendous amount to minor hockey and junior hockey, and he has invested a fortune in the Carolina Hurricanes.

I would like to jump ahead a few years for a moment, to April 13th, 1997, and say that it was incredibly sad for Karen and me to watch that final game played on Hartford Civic Center ice with the players, led by Kevin Dineen, raising their sticks to salute the Hartford fans. This team should never have been allowed to leave. In the best of times, it is extraordinarily hard to bring a major-league sports franchise to a city, but even harder to bring it to a small city like Hartford. It was truly the end of an era.

Since the departure of the team, Hartford has been on a steady decline, going from a lively and bustling place to a city that is deathly silent.

In 1988, when we left Hartford, the sport of hockey was thriving. The '80s were very prosperous for the NHL. The Islanders and then the Oilers were ruling on the ice, and teams were making money.

Looking back on the Hartford Whalers, I take great pride in the fact that we achieved so much success on and off the ice. Merchandise sales were through the roof, and the logo won many awards for creativity and design. The Whaler Booster Club is still active and vibrant. Hartford hosted not only a WHA All-Star Game, but also an NHL All-Star Game as well as a Whaler-CCCP game and Canada Cup games. We also hosted the Hollywood celebrity team on several occasions, the most memorable of which was the game in which actor Alan Thicke broke his nose.

The 1985–86 group of Whaler players was extraordinary. Joel Quenneville has won two Stanley Cups as a coach and is one of the all-time winningest coaches in the NHL. Kevin Dineen has coached in the AHL and the NHL, and most recently coached the gold-medal-winning Canadian women's hockey team in Sochi. Dave Tippett is a top NHL coach and is moving up on the all-time wins list as well. Ron Francis is a key executive with the Carolina Hurricanes. Other players, such as Ulf Samuelsson, Paul Fenton, Ray Ferraro, Steve Weeks, Dean Evason — seriously too many to reference quickly here — have gone on to play an important role in the world of professional hockey.

But those same storm clouds that were hovering over the skies in the early 1970s were about to re-gather in the 1990s. Little did I know at the time that I would have a very active NHL decade ahead of me.

PART FOUR

The NHL:
The Turbulent '90s

ЦЕНТРАЛЬНЫЙ СПОРТИВНЫЙ
КЛУБ АРМИИ

Back in the Game

Nineteen eighty-nine was a transition year for me and Karen. After I finished with the Whalers, we moved to L.A. in September and concentrated on the movie production business. By that point, we had made *From the Hip*, *Billy Galvin*, *Spellbinder* and a few others. When we left Hartford, we left with some money — our share of the sale of the Whalers was $2.7 million — and we were living off that money and also investing in films. Karen was finding success with the acting and writing, and we were expanding our film company, as we both liked living in California.

Although I was not active with my own team in the NHL, I'd stayed close to people in the league and had many friends and connections within it.

Jay Snider was running the Flyers at the time and, thoughtfully, had put me on their board, which to this day I still appreciate. As well, Karen and I developed a friendship with Bruce McNall, who owned the L.A. Kings. We had season tickets for the Kings at the Forum, and Karen even sang the national anthem prior to the Kings-Whalers game. There were 16,000 people there and she did a great job. I was so nervous that I was in the bathroom, sick to my stomach.

We were happy in Los Angeles, but I did miss what I had grown used to doing for over 20 years — running a hockey team. I missed the competition and camaraderie of it. For me, hockey was a safe haven; it was all I had done since I started my working life. I had been very fortunate because with the Whalers, from day one, I always had great partners, starting with Bob Schmertz and evolving into the corporate partnership. There was stability for me in hockey, whereas with the film business we didn't generate any income unless we made a film.

So I was at a place where I was eager to find a way to have a little more stability. And just as I will never forget that small WHA article in the *Boston Globe*, I will never forget the phone call from NHL president John Ziegler and Calgary Flames partner Norm Green.

It was the summer of 1989, and Karen and I were driving along the Pacific Coast Highway in Malibu when our car phone rang.

"Howard," John said, "the league would like to expand by at least two more teams, and we want to push westward. You're on the West Coast, see what you can find out."

John added that they wanted to establish a new benchmark price of $50 million for a new NHL franchise. Although I was a bit taken aback by the size of that number, I said I would see what I could do.

The call came a little less than a year after Peter Pocklington traded Wayne Gretzky to Los Angeles. I remember having a bet with Ed Snider after that trade. Ed was saying, "Oh my God, with that deal, L.A. will win the Stanley Cup this year." And I said, "I bet you Edmonton wins another Cup before L.A. does," because I felt Mark Messier was such a competitor that he was going to prove a point. And the Oilers did win, in 1990.

The Gretzky deal was sad for Canada, but for L.A. and the rest of the U.S. it was great. It triggered the growth of hockey on the

West Coast. You take the greatest player in the history of the sport, in terms of persona — you could argue that Bobby Orr, or even Gordie, was a better player, but Wayne was an absolute giant at the time — and put him in a star-studded city like L.A., and it electrified people.

Suddenly people started going to the hockey games in L.A. in record numbers. That trade single-handedly did more to generate interest in the NHL in the United States than anything that had been previously done. Wayne was the one star of the game who transcended it. Mario Lemieux, the other superstar of the time, was very reserved — a reluctant star. Mario was a great, great player, but he did not enjoy being an ambassador for the sport. Wayne was an ambassador for the sport and Bruce was a smart promoter.

Bruce immediately tripled Wayne's salary to $3 million per year. Bruce knew he had to get the front page, from a marketing point of view, and one of the ways he did this was to encourage celebrities to come to the games by placing them in prominent seats along the ice where the media could capture photos of them and where the TV cameras could pan to them during the game. On any given night you would see such luminaries as Ronald Reagan, Tom Hanks, John Candy, Sly Stallone, Kurt Russell and Goldie Hawn. Bruce made the games a place to go and be seen.

In the Hockey Hall of Fame, they have a Builders section that rewards key executives and owners who have made an extraordinary impact on the sport. Bruce should be in the Hall in that category, as he was a true builder. Granted, he had legal difficulties and he was punished for them, but that doesn't change the incredibly positive impact he had on the sport itself. When he did that Gretzky deal, it turned the whole hockey world upside down and put all the attention on the West Coast market. It made the NHL a coast-to-coast sport in the U.S. and opened up new markets to hockey. It brought Anaheim into the league in a couple of years, and it was not very long afterward that the league started to move into warmer, non-traditional markets like Miami, Tampa Bay, Dallas, Phoenix and San Jose.

There is no question that Wayne's trade prompted that call along the Pacific Coast Highway. In a follow-up call shortly after the first one, Norm and John suggested I go to the desert, to Palm Springs, to meet Morris Belzberg, a friend of Norm's from Canada who was interested in owning a hockey team. Morris had risen from being the first individual licensee of Budget Rent a Car in Canada to being chairman of the board and CEO. Morris and I liked each other from the start and agreed we would join forces to pursue a team. Morris would provide the principal financing for an expansion team on the West Coast, and I would spend the time to explore various markets.

During the late '80s, right when we were leaving the Whalers, I started working much more closely with Tom Ruta. Tom had always worked with us on our personal financial matters, but in the late '80s we formed a partnership that remains strong to this day. There is not a thing I am involved with where I don't reach out to Tom for his input and expertise. Tom and my older brother Michael are two business partners I value greatly. As well, Tom's brother Nick Ruta has worked with us on all business matters, film and personal. Tom is a brilliant financial mind and our alliance was fortuitous. I love to work with him because he has the ability to take some of my "creative ideas" and ground them in good business practices. It made us an effective team.

Morris, Tom and I began by looking at the San Diego and San Francisco markets, the two most obvious targets. To me, San Francisco was very attractive. I really liked it as a city. It has an East Coast feel to it. The city itself is absolutely beautiful and it had a history of hockey in the old Pacific Coast League, with the San Francisco Shamrocks. However, the politics of the city were such that it was quickly clear to my group that it would take years to get the support needed to build a new arena.

We also looked long and hard at San Diego. They did have a 13,000-seat arena that we could have used temporarily, but we didn't like the marketing radius of San Diego: it has the Pacific Ocean to the west, Orange County to the north, the desert to the east and Mexico to the immediate south. That location gave us great concern for its long-term viability as a hockey city.

Then I received a call from Jim Hager, a young lawyer in San Jose, who said he had read in the paper that I was spearheading the drive for an NHL team on the West Coast. He asked if I would visit him and the mayor in San Jose.

Jim, a terrific young fellow, met me at the airport, showed me around and took me in to meet the mayor, Tom McEnery. Tom comes from an old-line California political family and to this day is a very good friend of mine.

I knew instantly that San Jose was it. The team would be the only show in town, like in Hartford. It was an exciting up-and-coming city. They had all the financing in place to build a new arena. They were in the Silicon Valley area just as internet technology was exploding. It was a technology center for the world, just as Hartford was the insurance capital.

We engineered a very exciting and powerful deal for the NHL. The team was to be financed based on all the revenue streams we would generate from the arena. Part of the deal with the mayor was that the city turned the arena over to us. So we had the arena and the management rights to the arena to help finance bringing a hockey team there. I then went to Tony Tavares, who was running Spectacor Management Group, an arena management company owned by Ed Snider, and we put together a deal that set the bar for a new NHL team at $50 million, which became the expansion fee for the 1990s. We were able to generate additional financing by bringing Spectacor in as the arena manager — Spectacor advanced dollars to our partnership (Morris, Tom and me) against future arena revenues that it would earn. San Jose was pleased because they would get a top-of-the-line arena management company and an NHL team — a huge boon to the local economy. We were all very proud of this deal.

Karen and I had actually picked out a home and were prepared to move to the area. We were committed to the relocation and to running the team as we had in Hartford. It was close enough to Los Angeles that we could keep an eye on the film business, and if Karen had the right opportunity, we could easily commute for her to take advantage of it.

Then I got another phone call from John Ziegler and Norm Green. Norm invited me to Palm Springs to discuss an "exciting idea."

You know when you can sense it's *not* an exciting idea? So I said to myself, "Whoa-oh."

If anything, I tend to overly communicate, so I had been keeping John Ziegler and Bill Wirtz, who was chairman of the NHL, closely apprised of the progress I was making. The possibility of the NHL coming into San Jose was now known to the public. Of course, it was also known to the member teams of the NHL.

At the same time that our San Jose deal was coming together, Gordon and George Gund, the owners of the Minnesota North Stars, were making noises about wanting to move their team. When the Gunds became aware of the dynamic opportunity in San Jose, they started to put in a claim on what was essentially my deal. This created some serious debate within the league. On the one hand, there was an existing NHL ownership group which had lost a great deal of money in Minnesota. And on the other hand there was my group (Baldwin/Belzberg/Ruta) which had done exactly as asked by the NHL — create a new, exciting West Coast venue at a premium price to the league.

"We love the idea of San Jose," John Ziegler told me. "But we have a problem here. The Gunds want to relocate from Minnesota to San Jose and they are a member team."

The battle lines were drawn. There needed to be a compromise and there was: the Baldwin/Belzberg/Ruta group wound up owning Minnesota and the Gunds got San Jose.

I fought it initially, pointing out that I put the whole deal together, that I had sweat equity in the franchise and that Karen and I were prepared to move up there. Bill Wirtz and some of the other guys on the board were very loyal to me and said, "Howard found this," but there were other guys who said, "Yeah, but Gordon's in the league and he's lost a lot of money."

It wasn't going to go our way, so the solution was a swap.

The compromise deal was announced on May 5th, 1990. The Gunds would take their Minnesota team to San Jose as an expansion franchise, and the league would put an "expansion" team in Minnesota for us. We had a draft of the Minnesota players to split them up, and both teams would take part in the expansion draft.

San Jose paid $50 million to the league, and we paid $33 million to the Gunds. So an interesting way to look at it is that the Gunds got San Jose for only 17 million bucks.

That's the only deal that I was really disappointed not to get done. I thought we had San Jose, and it kind of pissed me off, but that's the way it went. It was sad for me because we loved the market and we loved the people.

So we created San Jose for the league, we created the $50 million benchmark and we saved their asses in Minnesota.

We paid less money for our franchise but to be candid with you, neither Karen nor I wanted to be in Minnesota. However, it was a good hockey opportunity, so we said we'd adjust our personal plans and go to Minneapolis and try to make it work.

The deal wasn't as good as the one in San Jose. We thought we had a deal for a new arena, but it didn't work out. They were building a new arena in Minneapolis for the Timberwolves basketball team, but at the last minute the owners of the NBA team decided they didn't want to share it with another prime tenant.

To further complicate the situation, Morris decided he didn't want to finance the team in Minnesota without an additional money partner. So, lo and behold, who does he bring in but his friend Norm Green?

I knew from the moment Norm set foot in Minneapolis that he wanted to run the team, and there was going to be conflict. The only opinion that mattered to Norm was his own. I had no issues working for somebody, but I wasn't about to start working for somebody who knew little to nothing about the business.

I don't think Norm behaved the way you're meant to behave. He thought he knew more than anybody, and he was a bully to people who couldn't fight him back. I remember he called the office once and couldn't get right through to me, and he had the receptionist in tears. It was at that point that Karen and I looked at each other and realized that our relocation to Minnesota was going to be a short one.

Another time, Karen and I were in our apartment early on a Sunday morning. Those were the days of the old fax machines that spun paper out like toilet paper, and I hear this thing going "Mmmmzzzz." I thought it was stuck or something, but when I went in the other room to check, there was a fax from Norm that stretched all the way to the bathroom, telling me, "Do this, do that." And I thought, "Mmmm, this isn't going to work." And of course it didn't.

Karen and I were in Minneapolis for only two or three months. We hired Bob Gainey as coach and Bob Clarke as general manager, but it was only six weeks later that I sold out to Norm and Karen and I went back to L.A. And Norm actually got lucky that season, as Minnesota made it all the way to the Stanley Cup final before losing to Pittsburgh.

One of my favorite Norm Green stories has to do with my cousin, Taylor Baldwin. Taylor came to work for me in the mid-'80s. His story is a fascinating one. Taylor's father, my father's older brother, was Peter Baldwin. After World War II, Uncle Peter settled in Bombay, India, rather than returning to Harvard. He was a physically imposing man, one of the last runners-up to Johnny Weissmuller for the part of Tarzan. Uncle Peter started his own airline in Bombay in the late '40s and it was a great success, so much so that eventually it was taken over by the Indian government. Uncle Peter was married to his fourth wife, Taylor's mother, an Indian woman named Myrtle, and he decided to leave India and move to Kabul, Afghanistan. In Kabul he was a highly successful businessman and did a tremendous amount of wonderful work in the country for the local people. Peter and Myrtle had three boys — Taylor was the middle child. Very sadly, Uncle Peter died playing tennis with the man who was then king of Afghanistan. My father flew over there to get Myrtle and the boys and bring them to the United States. Taylor was 11 when he was relocated to this country.

As he grew to manhood, Taylor reached the impressive height of seven feet and was a standout college basketball player at Maryland. When he left Maryland, I immediately hired him as a salesman for the Whalers. I remember with delight the first time Karen saw Taylor — she thought he was standing up behind his desk when in fact he was seated, and then he rose up in all his seven-foot glory! Everyone adored Taylor — he was a gentle giant.

When we left Hartford, Taylor came with us to Los Angeles, and then on to Minnesota with a few other Hartford employees. The one agreement I had with Norm Green when we left the North Stars was that he would give every Hartford employee that we had taken with us at least three to four months to prove themselves.

Needless to say, in classic Norm style, the minute the jet wheels were up and we were on our way to L.A., he called Taylor into his office and told him his "services were no longer needed." Norm was behind his desk. Somehow he hadn't twigged to the long reach of Taylor Baldwin's arm.

Taylor stood up as if he was going to reach for Norm behind the desk, pick him up, and give him a good shaking — which, believe me, Taylor could have done — but he was only trying to scare Norm. Norm flipped over backwards in his desk chair in fright, and Taylor proceeded to laugh hysterically as he exited the office and the city and came back out to L.A. to rejoin us in film.

Taylor went on to work for us in Pittsburgh, but tragically he passed away of brain cancer in 2000. It was a devastating personal loss to Karen, to me, to my children and everyone in our family, and to anyone else whose life Taylor touched.

The Penguins, Part II

Karen and I had kept our place in Beverly Hills, so when we returned to L.A. from Minnesota we went straight back to doing film work with our production company.

In the early fall of 1991, I received a call from Tony Liberati, who was then working full time for Ed DeBartolo Sr., the owner of the Pittsburgh Penguins. Tony had been with Equibank a decade earlier, when we tried to do the deal where the Whalers would buy the Penguins and jump leagues.

Tony said that Mr. DeBartolo wanted to sell some of his holdings because the real estate market had gone soft, and because he knew I'd done a couple of NHL deals, he wanted me to handle the sale of the Penguins. Tony flew into L.A. and we made a deal for, I think, 2 per cent of the purchase price, plus my expenses.

Paul Martha, who had played football for the Steelers, was running the Penguins, and he didn't like my presence in the sale. I knew Paul very well because I'd sat across the table from him at many NHL board meetings, and I said, "Look, Paul, Mr. DeBartolo wants my assistance, and I intend to try to help him."

To me, Pittsburgh looked to be a pretty good opportunity, in that whoever purchased the team would also get the arena management contract. I thought Peter Karmanos from Detroit or Bill Comrie from Edmonton might have an interest in the Penguins, and I had very good meetings with both gentlemen. (This was before Karmanos ended up buying the Whalers from the Gordon Group.) Both of them were genuine in their interest, but both felt the price should be between $30 million and $35 million, based on the performance of the team at the time. But it was clear to me that the franchise was underperforming and that there was a significant upside for any new buyer. I just had to convince Comrie or Karmanos of that fact. Both had a passion for the sport, and either would have made a fine owner. Peter had a junior hockey team in Michigan, and Bill's son Mike — whom I first met when he was about 12 years old — went on to become an NHL player and is married to actress Hilary Duff.

I had a great meeting with Bill up in Vancouver, which I invited Paul Martha to attend with me, as I needed him to give Bill the kind of information about the team and franchise that a prospective buyer would want. But instead of helping me out, Paul said to Bill, "Why would you want to buy this team?" and mentioned how the Penguins were always struggling at the gate. Instead of trying to help me sell the team, he's trying to talk the guy out of it! Paul clearly had his own agenda.

When I returned to L.A., the phone rang and it was Ed DeBartolo Jr., whom I'd never met, but whom I was excited to talk to because he was one of the owners of the San Francisco 49ers. Ed asked how the meeting with Comrie had gone and how Martha had handled himself, because I think they were suspicious of him. I told Ed that Paul "didn't contribute much," as I didn't want to get him in trouble with his bosses. Ed was a very perceptive individual and made it clear to me that I shouldn't worry about having Paul attend any more meetings. We had an unspoken understanding.

Ultimately, we were unable to conclude the deal with Comrie or Karmanos, as they were fixated on the $30 million price and undervalued the opportunity. Mr. DeBartolo, conversely, was rightfully fixated on a higher price, based on the new expansion model which we had created. That is: $50 million.

It was right after the talks with Comrie and Karmanos broke down at the end of the 1990–91 season, and as the Penguins were about to win the franchise's first Stanley Cup (taking Norm Green's North Stars in six games), that I received a call from my friend Ed Snider. He urged me to put together my own deal with Morris Belzberg and Tom Ruta and buy the Penguins ourselves.

I didn't know it then, but ironically that Stanley Cup final was between a team we'd owned briefly and one we were about to own.

Ed said that his arena management company, Spectacor, would do the same kind of deal we were going to do in San Jose — that is, turn around and acquire the arena management contract back from us, thereby enabling us to get the team for a number that was lower to us but still worked for Mr. DeBartolo. Morris agreed, and I called Mr. DeBartolo and asked if he minded if I was the bidder.

"All I'm worried about is getting the price," he replied.

It was a very creative deal: we spun off the arena end of the business in return for a large part of the purchase of the team.

But the league was unhappy with the way we structured this deal. They felt the value wasn't what it should be, based on the $50 million expansion fee that Ottawa and Tampa Bay had just paid, which, again, we had helped create. They wanted to see a higher value on paper.

The league objected to the structure because they felt it was lightly capitalized with very little equity money coming in from ownership. And frankly they were not wrong, but after successfully operating a team in Hartford for 17 years and looking closely at the Penguins' numbers, I felt that we could make up for the capitalization, because the revenue streams could be dramatically enhanced with reasonable price increases.

The deal we originally created was worth between $37 and $38 million, but we had to go back to the drawing board in order to get it to come in at $50 million to maintain the validity of the newly-established expansion fee. So we created a performance-based scenario relative to how the team did. If the Penguins made the playoffs, then we would pay a bonus. If the team made the second round, we'd pay a second bonus. Increased television revenues resulted in a bonus too. Mr. DeBartolo made every one of the bonuses and I was pleased about that because he had stood by us. He was a good man.

We closed the deal in October of 1991, and I was back in the National Hockey League with a team that was the reigning Stanley Cup champion and had two of the greatest players in the game — Mario Lemieux and Jaromir Jagr — plus my star player from Hartford, Ron Francis.

Bumpy Road Back to the Stanley Cup

We took over a tremendous hockey team which had just won the Stanley Cup, and which had so much talent that winning a few more was certainly not out of the question.

There were stars — and one mega-star — on the ice; Craig Patrick was doing a brilliant job as GM; and the coach, Bob Johnson, had created just the right atmosphere for a team on its way to the Cup. Bob, known as "Badger Bob" for his run of successes at the University of Wisconsin, was famous for the observation, "It's a great day for hockey!" which has become part of hockey's everyday language. You won't find anyone in hockey who didn't love Badger.

But in August of 1991, as we were still working on the formal deal to purchase the team, Bob suffered a brain aneurysm while he was preparing to coach Team USA in the Canada Cup. While he was in hospital, he was diagnosed with brain cancer and he was immediately flown to Colorado for treatment.

We opened the season with our assistant coaches Pierre McGuire, Rick Paterson, Barry Smith and Rick Kehoe as sort of a coaching committee, and Craig asked Scotty Bowman, our director of player personnel, to be the interim coach until, hopefully, Bob recovered. Craig's famous father, Lynn, had hired Scotty to coach St. Louis when they went to the Cup finals the first three years of expansion, and Scotty had coached Craig with the Montreal juniors in the mid-1960s. Of course, Scotty also had those five Stanley Cup wins in the '70s coaching the Canadiens, and in November of that year he was being inducted into the Hockey Hall of Fame. So with Scotty at the helm, and solid assistants, we were in good hands.

We got off to a quick start, going 22–13–4 before New Year's. What made that record even more commendable was that the players, who all loved Bob Johnson, were really worried for him. Bob was communicating with the team and coaches through faxes, and was sent videotapes of all the games, but sadly, on November 26th, Bob lost his battle to cancer. The whole hockey world, and especially our team, was devastated.

The players dedicated the season to Bob and wore commemorative patches on their left shoulders, bearing his nickname, "Badger," and the numbers 1931 and 1991, the years of his birth and death. Bob's catchphrase, "It's a Great Day for Hockey" was painted on the ice at both bluelines and remained there the whole season.

After our hot first half, we cooled off dramatically for a few weeks, managing to get only 14 of our next possible 48 points. On February 19th, when Craig Patrick traded Paul Coffey, who was going to be a free agent anyway, to Los Angeles for Brian Benning and Jeff Chychrun, a lot of fans thought we had given up. But that same day Craig sent Benning and Mark Recchi to the Flyers and we got some much-needed toughness back in Kjell Samuelsson and Rick Tocchet, plus a good goalie in Ken Wregget.

We were only three games over .500 at the time, and fell to an even .500 by the end of the month, with the playoffs in doubt. But we went on a 12–5–1 tear to end the schedule and head toward the post-season with a head of steam. Mario was incredible, leading the league in scoring with 131 points despite missing 16 games, and Kevin Stevens finished second with 123 points. Joey Mullen had 42 goals, and Jaromir Jagr, who turned only 20 in February, had 32 goals and 69 points, essentially a point a game (he played 70 games total). We led the league in scoring, with almost 4.3 goals per game, and were a lot of fun to watch.

Midway through that first season in Pittsburgh, there was a significant turning point in hockey history when the NHL Players' Association appointed Bob Goodenow as its executive director on New Year's Day. I happened to know Bob from some time earlier. During my first year with the Whalers, my father called to say that a friend of his from Harvard knew a young man who was writing his thesis on hockey and wondered if I would talk to him about the game. That graduate student was Bob Goodenow, and we spent a whole afternoon talking about hockey in general.

I liked him and we stayed in touch, and we still do.

It was a different game with Goodenow in control rather than Alan Eagleson. The collective bargaining agreement had expired at the start of the season, and on April 1st, 1992, with only a few days left in the season, the players association called a strike. It was the first general players' strike in NHL history, although the Hamilton Tigers did strike over playoff wages in 1925. (The team dissolved rather than pay, and Hamilton has been trying to get back into the league ever since.)

I kept hoping and praying that the strike would not happen. We had just taken the team over six months earlier, and I didn't want our year to end that way. There was tremendous pressure on us, as new owners and defending Cup champions. I said to the other members of the NHL Board of Governors, "Guys, if you don't have a Stanley Cup playoff, how are you going to sell tickets all summer? What are you going to tell your season ticket holders? We've got to play!"

And that's where I was out of step. Every strike, every lockout, I was out of step. As a member of the board, I was always looked upon as somebody who was friendlier to the players than other board members were. Remember, we came into the league not through the front door but through the back door, and we had to hammer it down too. With a battering ram. And I've always felt that too many board members didn't have the experience that comes from running their teams on a day-to-day basis like I did.

As the strike went into its second week, everyone was swirling around in unhappiness over it, worried that the playoffs would be cancelled. Bruce McNall was one of the leaders of the settlement group. I was on some of the calls, as were Peter Pocklington, and Bill Wirtz and Stan Jaffe of the Rangers. We were more vocal in that our teams had a shot at the Cup, but others wanted it settled as well.

We were all talking about how best to resolve this when John went ahead and made a deal with Bob Goodenow. John just made up his mind that we couldn't afford not to have the Stanley Cup, and he went into a room with Bob, put together a deal and then told the board about it. Everyone voted for it. The players would get better playoff bonuses and changes to free agency, and each team's season would go to 84 games with two games in neutral sites as market tests for future expansion.

Some of the owners were very upset with John because they felt he hadn't built the consensus to make the deal he made. I was adamant, though, that he did the right thing. If the Stanley Cup playoffs were not held, it would have been devastating for the sport. Sadly, the decision cost John his job.

Thanks to the fact that there *was* a Stanley Cup playoff, we had a chance to repeat as champions, which is exactly what we did. We were in a tough division, finishing third behind the Rangers and Washington but fourth overall in the east. The Capitals finished 11 points ahead of us and beat us in the first two games of the opening round of the playoffs, and then took a 3–1 lead after game four, but they never could beat us in the playoffs and we swept the next three games, with Tom Barrasso outstanding in a 3-1 win in game seven, right in Washington.

Then the Rangers won two of the first three games against us in the division final, but we took the next three to advance to play Boston for a berth in the Stanley Cup. We swept the Bruins, and then won the Cup final in four straight games against the Blackhawks, clinching the championship on their ice to become the first team since the 1988 Oilers to win back-to-back Stanley Cups. Our 11 straight wins to end the playoffs was also a league record. Mario, who had 34 points in just 15 games, won the Conn Smythe Trophy as playoff MVP for the second straight year. Just as in Hartford, in my first year in Pittsburgh we won the league championship.

Winning the Stanley Cup was an exhilarating experience. However, in my mind it almost came too easily, in that we had not had a long history with the Penguins franchise and we couldn't help but feel a little bit like passengers. Having said that, I was incredibly proud for my partners, for the players, and for the City of Pittsburgh.

I also knew that winning the Cup would make the job in front of us really difficult, moving forward. We had many expiring contracts and we were negotiating from weakness — it is tough to look a player in the eye when his team has just won two Cups in a row and tell him that we can't afford to pay him. Also, with Bob Goodenow in charge of the players, we were entering a whole new era.

Still, we were thinking we could defer some of the bigger contracts until our revenues caught up. We couldn't do it all at once, but we had a truly great product.

I felt we were right on track in our progress the first season.

Embracing Change

In June, after the Stanley Cup final, the NHL had its annual board meeting in Montreal. At that meeting we decided to make the change from John Ziegler to a new NHL president.

There was the usual run of phone calls and meetings leading up to it, all pretty well agreeing that it was time for change because it was clear that we were entering a new era. Bob Goodenow was at the helm of the players' union and, from the tough way he conducted himself during the strike, there was no question that there would be trouble ahead.

John was asked to stay out of the meeting, so he knew what was going on and I think he was ready for it, but I still felt John was treated very badly. He was never properly honored by the league and the board for his 16 years as president. And I'm partly to blame because I was a member of the board of governors. I've always looked back on that firing in regret and shame because it was not well done.

Being NHL president (or commissioner, as it is now) is a demanding job, and during his reign John Ziegler was a very good president. He was a huge believer in collaboration and had all the board members vested in the league by sitting on committee after committee. The question around John was whether he was going to be able to do it from the marketing point of view. And that was definitely a concern at the time.

The agreement at that board meeting was that Bruce McNall of the Los Angeles Kings would be the board chairman, with Gil Stein the acting president, and that they would run the league while we put together a committee to search for a new, permanent president.

That was what I called the NHL's defining Alexander Haig moment. Gil, whom I'd known since he was Ed Snider's lawyer with the Flyers, had always been in the background as league vice-president and legal counsel. And some people don't know enough to stay in the background. When we all left the meeting, everybody supported the plan of temporary leadership while we conducted our search, but within days Gil went out and *campaigned* to make the job his permanently. Gil clearly was bitten by the bug of wanting the NHL presidency. He was an outstanding legal counsel for the league, but unfortunately nobody envisioned him becoming the permanent president.

I wasn't on the search committee for the new president, but I did put forward the name of a good friend of mine, Senator Lowell Weicker of Connecticut, for consideration. They interviewed Lowell and they also interviewed two executives from the NBA, Deputy Commissioner Russ Granik and legal counsel and Vice President Gary Bettman.

Gary came in and just blew everyone away. He was extremely confident, and coming out of that NBA school of marketing he had a leg up, because they were very hot at that time. He said, "Look, this is what we did, this is how we did it, and this is what we can do here." He was very impressive, and he got the job. After 75 years of presidents, the NHL had its first commissioner. The reason for the title change was that the other three leagues were run by commissioners, so it was time for the NHL to make it clear to the sporting world that it too had a very strong leader. "Commissioner" has a stronger connotation. It was a change to be consistent with the other major leagues.

Meanwhile, I had a lot of work to do with the Penguins. We had our second Cup but we also had a lot of star players, including Mario Lemieux, whose contracts were up, and we felt that part of our ownership mandate was to keep this great team together.

Karen and I first met Mario when we and our partners, Morris Belzberg and Tom Ruta hosted a reception for players and staff after the first game of our first season. Mario arrived late with his beautiful French-Canadian girlfriend, Nathalie, whom he later married, and clearly possessed the aura of a star who transcended the sport of hockey. He and I formed an immediate bond that night and agreed we'd get together as soon as possible to discuss his future with the Penguins.

Throughout that first season Mario and I met for dinner from time to time with his agent, the very powerful, passionate and well-respected Tom Reich. Tom had a lot of gray in his hair and beard, but in his feelings he was all black and white. He either liked you for life . . . or didn't like you at all. He always fought fiercely for his coveted client, and despite that ferocity, he and I are friends to this day. Tom would often say that Lemieux was a "God" to him and that he would fight to the death for him. That might seem a little extreme . . . but so is Tom.

As soon as we arrived in town the media began speculating that we would quickly sell Mario or other stars to help defray the cost of purchasing the team. That began my frustration with the Pittsburgh media. It was during my tenure in Pittsburgh that I, a newspaper reader all my life, decided to stop reading newspapers. Why? Because in Pittsburgh, I learned the hard way that I wasn't going to let any members of the media influence my moods or decision making. I decided, better just not to read anything and to do what I thought was right than to read something and overreact.

We were working with Craig Patrick to re-sign a team that had won two Cups, and the public in Pittsburgh had already pre-judged me. Since I was from out of town, they figured I wasn't committed to Pittsburgh and would sell off this player or that player for whatever I could get. However, it wasn't my intention to sell anybody.

There were players on our team who would have been super-stars on other teams, guys like Kevin Stevens, who had just scored a hat trick in the first period of a playoff game against the Bruins; Joey Mullen, one of the top American players ever; Tom Barrasso, the All-Star goalie; Larry Murphy, who would be going into to the Hall of Fame; and Ron Francis, my favorite Whaler, who through the short-sightedness of the new Hartford owners became a Penguin in time to win the two Cups.

We knew we couldn't keep them all, so it was a challenge. We knew that among all those stars, we had two mega-stars in Mario and Jaromir Jagr. The dilemma was, how could we let either one go? If we let Mario go, we would have been horribly crucified. And if we let Jagr go and threw all our eggs in Mario's basket, we weren't even sure whether he'd be playing or not. His back was bothering him a lot and he was already missing games.

We had to find a way to keep them both. Jagr was only 20 years old and his contract was still low, so the first challenge was to sign

Mario. Although I had a close relationship with both Tom and Mario, negotiations were tough. But Mario was cooperative and was open to structuring his contract in a way that we could afford to pay him what he was worth.

Mario's contract was up and he was eligible for free agency. Salaries were exploding, and the Flyers had just signed Eric Lindros to a deal that gave him a $2.5 million signing bonus, two years at $2 million and another four at $2.5 million. How could I have Lemieux — who had achieved all that he had, and who had just won two Cups — not make more than Lindros, who had never played a game in the National Hockey League? Mario was the greatest player in the game at the time, and one of the very few who could put fans in the seats and drive TV ratings.

So Tom knew he had the leverage in the negotiations, and we knew it too, but in October of 1992 we were able to get Mario's contract done: $42 million over seven years.

I felt Mario's contract was reasonable because it was structured in such a way as to give us time to build up our revenues, which were way below the league average. The contract averaged $6 million per year over seven years, but it was weighted to the back end, so that the largest annual salaries came in the final three years. There were some deferrals of salary payments that would come due after the actual playing life of the contract.

We needed time to build revenues because when we acquired the Penguins, their revenues ranked 19th out of the 22 teams in the league, despite the fact that they had just won the Cup. What was gratifying was that, in slightly more than a year, we had increased revenues enough that we were among the top nine teams in the NHL.

Going back to my early lessons in Philadelphia and Hartford, we immediately re-scaled the house, enabling us to generate gross gates that would allow us to keep the team together on the ice. If a team can't do that after winning two Cups, it can never do it. We did get some pushback from fans, which was to be expected, but the answer was obvious: if you want to keep a championship team, you have to pay more.

We increased sponsorship. We were more aggressive on merchandising. We changed the logo. We were also among the first to put games on local pay-per-view. Our revenue stream immediately increased.

We certainly did try to keep our team together as much as we could. We could take no credit for the first Stanley Cup, but we certainly were an active participant in the second one.

It was frustrating in that the media assumed we were going to get rid of players and they criticized us in advance for it. We didn't do it, but then when we signed the players, the media were critical and said we paid the players too much. We were damned if we did, damned if we didn't.

I can defend every Penguins contract we signed during that period. We signed Ron Francis to triple what he had been making and everyone said we overspent on him, but Ron was a treasury bond. He finished in the top five or six scorers every year. By 1998, my last year with the Penguins, Ron's contract was about $1.9 million. The next year he went to Carolina for about $6 million. This proves the argument that players' values are based on the contracts they are able to generate. A player is worth what a team will pay him. It didn't make us wrong for not paying Ron that much, nor did it make Carolina wrong for signing him for that number. That's what they thought he was worth and it was their right to determine that.

Another contract we were really criticized for was the Kevin Stevens deal. In May of our second year in Pittsburgh, we were about three-quarters of the way to signing a new contract with Kevin. We were playing the Islanders in game seven of the second round of the playoffs when Kevin went into the corner, collided with Rich Pilon and was immediately knocked out. He couldn't break his fall to the ice and broke an amazing number of bones in his face. He required delicate surgery involving metal plates to help reassemble his face. It was one of the worst injuries I've ever seen. How could we have said to Kevin Stevens — who gave his face for the team — that we weren't going to pay him? A lot of people questioned whether Kevin could come back and play after that injury, but the very next season he came back and scored 41 goals and 87 points.

Mario's Battle

The team that went for the third Cup was the best Penguins team of them all. I've always said that, and so has Scotty Bowman.

That year we had five players (Lemieux, Jagr, Tocchet, Stevens and Mullen) with 30 goals and four (Lemieux, Stevens, Tocchet and Francis) with 100 points. We finished first overall with 119 points to win the Presidents' Trophy for the first time in franchise history. Mario started the year with at least one goal in each of the first 12 games and by January was threatening to break both Wayne Gretzky's goals and assists records for a single season.

Then, on the morning of January 12, 1993, I got a call from Mario while he was on the way home from the doctor.

"They found a lump and I have Hodgkin's disease," he said.

I was just stunned. I wanted to be there for him and immediately flew from L.A. to Pittsburgh.

Here's what most people don't know. Mario couldn't start his lymphoma treatment right away because he had an infection in his lungs and the doctors couldn't be sure that the infection wasn't more cancer. So for two weeks we were all very nervously praying for the lungs to clear. Fortunately they did, and Mario began a series of 22 radiation treatments.

It was a difficult, frightening time for Mario and his family, and also for everybody in the franchise, but the players managed to play a game above .500 and hang onto first place in the division for the six weeks that Mario took treatment.

Mario got his last treatment on a Monday, and two days later he was on the ice in Philadelphia. The Spectrum is not known for its friendly fans, but before the game they gave Mario a huge standing ovation. Unbelievably, after 52 days off the ice and weakened by radiation, Mario scored a goal and an assist. Unfortunately, we still lost that game.

We lost again three nights later in New York but then didn't lose another game for the rest of the regular season. We set the NHL record, which still stands, with 17 straight wins before ending the schedule with a tie. Mario was out of this world. When he came back he was 12 points behind Pat LaFontaine in the scoring race, and he ended up winning by just that, 12 points. Pro-rating his points-per-game and goals-per-game percentages, if he'd played the entire schedule he would have broken both of Gretzky's records.

We beat New Jersey in five games in the first round, but never got a chance to go for the third Cup because the Islanders took us out in game seven of the division final when David Volek scored in the sixth minute of overtime.

I don't think anyone in professional sport has ever come close to doing what Mario did in 1992–93. Being diagnosed with a disease that could have ended his career, and maybe his life, then coming back to play the way he did after 22 radiation treatments. It was superhuman.

However, he may have come back too soon, because when we started the next season, we could see that things weren't right with him. He had had his second back surgery in the summer, and missed the first 10 games of the season, recovering. After he came back, Howard Jr. came out to a game in Anaheim with me, and by this point it was always tenuous whether or not Mario was going to play. We were sitting up in a box when the players come out for the second period . . . and no Mario.

I asked Howard Jr. to go down to see what was going on, and Mario was sitting in the back of the team bus, pretty emotionally distraught. Tom Reich soon came to me and said Mario was going to have to take a break, and I supported that idea. As a friend, I wanted to be very sensitive to Mario, as the past year had been an immensely trying one for him, both physically and emotionally. Mario never properly fully rested after the cancer treatments. Mario played only 22 games that year, 1993–94, but as a testament to his ability, he had 37 points in those games. He came back in February, and from that point on, I felt, he was always a reluctant participant in the sport. That was something that always ticked off Roger Marino when he became my partner a few years later.

Mario got seven points in the first playoff round, but Washington, the team that could never beat us in the playoffs, eliminated us in six games. That was the spring that the Rangers finally won the Stanley Cup after 54 years, with Mark Messier publicly guaranteeing that the Rangers would win game six of the Eastern final, then scoring a hat trick to make sure it happened. That's what superstars like Messier, and Gretzky, and Mario could do.

The First NHL Lockout

Most people in the sport will tell you that once their team gets eliminated in the playoffs, they are reluctant to watch any more hockey that season.

However, I watched the 1994 Cup final between the Rangers and Vancouver because it was so electrifying for the league. Messier made that incredible prediction the previous round, then single-handedly carried the Rangers to the Cup.

We had played the entire 1993–94 season without a new collective bargaining agreement between the league and the players' association. The CBA we signed to end the short players' strike in April of 1992 was a two-year deal, but it dated back to the start of that season. That led to a lot of media speculation that the NHL would lock the players out before the 1993–94 season, but we played that season without any interruption and went into the summer hoping we could hammer out a new agreement.

I was on the league's negotiating committee and we had a lot of meetings over the summer, trying to work out a new deal. It was a difficult process involving a lot of discussions because there were a number of complicated issues involved. We actually agreed on one of the most fundamental points, though: that it was important to find a way to keep the smaller-market teams alive in an era of changing economics. The two sides came at it from vastly different points of view, of course.

Essentially, in the negotiations, the NHL was proposing a payroll tax and a salary cap, along with some changes to free agency and salary arbitration. The players, meanwhile, were suggesting revenue sharing among the teams as an answer to economic issues.

We were having meetings every other week to discuss the potential work stoppage, and I really did not enjoy them. The owners who were pro-lockout felt the only way to do it was to shut the game down and force the players' hands.

As I've said, I've been out of step on every strike and every lockout, and to this day I feel that this was the most ill-advised lockout this league has ever had. There are a number of reasons for this. With the Rangers having just won the Cup after five decades without it, there was a renewed public interest in hockey. We had just signed a new TV deal with the emerging Fox network, which appealed directly to the NHL demographics. As well, Major League Baseball players went on strike in August, which eventually cancelled the World Series, thereby putting us in a position of not having to compete with baseball for media attention. It moved us up to right after the NFL on the nightly sports news, so even our *exhibition* games were getting on ESPN and in the sports pages.

Some owners thought that my objection was because we weren't financed properly in Pittsburgh and couldn't afford a work stoppage. They were partly right, but 60 per cent of the other teams were in the same situation.

My point of view was, "Look, we've got momentum, and that's the hardest thing in the world to get. We've captured the eye of the general sports public, not just hockey fans. We are on Fox, and to make it even better, there is no baseball." And history has proven me right, because it took years for the game to regain the momentum we had before we locked the players out.

Right after training camp we took a vote at the Waldorf in New York, and my vote was one of only four against initiating the lockout.

I remember walking out of the Waldorf ballroom after the vote with Bruins owner and chairman of the Board of Governors, Jeremy Jacobs, and John McMullen of the New Jersey Devils, both of whom I had tremendous respect for and still do. John put his arm around me and said, "Howard, don't worry about a thing. These players will miss a paycheck and they'll be back right away." I answered that we were all forgetting why we overpaid players: they're competitive, and do not want to lose. They were going to want to beat us.

At the meeting, one of the lawyers had passed around Marvin Miller's book *A Whole Different Ball Game*, which describes what happens during collective bargaining. I didn't read it until the entire process was all over, and then I wished I'd read it when they gave it to me, because it warns you not to think that a deal will get done until it is the 11th hour. Each side knows that their best deal isn't going to be extended until the last possible minute, and that is exactly what happened.

The longer the lockout went on, the more people started to object to it. This was the first lockout in the history of the NHL, so nobody knew what to expect and nobody was prepared for it. While some teams laid off staff, we continued to pay all our employees and didn't lay off one person. My feeling was that it wasn't their fault that there was a lockout.

There were a lot of hawks amongst the governors: Jacobs, McMullen, Richard Gordon in Hartford, Abe Pollin in Washington. I couldn't get mad at Abe Pollin — he was a wonderful man and was always good to me. I remember during one vote he was sitting next to me and he said, "Howard, I know you think I'm an asshole, but I've got to vote no." I said, "Abe don't worry about it. I don't think you're an asshole, I just think you're wrong."

The lockout was crippling us and kept going right through Christmas. I was really apprehensive that it might not end and we could lose the whole season. It went right to January 11th, and I remember walking around the Civic Arena concourse while the vote to end the lockout was being conducted by telephone, and saying a prayer to myself, because if we had lost the whole season we would have been in trouble financially, along with a number of other teams.

The vote to end the lockout just squeaked by, and we executed our plan to launch a 48-game season. You couldn't really do it with any fewer games than 48.

We did manage to get a rookie salary cap in the settlement, and rookies had to sign two-way contracts, but there was no overall salary cap — and there wouldn't be one for another decade. There are those who say we didn't accomplish enough, and who are critical of teams like ours who couldn't afford to lose the season financially and so voted to end the lockout. As far as I am concerned, history has proven that I was right with regards to my position on the first lockout. Momentum is really hard to generate in pro sports, and we had it going for us, only to see it dissipate. All you have to do is look at the franchise problems that occurred after this particular lockout, and you will understand why the lockout was so ill-advised. There was a significant number of changes in ownership after the 1994–95 lockout.

When we finally got back on the ice in January of 1995, it was without Mario, who had decided to take the year off to rest emotionally and physically. But Jaromir Jagr helped compensate for Mario's absence with his first of an eventual five NHL scoring titles. We won 12 of our first 13 games and tied the other one, before cooling off for the rest of the schedule and finishing second to Quebec in the Northeast Division. In the opening round of the playoffs, Washington went up on us three games to one, but for the second time in four years we rallied to beat them out in seven games. Then we lost in five games to the Devils, who went on to win their first Cup.

The 1994–95 lockout was the first lengthy work stoppage for the NHL. It was a learning experience for everyone, including the players. The next work stoppage would be in 2004–05, when the NHL lost the entire season, including the Stanley Cup playoffs. Then there was the 2012–13 lockout, which also resulted in a 48-game schedule.

Each work stoppage made for a far better working environment for ownership and, as far as I am concerned, for the players as well. Without the type of structure that came out of the stoppages, we would have had a league of 12 to 16 teams. The players on those teams may have been richer, but there would have been a lot fewer of them. The NHL is only as strong as its weakest link. Of course Toronto, New York, Montreal and other traditionally robust franchises do well, but the Nashvilles, Carolinas and St. Louises of the league need the opportunity to succeed in markets that are considerably smaller. Under Gary Bettman's leadership, a CBA has evolved that allows both players and owners alike to grow as the sport grows.

Sudden Death

During the 1994–95 lockout we were also filming a movie called *Sudden Death*. The lockout made the shooting more difficult, as we were counting on actual sold-out games to film crowd scenes, and there weren't any.

Karen wrote the treatment for the film, and Gene Quintano wrote the screenplay, which was about a terrorist group that planned to blow up the Civic Arena just as the seventh game of the Stanley Cup final between the Penguins and the Chicago Blackhawks ended. Jean-Claude Van Damme was the star and the director was Peter Hyams, who had done *The Star Chamber, 2010* and *Timecop*.

In the script, the opposing team was Chicago, so we were planning on filming the game from every possible angle when they came to town. Of course, that plan went out the window after the games were cancelled.

Fortunately, I had a pretty good relationship with Bob Goodenow, the head of the players' association, and I asked him to let me have the Cleveland Lumberjacks, our farm team, play an exhibition game in Pittsburgh dressed as the Blackhawks, as our guys on the Penguins had agreed to help us out and play. Bob agreed to this, too, and we wound up with close to a sellout crowd.

What we hoped to do with *Sudden Death* was create a movie that was very commercial and would draw people to hockey. And we wanted to tie our Penguins merchandise to the movie, to drive sales.

The movie itself is essentially *Die Hard* in an arena. It opens with Karen as the director in the ESPN truck, and from there all the action of the movie is tied to the ticking clock in the arena. We cut from scenes around the arena, to things going on outside, to action on the ice, with the scoreboard joining everything together as it dramatically winds down to 0:00, when the arena will blow up.

Bill Wirtz loved the movies, so when he heard we were making *Sudden Death* he asked what it was about. I showed him the script, and then told him that he was in it! He said he would love to play himself. Bill then realized that it would be a three-week commitment for him on the set, and that ended that. We had to use a real actor.

Sudden Death was a modest success. It made about $75 million worldwide. It was, in its way, a testament to the old Civic Arena: the inspiration for the film was the fact that the roof of the arena could actually be opened up, although the hydraulics never were consistently reliable. When it was built in 1961, six years before NHL expansion, the Civic Arena was the first sports facility in the world with a retractable roof and was considered a major architectural feat at the time.

The Russian Penguins

By now, people in hockey recognized that I like doing things a little differently and am naturally attracted to situations a little off the beaten path. I think that's what inspired Mike Barnett to present me with the most unique investment opportunity I'd ever seen in hockey.

Much later, Barnett would become the general manager of the Phoenix Coyotes, but in the early 1990s he was running the hockey branch of the International Management Group, the largest sports management agency in the world. And he was the agent for Wayne Gretzky, among many other players. He had a lot of clout in the sport and was also a good friend.

As we were coming to the end of our first year in Pittsburgh, Barnett came to me and asked, "Would you ever think about getting involved with the Red Army team?"

The Iron Curtain had lifted less than four years earlier, and everything was changing dramatically in Russia. It was the Wild West, and some of the biggest institutions of the communist era were having trouble adjusting to life in the new world. One of those was the CSKA — the Central Sports Club of the Army, better known as the "Red Army." The Red Army had always dominated Russian hockey, wearing the iconic red jersey with the letters CCCP, and had supplied most of the players for the USSR's powerhouse international team.

Mike was working with a fellow named Paul Theofanous who was fluent in Russian and really knew his way around the Iron Curtain countries. Theo was bright as hell and had an excellent knowledge of the inner workings of the Russian world. Mike and Paul were representing the Red Army, which had fallen on hard times in the Russian Elite Hockey League. You have to understand that Russia was just coming off communism, and while I wouldn't say it was becoming a democracy, there was certainly a cultural revolution and the Red Army didn't have the ability to do the things it used to do. For decades, if you were a great player in Russia and the Red Army wanted you, even if Spartak or any of the other teams wanted you too, the Red Army got you because they just enlisted you in the army with a one-time draft. So the Red Army got all the players they wanted. They had the crème de la crème of Soviet Hockey.

Once that changed, it became a competitive environment, and they, of all teams, didn't know how to compete. They had to buy players and didn't have the money or know-how to compete for them because they had never had to — it was counterintuitive to communism. So they were looking for ways in which to create a business, and they came to us.

We did the deal with Viktor Tikhonov, who was the Red Army coach, and Valery Gushchin, who was the general manager. Gushchin was a genuine character, and perhaps it's a cliché, but he sure looked like he enjoyed his vodka. Tikhonov was stoic, didn't smile much and was very serious about the game and how it had been traditionally played and presented. He had zero interest whatsoever in anything other than what was happening on the ice, and winning the game. He didn't have a marketing bone in his body. He had been, by far, the most famous coach in the old USSR and had driven the Soviet national team to eight world championships and three Olympic gold medals. During the communist years, he had the rank of Red Army general and he controlled his team like a dictator, keeping his players isolated in training camp 10 or 11 months out of every year. He had to try to adapt to the new situation when players began to have freedom of movement, but it was a very difficult adjustment for him. He also had an extremely difficult time dealing with the multitude of promotions and marketing techniques that we brought to the situation.

Tikhonov and Gushchin flew over to the U.S., and after meeting with them we got excited and decided to do the deal. We announced it in Pittsburgh, and it generated a lot of interest and speculation. Everyone was immediately suspicious of what we were up to.

On our side the partners were Karen and me, our hockey partners Tom Ruta and Morris Belzberg from the Penguins' ownership,
our film partner Richard Cohen, the Canadian actor Michael J.
Fox and Mario. It was a 50-50 deal between us and the Red Army,
and I think we originally put 350 grand into the program. We had
a legitimate Russian lawyer paper the deal, and their minister of
defence signed the document.

We were repeatedly asked why we were entering into such an
agreement. We had four reasons.

1. It had never been done before.
2. We thought it would give us an edge on inside knowl-
    edge about potential Russian talent for the Pittsburgh
    Penguins.
3. We thought it could be profitable because there was
    great interest in American products being sold in Rus-
    sia, now that the Iron Curtain had been lifted.
4. Any Russian player drafted off the Red Army team
    would generate a substantial transfer fee from the NHL
    to us.

We hired Mark Kelley, Jack's son, as our on-site GM. He was
there to be our hockey eyes and ears and to find players for the
Penguins. This was a time when NHL draft choices were worth
something to the teams they were chosen from. If you were drafted
number one, your team got 250 grand and there was a declining
order of payments after that. So we said to ourselves, "Hey, this
is a) a way to make money and b) a way to get a little edge in the
NHL." This was the old Branch Rickey theory of operating a minor
league team: find the best players, put them on your team with
good coaching, and when they get selected by the NHL you end up
with a high fee for your efforts. Then the NHL changed the rules.

Any money changing hands between the league and an international federation would now have to go to the federation. Prior

to this, if the Red Army had a player drafted in the first round, they were the direct recipients of $250K. For a second-round choice that number decreased but was still paid directly to the team. Under the new deal, the NHL just paid one flat fee to the IIHF (International Ice Hockey Federation), which was then shared equally amongst all the international federation teams. Therefore we lost the most valuable profit center for the Russian Penguins. That was the stupidest deal the federations ever made and they realized that . . . after the fact. It took away all the incentive for people to do a good job. Originally, club owners had been incentivized to develop as many number one draft choices as they could because that was their money, right there. Then that got taken away.

We happened to introduce this Russian idea to Michael Eisner, the CEO of the Walt Disney Company, who had just acquired an NHL expansion team and called them the Mighty Ducks of Anaheim. The Disney folks wanted to get involved as a partner in the Russian deal too — Michael was really excited about it. They actually designed an amazing uniform for us and sent a young executive named Kevin Gilmore to join us on our Russian journey (Kevin is currently the chief operating officer of the Montreal Canadiens). The uniform created by Disney was fantastic but never used because we never could finalize the deal with them.

Karen eventually designed a new logo and uniform in red, black and white. The red was the basic CSKA color, and the black and white came from the Pittsburgh uniform. The logo was a menacing-looking Penguin with a military cap and skates. When Tikhonov and Gushchin first saw the logo, they were hysterical with laughter. When we pressed them on what was so funny they admitted it looked like the general who had just been put in charge of all Red Army sport.

We put in a young marketing whiz named Steve Warshaw to run things for us. If you were going to cast a movie, he'd be the Ben

Stiller type. A shorter Ben Stiller. The idea was for Steve to show the Russians the culture of filling your building and doing all the cool things around an arena that we do over here — hockey, North American style.

Candidly — and Steve would probably laugh at this — he had worn out his welcome at various other sports franchises. He lacked a bit of tact and he kept coming up with crazy ideas, but crazy ideas and someone who would not be deterred were just what the doctor ordered for this unusual situation. So we sent him to Moscow, where we thought he would be tolerated . . . or at least we wouldn't have to hear about it. We figured the language barrier might work in our favor. It was a plus to not fully comprehend what Steve was saying. He was the proverbial "gum on a shoe" director of marketing. Sometimes he went too far. For instance, after a dinner in New York City with Michael Eisner and his wife, Jane, at the 21 Club that somehow Warshaw invited himself to, he sent Michael a follow-up e-mail which began "Dear Comrade Eisner." I called Warshaw and said, "Stevie, Michael Eisner is head of one of the most important entertainment businesses in the world. He's not your comrade, he's 'Mr. Eisner.'"

It was a time of unrest over there. They wanted American money but they didn't necessarily want Americans in their faces messing around with their way of doing things. Keep in mind that until our arrival on the scene, Tikhonov could have cared less what size of crowd they drew. Actually, they never had a crowd. They might have gotten 500 people on the best nights.

It was hysterical to watch Steve and Tikhonov interact. With Tikhonov, it was all about the game on the ice, and winning. Period. With Steve it was all about cutting-edge promotions, and he could care less about the actual games themselves.

For the first few games, nobody showed up except people who wanted to get out of the cold. Then, as Steve started doing more interesting and creative promotions, people started to take notice and they began buying tickets. Sponsors were sponsoring events once they saw the crowds starting to increase. It was starting to work. We had a Toilet Paper Night, a Razor Blade Night, a Toothpaste Night. People needed the basics and they came to the game for them. We drew a sellout crowd for a Free Beer Night promotion with Iron City Beer out of Pittsburgh, with cans featuring the Russian Penguins logo. Unfortunately we made one mistake: we gave out the free beer before the puck was dropped. Needless to say, as soon as the first goal was scored and there was a stoppage in play, 6,000 empty beer cans were thrown onto the ice. Watching Tikhonov's reaction from the bench? Priceless.

Then you had the cheerleaders. There had been no cheerleaders at Russian games before we arrived — in fact, there were no cheerleaders at U.S. games either. But Steve wanted to try something new. Near the arena complex in Moscow was a strip bar, and Stevie figured maybe the girls would want to make a little extra cash on the side, so he proposed that they come and cheer at the games. Remember, he spoke no Russian. So he hired some of them to entertain our crowds, and on the first night, the cheerleaders were going to perform their dance on the ice between the first and second periods. The crowd was excited and Steve was sitting in the stands feeling smug about his new "event." The music began and the next thing you know our cheerleaders started shaking, and then began shedding their cheerleading outfits. Even over the sound of the music and the fans hooting and hollering, you could hear a primal scream from Warshaw in the stands as he shot out of his seat and raced onto the ice to pull the plug on the "inevitable" outcome. He was absolutely aghast and felt there needed to be a premium charged for that much entertainment! As a postscript, the next game was a sellout. The cheerleaders were retired, but they'd had the desired effect. Thank goodness Tikhonov was in the locker room at the time, or we would have had to resuscitate him.

We chartered a private plane for our own personal visit around February of 1994. It was highly recommended that we bring security with us, as it could get dicey over there. Our security was provided by a friend of Theo's named Billy McClain. All we had to do was look at Billy to know we were safe. Also on the trip were Tom Ruta, Ken Sawyer (the former NHL CFO who consulted with us), and Kevin Gilmore of the Mighty Ducks.

It was dicey all right. There were people getting shot. Rich Americans were being kidnapped for ransom. We stayed in a beautiful hotel, but there were cement barriers all around it with guys carrying machine guns on patrol. When we went to Red Square, where all the markets were, there were all these American knock-offs, and Kevin Gilmore was taking pictures of it all. I asked him, "What the hell are you doing?" "Well, I gotta send these back to Disney, they're illegal." I said, "Kevin, you and what army are coming over here to tell the Russians they can't sell merchandise featuring Mickey Mouski?"

We had landed a major sponsor, American Motors. They wanted to promote the Jeep Wrangler in Moscow and were raffling one off through a lottery system that Warshaw ran all season. The game that we attended that February was the game when the winner of the Jeep was to be determined. The building was packed, and to Tikhonov's utter dismay, the people were way more interested in who was going to win the Jeep than who was going to win the game. Remember, maybe one-tenth of the Russian population at the time even knew what a Jeep Wrangler looked like, and owning one was completely out of the question for almost all of them.

The plan was that between the first and second periods there would be a selection process to go from 10 semi-finalists down to 2. It was just electric in the building, especially when they drove the Jeep out between the first and second periods. The place was going crazy. Everybody was cheering and yelling as we got down to the two finalists: an older couple, and a young man about 19 or 20 years old. Each was given a key, one of which would start the Jeep, one of which was bogus.

The young man had never driven a car, but with the help of the ice crew, he got the key into the ignition and cranked it. It started, the engine revved and there was pandemonium in the stands. In all the excitement, the young man shifted it into gear, the car started to spin around the ice and went right through the dasher boards. They patched up the boards with something or other, and Tikhonov was incensed, of course, absolutely beside himself with rage. But the kid got his Jeep. And Warshaw had outdone himself again.

That night, Vadislav Tretiak, one of the world's all-time great goalkeepers, hosted us for a delightfully memorable authentic Russian dinner, and we all had a good laugh over the Jeep.

The next day we went to the rink, and Tikhonov and Gushchin told Tom and me that the general who had just been made sports minister of the Red Army, and who had just come back from the Afghan front, wanted to meet us. Apparently he wanted to express his appreciation for our investment in the Red Army team, and also wanted to see if we would come in on soccer and basketball and other sports under the Red Army umbrella. We said we would be delighted to meet and consider any rational proposal.

Tikhonov and Gushchin said to me, "Now, Howard, do us a favour. If you are going to come in on soccer and basketball, it would make us look really good if you say that you want us involved." I figured that would be fine. Theo was meant to be my interpreter, but he had evaporated for the afternoon, so we got an executive from the office instead. Our group — Tom, myself, Gushchin, Tikhonov, Steve Warshaw, and Billy McClain for security — were escorted over to the general's offices and into a secure room with a massive conference table. There were a number of well-armed military personnel around. The head of the table was clearly reserved for the general, and I couldn't help noticing Gushchin and Tikhonov at the farthest end of the table, looking very uncomfortable. I wondered, "What's up here?"

The general entered the room, shook my hand, then Tom's, and barely acknowledged anyone else. He welcomed us in Russian, the executive doing the translation. He then proceeded to say exactly what Tikhonov and Gushchin had prepared us for. "We love what you're doing, and we really would love to have you invest in other sports teams. We hope you'll stay with this." So then I did what I said I would do, expressing great appreciation for the privilege of being allowed to be part of such an historical and exciting venture. I then said that we would welcome the opportunity to pursue soccer and basketball involvement and that we would like Mr. Gushchin and Mr. Tikhonov to be involved as well.

There was complete silence in the room. The general looked at me expressionlessly, then glared at Gushchin and Tikhonov, who were now practically shaking with fear. All of a sudden the general stood up and raised his fist — and I was thinking, "Is he going to hit me?" — then slammed it down on the table and yelled, "Wrong answer!" in perfectly good English. He looked at Gushchin, who was practically ready to die, and said, in English, "Gushchin, you drink too much and you've never been in the army. If you aren't careful, I'm going to see to it that you're drafted tomorrow." He was more respectful of Tikhonov, but he admonished him too. "Your team isn't doing well at all, and if that team doesn't get going, *you'll* be back in the Army." He went on like this for a while. Tom and I looked at each other thinking, "What the hell have we gotten into?" and "Thank God we have a charter plane to take us home."

Then the general very calmly sat down, his whole demeanor softened, and he said, "Now, please, Mr. Baldwin, how is Mario Lemieux feeling after his bout with Hodgkin's disease? You must tell him that all Russian prayers are with him." Which was actually incredible, because all during the Soviet era that had just ended, officially there was no religion in Russia.

We proceeded to have a delightful meeting.

When we left, Gushchin and Tikhonov practically sprinted back to our office. Most offices have a desk and filing cabinet, but this one had a locker, and it was full of vodka. That vodka came out and they were just . . . well, it was a typical Russians-drinking-vodka scene. The fact of the matter was that the army could still do whatever it wanted, even after the fall of the communist era. Tikhonov and Gushchin were relieved to get away with nothing more than a severe admonishment, but I think the general just got there in a bad mood. The guy had just come back from the Afghan front and that was not a good time for the Russians. And I think he also felt that Gushchin and Tikhonov were out of line — which they were.

On the ice, the team was still pretty average, but it was better than it had been when we got there. In 1992–93 CSKA finished second-last overall, with a 7–28–7 record. After we took over, the 1993–94 team climbed just over .500, to 21–20–5, and 14th overall in the 24-team league.

It was a young roster, with about 17 or 18 teenagers playing at least one game that year. Nikolai Khabibulin was probably our most recognizable player; he had already been taken by Winnipeg in the 1992 draft. Sergei Brylin went to the Devils in the second round that June, and Yan Golubovsky went to Detroit in the first round even though he had only played eight games for us after coming from Dynamo's second team. Golubovsky didn't have much of an NHL career, but at least he played a few dozen games in the league. We, like most other teams, had a lot of players drafted who never played in the NHL and some who never even came to North America. But now that they could finally get players out of Russia, NHL teams were drafting them like crazy.

Over our two years there, we drafted a handful of players from CSKA for Pittsburgh, like Valentin Morozov, Oleg Belov and Alexei Krivchenkov, but they turned out to be AHL types who never made the Penguins. But by being there we knew all about Alexei Morozov, who played for Krylja Sovetov, and we took him in the first round of the 1995 draft. He had a 20-goal season for us seven years later.

That first year, the 1993–94 season, we toured the Red Army team, billed as the Russian Penguins, through the U.S. We played 13 games against International Hockey League teams, with the games counting in the IHL standings. We won two games, tied two and lost the other nine.

In the 1994–95 season, our second year, we got up to 25–20–7 and finished 6th out of 14 teams in the new West division, but the main thing was that by the middle of that season we were really starting to make money. Warshaw and his crew were doing a terrific job. The team was playing to full capacity on a regular basis, and we were doing over a million bucks in sponsorships, mostly from American companies. The whole idea was that American companies were itching to get into Russia and were looking for vehicles to get their products there. So we introduced North American culture to the Russians . . . through hockey. It made a profit for CSKA, and for us — which, ironically, is what led to our departure.

We got more publicity from the Russian Penguins than from anything else we did. *The Today Show*, the *Wall Street Journal*, *Good Morning America*, a feature in *Penthouse* magazine — everything. We were mentioned in a speech by Al Gore about how more Americans should go over to Russia; he used us as an example of how Americans could blend into their culture. But all the attention was a double-edged sword. It woke up the wrong Russian elements to our venture, even in our own office. Periodically, Gushchin would send a message asking for an additional $5K or $10K here and there for "hockey" expenses. The final request was a Mercedes for Gushchin, to "make the team better," to which we said, "*Nyet!*"

At the end of that year we had our usual "owners'" meeting in New York, and we requested that Gushchin and Tikhonov bring an accounting of how the money had been spent. It was Tom Ruta, Karen and me, and we did what we always did: we went to Morton's for dinner and the meeting. Gushchin and Tikhonov met us there, but this time they brought with them two guys, both young and pockmarked, with slicked-back hair, gold Rolexes and black shiny suits. Instead of financial documents, Gushchin produced Polaroid photos — in color! — of his new office and Tikhonov's new office, complete with a high-tech sauna between them. This was their version of accounting for where our money went.

And then they put the arm on us. It was very simple. It was really obvious that their companions were thugs, but Gushchin and Tikhonov introduced them like this: "These gentlemen are our bankers, and they're our partners now, and in order for this to continue the way we hope, we hope you'll invest money with them to be able to continue to maintain the program we have together." This was right in the restaurant. It was a complete shakedown and we'd have to have been pretty naive not to get that. That kind of intimidation was a rampant phenomenon in the "new" Russia. We politely declined to make any payoff, but we also got the message. We would be saying "*Do svidaniya*" (goodbye) to Russia.

We finished dinner, picked up the tab, said our goodbyes, and the minute we left the restaurant Tom and I looked at each other and said, "We have to get our people out of there, *now!*" It was getting dangerous, and we didn't want to jeopardize the safety of our people.

We brought Stevie Warshaw and his crew home from Moscow as soon as we could. To underscore the danger, the concession company at the arena would not acquiesce to any payoff either, and sadly, right after we got Stevie out of there, their concession manager was gunned down right in front of the building.

So you see, we hit it at sort of the perfect moment, and while it is more stable there now, we got out at the right time.

I loved the experience, and I was very proud of it because we were the first. If the rules hadn't changed, we might still be there today. Tikhonov and Gushchin were great, fun characters, and Tikhonov, to this day, is one of the great hockey coaches of all time, and not just in Russia. The general who everybody thought was going to shoot us? I'm not sure what happened to him but would love to find out.

It was one of the more interesting chapters of my life. I'd like to think we made a difference in a transitional period for Russian hockey. If you go to a game there now, they are doing all of the same kinds of promotions, plus more.

To this day we still have the rights to own half CSKA if we wanted to. Once a year or so, we get an e-mail: "Come back." But now that they've got the KHL, they don't need us. On a number of occasions quite recently, Gushchin has reached out to Stevie Warshaw to see if we might consider returning.

I guess they need a new Jacuzzi.

Reluctant Bankruptcy and Leaving the Penguins

My final two years with the Pittsburgh Penguins were sometimes dramatic and almost always difficult.

On the ice, Mario decided to retire after the 1996–97 season, despite winning his sixth Art Ross Trophy as NHL scoring champion, blaming his back problems. In his final season, the Flyers easily eliminated us from the first round of the playoffs in five games. GM Craig Patrick was behind the bench after relieving Eddie Johnston of his coaching duties late in the season. Kevin Constantine took over the next year and, without Mario (who was fast-tracked into the Hockey Hall of Fame that November), instituted more of a defensive style, and we finished a very strong second in the East with 98 points. Ron Francis had taken over as captain, and Jaromir won the NHL scoring title with 102 points, 11 more than anyone else. But the Canadiens, who had finished seventh, upset us in six games in the first round of the playoffs.

Off the ice, I got a new partner, Roger Marino, and that eventually led to the Pittsburgh Penguins declaring bankruptcy in October of 1998.

I took a lot of criticism in the Pittsburgh media for that, and still do. I get a little sensitive about the bankruptcy. It did not occur because we *had* to go bankrupt. It occurred, I would argue, because of three commitments — Spectacor Management Group's stranglehold on the arena income, our Fox TV deal and Mario's contract.

After the lockout in 1994, Morris Belzberg, at this point a reluctant partner, asked me to get him out of his share of Penguins ownership. He was retired and said he didn't need the pressure of having to make payrolls any longer. So I contacted my close friend and lawyer from the Whaler days, Bob Caporale, who had founded Game Plan LLC with the former NFL star Randy Vataha. A large part of Game Plan's business was putting buyers and sellers of sports teams together. They introduced me to Marino, a Boston businessman who made his fortune as one of the founders of EMC, a major computer technology business. He also owned the Worcester IceCats of the American League.

Roger bought out Morris, and Tom Ruta as well. I had honored my commitment to Morris because as a result of this transaction he was no longer liable for putting more money into the team, and he got all of his investment back. Roger's cost came to $15 million, plus a line of credit for team operations.

Roger and I then began a partnership that would eventually turn into a match made in hell. We became like Michael Douglas and Kathleen Turner in *The War of the Roses*. Roger wasn't what he appeared to be. He could be a charming fellow, but in many ways he could be a contradiction. You'd have a great meeting with him and think you'd made some sense, and the next day he'd do whatever the hell he wanted. I believe he cost himself the franchise, he cost me the franchise and he cost a ton of money and aggravation to everybody else.

The new partnership deal closed in May of 1997, just a few weeks after we had been eliminated from the playoffs. Under our partnership agreement we had joint control — I could block him on decisions and he could block me. But make no mistake, he was the money. I had as much power as the money because I had a veto, but I would lose that power whenever we needed extra money because I couldn't put it in, and that was clear to Roger when he made the deal with us.

Before Roger arrived on the scene, we had structured Mario's 1996–97 season so that it didn't come across as a permanent retirement when it ended. We didn't want the bottom to fall out of ticket sales, and we were all still holding out hope that once Mario had a chance to rest a bit and recover, he would want to come back and play. Everyone felt his desire to retire was a temporary reaction to the trauma of cancer and treatment. But Mario retired because of his back problems.

My own feeling was that he could have and should have played — that it wasn't his back, it was his mind. But I had no way of knowing, so I was at his mercy. We had to accept Mario's word on his back because there was no other method to gauge how healthy it really was. There was no way to visually decipher his pain. His doctor, Bob Watkins, from Los Angeles, was one of the most renowned back doctors in the world. He worked on a large number of pro athletes and he did some work on my back too. Bob told me, "If Mario decides he can't play because of his back, there is no way you can judge that he can't."

We had no insurance if he didn't play because of his back. And therefore we were screwed on his contract. It was serious money, and the deferred portion of it was accumulating too.

That helped cost us the franchise, because from a marketing standpoint, we couldn't build around Mario, yet at the same time we still had to pay him.

In January of 1998, Roger, Penguins president Don Patton and I met, and we realized that attendance was not holding up. We were doing 11,000 or 12,000 a night, and that would be disastrous on the bottom line.

It was clear we had a problem, and it was about then that Roger became fixated on claiming bankruptcy, and our relationship, which had actually been pretty good, became rocky and started to erode. He felt that the only way to avoid bankruptcy was to redo three deals: our arena management deal, our local TV deal and Mario's deal.

Roger hated our contract with Spectacor Management Group, and he was absolutely right about that. But when I originally made that deal with SMG, it enabled us to acquire the Penguins in the first place. At the time, Ed Snider was the primary owner of SMG, but it was now under new ownership and they were inflexible about trying to help us through our problems.

As well, we weren't making enough from our regional TV deal with Fox. So Roger flew to L.A. and we met with the Fox people, with whom I had a close relationship. I'll never forget it, because it was right out of a comedy movie. Fox was great about it, and we rewrote the contract and Roger was like a kid. We walked out of the office and he jumped in the air and clicked his heels like Charlie Chaplin. I was kind of amazed that he performed the move so well.

I thought everything was all settled, but it wasn't long before Roger said, "You know what? I don't like the Fox deal." And he'd already clicked his heels over it. So we went back to Fox and got an even better arrangement.

Next Roger said, "Now we've got to attack the Lemieux contract. And the way to do that is go to battle."

I said, "We're going to lose that battle. Don't pick on the biggest star in the world, particularly in Pittsburgh."

I had already talked to Mario and Tom Reich about making some adjustments to his contract, and I told Roger that, but he didn't listen.

It was at this point that the bankruptcy discussions increased in intensity. I was just as intense as he was in my refusal to sign off on a bankruptcy. Bankruptcy wasn't the way to solve our problems. We had solved Fox and we could have solved Mario too, without reverting to that.

We were at an impasse, and Gary Bettman called and said, "Look, we have to end this thing, Howard, because he has the money and you don't."

So Gary brokered a meeting at Boston's Logan Airport in the first week of July. We all met with Roger, and I sold out to him. I was to receive $500,000 a year for 10 years, which was a lot of money to me, plus the practice facility. And I got the dormant American Hockey League franchise that we had bought from Colorado.

We shook hands on the deal, I thanked Gary Bettman and Bill Daly, and off I went back to my home in Massachusetts, figuring I was done in Pittsburgh. But later that month Gary called and asked if I'd received any paperwork on the deal yet, which

I hadn't. Nobody could reach Roger, and the next thing we knew, we were reading in the paper, "Roger Marino, owner of the Pittsburgh Penguins, flies to Houston, and then to Kansas City."

He was looking to move the team out of Pittsburgh. And to me it seemed clear that he wasn't going to honor the deal we had made.

Quickly, I got calls from Tom Reich and from Gary, saying that I was the only guy who could block Marino and would have to fight him on the bankruptcy. The deal with Roger wasn't done, so I still had co-control of the team.

Mario did not want the team to move, and he had a lot of deferred money that he was owed on his contract, so I had a number of meetings with Mario and said that I would fight for him. I could have walked away. I had a pretty good deal, on a handshake, from Roger, and I could have just said, "Screw you guys" and stayed away. But I gave up that deal and came back to the Penguins — and Tom Reich will back me up on this — to fight for Mario in any way I could.

And that was when it *really* became *The War of the Roses*.

With Mario not playing, one of our primary goals had been to sign Jaromir Jagr, our other mega-star, to a long-term contract, and I was working closely with his agent, Mike Barnett. In the fall of 1997, we were close to signing Jaromir to a five-year deal at $5 million or $6 million per year. But then the Flyers extended Eric Lindros's contract for two years, with his salary going up to $8.5 million per year in 1998–99. And right away I knew I was in trouble.

Then, in December, after Paul Kariya had held out for 32 games, Anaheim signed him to a short (two-year) deal too, that would pay him $8.5 million in 1998–99. It was clear that agents felt that the value of free agents would keep going up, so they wanted shorter terms. I talked to Jaromir about the value of a longer guaranteed deal over a shorter one, and he was good about it, but with those two deals out there, I knew we weren't going to be able to sign him.

Late in the 1997–98 season, Roger and I made up our minds that the only way that we could survive and get our debt paid off was to do a sell-trade with Jagr, the way Quebec did with Lindros and Edmonton did with Gretzky. In a sell-trade you get cash, you get draft choices and you get whatever else you can.

So Craig Patrick and I divided up the teams we thought could afford Jagr. One of the teams I took was the Rangers. On my very first call, Rangers president Dave Checketts said, "Okay, $12 million, a couple of number one draft choices, and a couple of young players."

It took only one call. But Gary got wind of it and said that wasn't going to happen under his watch.

I said, "Gary where do you think Jagr is better off playing? In New York City, where he'd be a marquee star? Or in Pittsburgh, where we're dying? We can't afford to keep these kinds of payrolls here."

But Gary put a cap of $4.5 million on the cash we could get back for Jagr, so we were screwed. In order to hang on to the franchise, we had to have more money than that. The only issue I ever really had with Gary was that we were unable to do what Marcel Aubut did in Quebec with Lindros, and what Peter Pocklington did in Edmonton with Gretzky, which was to take an asset that they owned and turn it into a bigger asset — cash and players.

Then we had a number of meetings in Gary's offices about bankruptcy. I'll never forget the one meeting when Mario, his lawyer Chuck Greenberg, Tom, my lawyer Steve Lynch and I were in one of the offices and Roger came into the room. When he saw us he took a Coke can and just threw it. It was childish.

Roger and I fought each other right up to the first payroll of the 1998–99 season, when Gary called and said that the only way the payroll could be met was if we filed for bankruptcy. Then, under debtor-in-possession rules, fresh money could be borrowed, because it would be in the first position.

Gary said, "Howard, Roger is the money. You're going to have to give in to him — as bad as it is, you're going to have let him file." I know that Gary didn't like it any more than I did.

In early October, 1998, Roger filed to put the Pittsburgh Penguins into bankruptcy.

Once he did that, I knew I was done in Pittsburgh. I knew I would get crucified by the Pittsburgh media for the bankruptcy, and I just wanted to be finished with the whole situation. I knew there was nothing that I could say to the media that they would accept and that wouldn't sound defensive.

The bankruptcy settlement took until the end of that season, and it was after that that I got mad, because the media all forgot that I'd fought for Mario. Part of the commitment I was looking for was for someone to say the right things — that I was an ally of Mario, and that I was an ally of the franchise, because I had tried to do the right thing by both. And when we were going through it all, the Lemieux people, led by Tom Reich, had been very appreciative.

I said to Mario, "Mario, I don't expect you ever to give me a dime. But when people criticize me, don't lump me in with Roger Marino, because that isn't fair."

At the time I was really pissed, but history will judge whether what I did was good, bad or indifferent.

Tom Reich was a hero of that bankruptcy. He's the one who brought Ron Burkle in with new money for the team, and he's the one who fought every second for Mario.

In Mario I was dealing with a man that I truly had genuine affection for. And who could not admire the skill level of this extraordinarily gifted athlete? I only hope that Mario and a few others realize how hard we did try on his behalf and on behalf of the franchise. People were quick to forget that at the time we acquired the franchise there was considerable speculation that it would be purchased and relocated.

The bankruptcy was conditionally settled in June, with Mario, the largest creditor, proposing to turn $20 million of his $28 million in deferred payments into equity, which would give him controlling interest. And in September, the NHL approved his application for ownership. In the end, as part of the bankruptcy settlement, I was able to keep the dormant AHL franchise (which eventually became the Manchester Monarchs) and a small residual interest in the team.

Postscript to Pittsburgh

On reflection, the 1990s was a very rough decade for me and for hockey.

Personally, I had the thrill and excitement of being part of a team that had Hall of Famers and some of the greatest players in the world at the time: Mario Lemieux, Ron Francis, Paul Coffey, Tom Barrasso, Joey Mullen, Kevin Stevens and, of course, Jaromir Jagr, who is still playing today and who will be an instant first-ballot Hall of Famer. We won the Stanley Cup, a Presidents' Trophy, and many other wonderful awards.

Financially, however, it was an incredibly difficult period to operate an NHL franchise. We were forced to suffer the indignities of a bankruptcy that I never wanted. That was heartbreaking for me.

There was new leadership in the NHL with Gary Bettman, who I think was the perfect man for those difficult times. Bob Goodenow was head of the players' union and he represented the players well. There was no longer the "overly chummy" relationship that the league had enjoyed for so long between the players' rep, Alan Eagleson, and the old-line owners. The players were very cognizant of the agreements the other three major leagues had between their unions and management. No longer were the hockey players going to just roll over.

On a personal level, I felt that I did some really good things. We held the Penguins together as a team. If they are put into their proper perspective, some of the contracts that I have been criticized for don't deserve the criticism. I took a lot of heat for the Lemieux contract from other owners and GMs. Yet those very same critical owners and GMs were guilty of contracts that were just as onerous as any contract I ever agreed to — if not more so. All one has to do is look at history to see that is a fact. And lastly on this issue, how could we not have paid the greatest player in the game at the time, and one of the very few drawing cards that the league then had, especially after we won back-to-back Stanley Cups?

The problem with some of the critics was, and still is, not understanding that there's more to it than just selling tickets. As we got into the 21st century, it was television and the worldwide appeal of the sport that would make the revenues grow dramatically. And that world is driven by stars.

I do feel, however, that I could have done a better job of managing other expenses and of building up the cash reserves of our company in the beginning, when we were doing well financially. We would have been better prepared for the "rainy day."

I also felt that we made too many changes at the top of the Penguins organization. That falls on me. There is no other way to say it — I was just unwilling to relocate to Pittsburgh full time. I feel strongly enough about my own abilities to operate a business to think that if I had been there day to day we would never have had to file for bankruptcy. Subsequently, when the ownership profile changed and Morris left and Roger came in, I was dealing with somebody who had his own point of view and was totally unwilling to listen to anyone else's — mine included.

I think another problem we had as owners was that we were always perceived as outsiders — which we were. However, the people in Pittsburgh were incredibly supportive of us as well as the team, and were so nice to us. Pittsburgh is a great city, and having Mario Lemieux as a local owner as well as the financial savvy Ron Burkle brings to the table as the lead money partner is huge for the franchise. Mario gives the franchise a great face not only locally but in the sports world at large. Ron Burkle gives the franchise immense financial credibility. It makes us very happy to see how well the team is doing now.

PART FIVE

Hollywood —
The Glittering '00s

A Taste for the Movies

I was introduced to the film business through my involvement in developing *Flight of the Navigator* with my great friend Bill Minot. Then I got a further taste of the business through my very dear friend from hockey, Johnny Bassett. The first two film projects Johnny and I worked on together were both scripts — *The Bill Tilden Story*, the proposed biopic of tennis legend Bill Tilden based on the book written by Frank Deford; and the story of Rommie Loudd, the African-American football executive who ended up going to prison for selling drugs in order to meet his team payroll.

Around that time, in 1974, I became intrigued enough with the business that, through a casting director friend of my brother Michael's, I got a bit part in a movie called *The Happy Hooker*. It may not sound like it, but it was a legitimate film, starring Lynn Redgrave and Jean-Pierre Aumont. I figured, what the heck, it was only a day, and I could have a little fun doing the part. I knew nothing about the filmmaking process and I was curious. The day I had to film my scene drove me nuts because it was so monotonous. We were mostly just hanging around and waiting for the scene to be set up. It was 10 hours after I arrived when they actually filmed me. My role was to play a "john" waiting in a lobby with other johns for a night of supposed entertainment. Once the film-ing was done, back to Hartford I went, and I never gave it another thought. To this day I have not seen the actual movie!

Cut to three years later, when the Whalers were playing badly and a critical column was written about me in one of the local papers. Unbeknownst to me, *The Happy Hooker* had come out in theaters, and this particular sportswriter had seen it. He wrote in his column that the problem with the Whalers was that the man-aging general partner of the team was off moonlighting as a movie extra. Caught!

The Kelley Connection

I've known David E. Kelley since he was a young boy. We even have pictures in the family photo album of him when he was eight or nine years old. David is the son of Jack Kelley, who coached Boston University during my brief stay with the varsity team, was our first Whalers head coach and GM and, starting in 1993, was president of the Penguins. David was our stick boy in Hartford and later played hockey at Princeton before studying law at BU and joining Phil David Fine's firm, where my close friend Bob Caporale also practiced.

One day in the mid-1980s, when I was still running the Hart-ford Whalers but also just starting to get some connections to the film business, I was watching a game with Jack in Hartford and he mentioned that David had written a movie script in his spare time and would love for me to look at it.

From the Hip was about a young lawyer who uses unethical practices during a civil case so he can rise quickly in his firm. He's faced with a moral dilemma during a criminal trial and, ultimately, makes the right decision. I thought it would make a good movie and sent it to my lawyer friend Stuart Benjamin and to Bill Minot in L.A. They both thought it was really good, although at 75 pages it was too short (a script should be about 110 pages long).

We optioned the script for $10,000, which meant that we had the exclusive right to try to make the script into a film. Bill Minot suggested that we talk to our old neighbor from Westport, Massachusetts, Bob Clark, who had directed the *Porky's* films and *A Christmas Story*. Bob loved it and agreed to direct, and then collaborated with David to make the script longer.

Within six months we were shooting at Dino De Laurentiis's studios in North Carolina with Judd Nelson as the lead and Elizabeth Perkins, John Hurt and Darren McGavin also in the cast.

From the Hip became the first movie that we did from soup to nuts, and that script eventually got David the job on *L.A. Law*. He took a leave of absence from the law firm, but I told Cap he might as well get another litigator because David was never coming back.

L.A.: The Early Days

The 1985–86 season in Hartford was a turning point for the Whalers on the ice and financially. We were up to 12,000 full-season tickets, had just made the NHL playoffs for the first time, and the team was clearly stabilized with Dave Andrews on the business side, Bill Barnes on the marketing and sales side and Emile Francis on the hockey side all doing a terrific job.

This all enabled me to finally catch my breath and reflect on what my future would be in the business world. Karen and I were to be married in October of 1987, and the film business was

becoming more and more prevalent in our lives. My Whaler partners were ready to sell the team now that it was profitable. I didn't
have much choice to stay with the team once the partners decided
to sell. I had to represent the partners and get them as much as
I could for the team, and I didn't have the financial capabilities
of buying the team myself. At the same time, Karen was finding
success in acting in Los Angeles and I was enjoying the film business and was ready for a new challenge. So in 1988 we relocated
to L.A. It was hard for both Karen and for me, as we both adored
our families and I had three children, but we felt we could make
it work.

We started a film company called Indian Neck Productions. Initially, there were three partners in the company — Bill
Minot, ourselves, and Brian Russell, who was married to Cheryl
Ladd of *Charlie's Angels* fame, and who had a solid production
background — but then Bill Minot left the company and Richard Cohen came on board. We met Richard through Brian and
Cheryl, and Karen and I took an instant liking to him. Richard
became one of our closest friends and was a wonderful partner.

Indian Neck Productions made two films — *Spellbinder*, starring Kelly Preston and Tim Daly, and a lower-budget horror film
called *The Cellar*. We invested heavily in these two films and pretty
quickly learned our first lesson in Hollywood: it can be a money
pit. We lost money on both films, and Brian left the company as a
result.

Richard, Karen and I licked our wounds and regrouped under
the banner of Baldwin/Cohen Productions. We then went on
to produce several successful films together, including *Sudden
Death*; *The Patriot*, starring Steven Seagal; *Resurrection*, starring
Christopher Lambert; and *Gideon*, starring many Oscar- and
Golden Globe–winning actors, including Charlton Heston and
Shelley Winters.

And while we were going through all the Penguins turmoil with Roger Marino, Richard, Karen and I made our fourth film together: *Mystery, Alaska*.

Mystery, Alaska

If you're in the hockey business and you're also in the film business, it only makes sense that occasionally you would combine the two.

The first time we did that was with *Sudden Death,* in our first year with the Pittsburgh Penguins, and the second time was with *Mystery, Alaska*, which is my favorite among the hockey movies we've produced.

Mystery, Alaska was released in October of 1999. But the seeds for the movie were planted when Karen and I had lunch with David E. Kelley at Delmonico's in 1996, when I was still immersed in running the Penguins.

By then, David had become an extremely successful producer and writer, first with Steven Bochco on *L.A. Law* and *Doogie Howser, M.D.*, and then with his own shows, *Picket Fences* and *Chicago Hope*. And he was about to debut both *Ally McBeal* and *The Practice*.

David is one of the most wonderful people on this planet, and one of the most creative. When I suggested at Delmonico's that day that we should try to come up with the ultimate hockey movie, he told me a story about the town of Shelby, Montana. It was an oil boomtown for a while, but its fortunes began to sag, and in 1923, trying to get publicity and revive the economy, the townspeople decided to raise the money to put up a purse for a title fight between Tommy Gibbons and the legendary Jack Dempsey. David suggested we do a hockey version of that theme.

David was very busy, so we agreed that he would get his friend from Princeton, Sean O'Byrne, to write the script, and then David would do the final rewrite. Our idea was to set a hockey game in natural elements to show people the roots of hockey, because in the 1990s everything in the game was perfectly packaged and temperature-controlled. That's how we came up with the idea of Alaska as the site for a televised exhibition game between the New York Rangers and local players.

Remember, at that time the NHL hadn't yet started their outdoor Heritage Classics, and I believe *Mystery* absolutely had an influence on the league staging those games.

In the fictitious town of Mystery, the Saturday hockey game on the outdoor rink is the major weekly social event, and it is considered high praise just to be invited to play. The story was built around the sheriff, who is asked to give up his spot in the Saturday game to a younger player. A former resident of the town is working for a major sports publication in New York City, and he takes it upon himself to issue a challenge to the New York Rangers to come to Mystery, Alaska, to beat the Mystery Boys on "the pond." This comes as a surprise to the town, as they have no idea he's doing this — and they are even more shocked when the Rangers agree to the challenge. The story revolves round the town getting ready for the big game.

Only a week after we got the final script, we signed what's called a pay or play deal for $30 million with Disney. The definition of "pay or play" in this case meant that Disney committed to make the movie, subject to cast and director and the budget coming in at $30 million or less.

The director we all wanted was Jay Roach, who had directed the first Austin Powers movie. It was a bold decision, because Jay didn't know hockey at all. He turned out to be a great choice because he had to really study and explore the game to understand it.

The Disney people said they thought Russell Crowe, who was coming off *L.A. Confidential*, should play the sheriff. They really wanted us to meet Russell, so Karen and I had dinner with him at Mr. Chow.

Russell turned out to be a wonderful guy. He brought a date to dinner and we all had a nice time, and then we figured it was time for us to turn in. When we told Russell we were leaving, he said, "Not when you're with me, mate. I've got a bunch of mates over at the Peninsula Hotel and we're all going over to meet them there." We were there until three or four in the morning, and it took me about a month to recover. He's a great guy.

In early December of 1997 we invited Russell to come to dinner with the Penguins because he had said, "I want to meet the players. I need to get the feel for it, mate." Every year Karen and I would take the Penguins to the Palm when they came to L.A. to play the Kings. We had also done the same thing when we had the Whalers. So there we were in the back room of the Palm when Russell came in, and everybody was having a great time. At the end of dinner, though, I saw that he had gone. I saw that Barrasso had gone, and Jagr, and Ronnie Francis. I was thinking, "Uh-oh." We took care of the bill and on the way out I saw that Russell was at the bar with the guys. I asked if everything was okay and he said sure, and invited us to join him. But we politely declined, because I didn't want to spend another month recovering.

The Penguins were on a West Coast swing and we had arranged for Russell to travel with the team to Anaheim and Phoenix. Three days later, I got a call from Ronnie Francis and he said, "It might be time for Russell to go home or we may not win another road game."

When we started filming *Mystery* in Canmore, Alberta, in February of 1998, Russell rented Glen Sather's house right under the Three Sisters mountain peaks. The weather had been absolutely freezing, but when it came time to film the hockey scenes on the outdoor rink we had built, a chinook blew in and the ice melted. So we called up NHL ice-maker Dan Craig, and he arranged for paneled ice to be brought out from San Diego.

We worked our butts off on the hockey authenticity of that movie. Jack Kelley was there as a hockey consultant, and he made damn sure the hockey looked great. Brad Turner, who played in Europe and had three games with the Islanders, was a great skating double for Russell. He even looked like him.

Russell was great because he really wanted to learn how to skate and play hockey. As an Australian, he was totally unfamiliar with the sport. But what makes Russell a brilliant actor is that he has the ability to study all the nuances of what his character is meant to be. If you saw him in *A Beautiful Mind*, *Gladiator* or *The Insider*, you know that he becomes the character he's portraying. Russell's brilliance in *Mystery* was that he totally felt he was a hockey player and was able to portray it clearly. Then when we had the actual skating scenes, we used Brad Turner.

Glen Sather's son Justin was in the movie, and so was Marty Lacroix, the son of Colorado GM Pierre Lacroix. Pat Brisson was in the movie, long before he was Sidney Crosby's agent. Phil Esposito made an appearance, and the extras had all played at a good level of hockey. Mike Myers had a cameo, playing the role of the colorfully iconic Canadian broadcaster, Don Cherry. Glen Sather, who was running the Edmonton Oilers, came to the set and spoke to the *Mystery* team as well.

There was only one thing that infuriated me and I'm still mad at myself that we didn't catch it. When Little Richard came out to sing the national anthem and the camera scanned the players' feet, one of them had black laces in his skates — and we all know that doesn't happen.

We made a mistake in making *Mystery* an R-rated movie instead of PG-13. We should have cut some of the language out so it would be suitable for more people. Disney also made a change in administration and brought in a new marketing director who didn't have a clue what the movie was about, and that hurt us. *Mystery* did $20 million at the box office, when it should have been $60-70 million, but it did great DVD sales.

Mystery, Alaska has become a cult film. It's a good movie, wonderfully acted, with a wonderful story and a wonderful set. It was ranked by the major website, bleacherreport.com as the fourth-best hockey movie ever made.

I'm extremely proud of that movie.

Crusader Entertainment

On May 27, 1999, tragically and unexpectedly, our dear friend and partner Richard Cohen died. Our lives were really in a state of flux at this point. We were mourning the loss of our partner and fighting the battle in Pittsburgh.

At the same time, we were introduced to a new member of the NHL, Philip Anschutz, who had recently acquired the Los Angeles Kings. Phil was a soccer enthusiast who owned several MLS teams and was interested in learning more about *Mystery, Alaska*, as he wanted to develop a film that promoted soccer. One thing led to another and we formed a company with Phil called Crusader Entertainment.

Karen and I really liked Phil and appreciated his immediate commitment to fund a film company properly, not only with development financing but with production financing as well.

We had a challenging mission statement at Crusader, but one we believed in and that made economic sense. The mission was to make G and PG films that had some message which went beyond pure exploitation. The first two films we did with Phil were smaller pictures called *Joshua*, starring Tony Goldwyn, F. Murray Abraham and Giancarlo Giannini, and *Children on Their Birthdays*, a Truman Capote adaptation.

Under the Baldwin/Cohen banner, we had developed a few projects that Crusader acquired but that we knew were not suitable under the mission statement. One of those films was *A Sound of Thunder*, based on Ray Bradbury's famous short story. We made a deal with Franchise Pictures for them to take this project over. The movie starred Ed Burns, Sir Ben Kingsley and Catherine McCormack, was directed by Peter Hyams and was released by Warner Brothers.

As a result of the development of this film, we established a wonderful relationship with Ray Bradbury, who was a magnificent mind. He gave Karen the honor of introducing him at an award ceremony for him at the University of Southern California.

We then made two films for Crusader in Australia, *Swimming Upstream*, the story of swimmer Tony Fingleton, starring Geoffrey Rush and Judy Davis, and *Danny Deckchair*, which was a fun, uplifting comedy starring Rhys Ifans and Miranda Otto. *Swimming Upstream* was nominated for five Australian Film Institute Awards, and *Danny Deckchair* had the honor of being the closing picture at the Toronto Film Festival in 2003. We did a few other smaller films and actually fulfilled Phil's hopes for a soccer movie, with *The Game of Their Lives* (a.k.a. *The Miracle Match*), about the 1950 U.S. World Cup team, and a project that reunited David Anspaugh and Angelo Pizzo, and starred Gerard Butler.

The two big films we did with Phil under the Crusader banner were *Ray* and *Sahara*.

Ray

The original title of *Ray* was *Unchain My Heart*. We had started working on this project at Baldwin/Cohen with our good friend Stuart Benjamin, and then brought it into Crusader. We put up the money to get the first draft of the script written, but Stuart had already been working on it for nine years.

Ray is a great example of how long it can take to get a movie made. By the time it was released in October of 2004, Karen and I had been involved for four years, but for Stuart the journey was more like 13 years.

Stuart had become a friend of Ray Charles and had obtained the rights to Ray's story. His relationship with Ray was very important to him and he had nurtured it for years.

Everybody knew Ray Charles's music. I had always liked it, and Phil was an avid fan. *Ray* was a hard movie to get made because it was a period piece and its subject was African-American, so there wasn't much overseas sales potential, or at least we didn't think there would be.

We all knew that Taylor Hackford was the right choice to direct because he had a passion for Ray Charles as well. Stuart and Taylor had been friends at USC and had worked together in the film business for years. Taylor's first big hit was *An Officer and a Gentleman* in 1982, and he had also directed *White Nights* and produced *La Bamba* and *When We Were Kings*, among many other credits.

Taylor's agent Jim Wiatt, a great guy who was head of the famous William Morris Agency, told me Taylor was reluctant to do the film because he was concerned about telling this story in a soft PG-13 manner. After a lengthy negotiation that dealt not only with finance but also with creative issues, we came to a fair agreement.

After Taylor agreed to direct, Jamie Foxx was quickly attached as the lead. Besides being a great actor, Jamie had a musical background. He sang in a band called Leather and Lace when he was young, and he went to United States International University on a classical music scholarship. Everyone was familiar with his TV work on *In Living Color* and *The Jamie Foxx Show* in the '90s, and he had moved into movies with *Ali* and *Any Given Sunday*. He was obviously the right choice to play Ray Charles, and in the end his incredible efforts and outstanding performance were rewarded with the Academy Award for Best Actor. When he also got the Best Supporting Actor nomination for *Collateral*, which he did with Tom Cruise, Jamie became just the second male actor (after Al Pacino) to receive two Academy Award nominations for two different films in the same year.

Ray was alive when we started filming, but sadly, he died of cancer in June of 2004, four months before the movie was released. The first time Phil and I met him, we had received very precise instructions to go up the studio's back stairs, which were like a fire escape, and ring the bell. We could hear someone coming down the hall saying, "Hang on, here I come," and it was Ray himself. It was pitch black in there, and I'm thinking, "We ought to turn some lights on," and then I realized Ray didn't need any lights. So Phil and I slowly followed Ray down the hall in the dark. It was the blind leading the blind.

Near the end of filming, Ray came onto the set with a lot of his kids and everyone got confused because Jamie, being the actor that he is, had stayed in character. The kids were calling him Ray and Dad, and I was calling him Ray and Jamie . . . it was surreal.

When Taylor showed us the first cut on a big screen, it ran two hours and 32 minutes, which is, by industry standards, too long by 30 or 40 minutes, but it was unbelievably good.

We screened it for Phil in a theater on the Warner Brothers lot; that was like being in a big living room. We were all apprehensive about some of the scenes in the movie, but to Phil's great credit, he was as excited about the quality of the film as we all were. There were changes that had to be made in order to satisfy the mission statement, but they were minimal and reasonable.

Then we had to sell the movie. I won't bore you with the mountain of details about how that's done, but in general in those days, you could use foreign-sales projections to help capitalize your film. The projections we got, though, were for a total of only $11 million. All the studios passed except for Warner Brothers — which offered a "P and A" deal, which only pays for the marketing — and Universal Studios. So we did the deal with Universal which guaranteed the $11 million to Phil (he had already put $36 million into it) in return for the worldwide rights.

Stacey Snider, whose ex-father-in-law is Ed Snider, was chairman of Universal's film division and said that the movie was just too long. But we told her it "played great" at the two screenings we had in Kansas City — one for a predominantly African-American audience, the second for more of a mixed bag. Stacey said we should screen it again, so we recruited an audience for a Monday night at Marina del Rey. We had the usual security there going up and down the aisles wearing infrared goggles to check for recording piracy, and one woman sitting directly in front of me got thrown out.

The Universal executives got there 30 minutes late, and when that happens it's usually the kiss of death for a testing, because having to wait aggravates the audience. But instead, it was one of the most exhilarating experiences of my life. During the movie, people were standing up and applauding. When a screening ends, the studio executives, producers and directors always huddle in a corner to discuss it, and when we did, Stacey Snider looked at us and said, "Don't change a thing. It's great!"

Ray has grossed almost $300 million, including about $60 million in foreign sales, which shows you just how smart the projections were.

The early part of each year is award season. Everyone, not only in Los Angeles but around the world, anticipates who the nominees will be. The Golden Globes are first, then, a few weeks later, the Oscars.

The Oscar and Globe nominations are announced at 8 a.m. Eastern Time, so in L.A. you have to get up at 6 a.m. to watch. The year *Ray* was in contention, we awoke that early! We were really nervous, because although people think you know beforehand, you actually have no idea if your film will be nominated. The Best Picture Award nominations are always last. Jamie was nominated for Best Actor and Taylor for Best Director, and we also got nominations for editing, sound, and costume design, before it was time for Best Picture.

When they finally said the word — *Ray* — Karen and I were overjoyed and felt incredibly honored. At that point the Academy Awards had been going on for 76 years, and almost 600 movies had been nominated for Best Picture. And how many did they have to select from? Probably more than 10,000.

If you want a measure of how much my 32 years in hockey still influence me, I wore my Whalers championship ring to the Academy Awards for good luck — and I never wear it anywhere. We were sitting with Adam Sandler and his wife, and as you heard in the introduction to this book, Adam, a huge hockey fan, became fascinated by the ring.

Sitting six seats down from us on the aisle was Martin Scorsese, whose *The Aviator* was up against *Ray*, *Finding Neverland*, *Sideways* and *Million Dollar Baby* for Best Picture. Scorsese's film started out the night by winning three of the first four awards, and then I noticed that he pulled out this little piece of paper: his speech. Being a sports guy, with all our superstitions and habits, I immediately figured, "That's killed it, he isn't going to win. You just don't do that, it's bad karma." Scorsese's film didn't win and neither did *Ray*. Clint Eastwood's *Million Dollar Baby* did.

We would have loved to have won the Academy Award for Best Picture — but it is not cliché to say it was a huge honor to be nominated.

Much has been written about who did what on *Ray*, but here are the facts: Stuart Benjamin had this project under his wing for 13 years and had the passion and commitment to not let it die. Karen and I are immensely proud that we were able to play a part in *Ray* by bringing it into Crusader, working with Taylor and Stuart to develop the script, and backing the project. Phil Anschutz deserves huge credit for the guts to write out a $40 million check to finance the film. Of course, creatively, Taylor, Jamie and the other members of the cast and crew deserve credit and accolades for their performances and fine work. Ron Meyer, Stacey Snider, Mark Shmuger and the team at Universal should also be applauded for taking the chance they did on the film when other studios were reluctant to do so. Most importantly we have to thank Ray Charles for his participation in the film and the extraordinary life he led.

In 2006 the American Film Institute put *Ray* in their "100 Years... 100 Cheers" list of the top 100 inspiring American films — "films whose 'cheers' continue to echo across a century of American cinema."

Sahara

Back when Karen and I first decided to move out to Hollywood, a good friend of mine, Senator Lowell Weicker, told me we were crazy because "those people are thieves." I assured him that I was still going to give it a try, and he said, "Okay, then you ought to buy the Cussler books."

If you're not familiar with Clive Cussler, he's the famous author of many wildly popular action/adventure books, one series of which features the hero Dirk Pitt. Cussler writes one Dirk Pitt novel about every two years — it's his brand like Ian Fleming's brand is James Bond.

Everyone in Hollywood looks for a book series, a good one, because there is the potential to do a number of movies off it.

Lowell and Clive share a love of the ocean. Clive's books all have to do with adventure on the ocean, and he and Lowell actually went on a couple of dives together. The two of them were also on a submarine for three days, and how they didn't end up killing each other, I'll never know.

Clive Cussler can be an incredibly difficult man, but I had always wanted to get the rights to his books.

So around 1995 Karen and I started meeting with Clive in Arizona, where he lived, and with his agent, Peter Lampack, in New York City. We were trying to reassure Clive that we respected his work, and slowly but surely he became comfortable with us. Clive drove a tough deal and we spent a fortune on the option, but we knew that if the movies did well, we owned the franchise. We had the rights to do a movie on what's called a revolving option. If you make one movie, you get two-and-a-half years to do another.

The book we chose was *Sahara*. We all agreed it was the best one because it would be manageable in terms of budget: there was not as much action on the water as in some of his other books. Scenes on water cost a lot more money because you either have to do them in reality, on the water itself, or you have to do them by CGI, computer-generated imagery, which is not easy.

After we got the deal done, we were into the difficult details of "approvals." As the author, Clive had a lot of approvals: over the script, over the director and over the two leads. Once those were all in place, our position in the deal was that we then had control of the film. Karen had the responsibility of dealing with Clive, and she deserved combat pay for this role. She was put into an impossible position.

After we got the script done and approved, there were several iterations of director and leading actor before we came to the Breck Eisner–Matthew McConaughey combination. The first actor we interviewed to play Dirk Pitt was Gerard Butler, but he was not a big enough name at the time, though he sure is now. Then we interviewed Hugh Jackman, who was an emerging star. When his agent gave his quote of $5 million, we agreed. It was pricey, but we were building a franchise and it was within our budget. We were delayed for a while because Hugh was travelling, and then he took the lead in *X-Men*, playing Wolverine, which put him out of the picture for us. We didn't want to have to hold up production for the lead actor, and Wolverine became his franchise, so he would be doing more than one.

Rob Bowman, who had done one *X Files* movie, was interested in directing. With Rob, we had Christian Bale interested in the lead role. We all loved Christian, but Paramount didn't think he was an "action hero." Ironically, he went on to play Batman.

Then Rob Bowman dropped out. We were close to getting another director, Jay Roach, who had done *Mystery, Alaska* for us. Tom Cruise was potentially interested with Jay directing. Also, on a weekly basis Matthew McConaughey's reps would be calling Karen to tell her how much he wanted to be Dirk Pitt.

Eventually, we ended up hiring Breck Eisner, Michael Eisner's son, to direct.

Then we got a call from the agent for Penelope Cruz. She wanted to get together to talk about the role of the female lead, Dr. Eva Rojas. Karen and I met Penelope and loved her. She was living with Tom Cruise then, and when she took the script back to the house, she left it lying around and Tom read it. So then we got the call from Tom's agent. He really wanted to play the role of Dirk Pitt. We met with Tom and told him to be sure to call Clive Cussler, because Clive was very opinionated on who should play the lead. Clive felt that Tom, who is short, didn't have the right physical stature to be Dirk Pitt. So Karen had to get on the phone and do what only Karen could have done: convince him that to get the biggest movie star in the world is actually a good thing. She pulled it off, and Clive approved Tom.

We kept telling Tom to call Clive, and he assured us he would. Every fourth day Clive would phone and say Tom still hadn't called. We told him Tom was filming a big movie, *The Last Samurai*, a great movie, and that he was travelling all over the world. Despite our promises that Tom would contact Clive, the days kept going by and he didn't call.

Then Clive's wife, Barbara, who had been terminally ill, died. Clive then became more difficult to deal with. Sadly and understandably, this period of time was extremely difficult for Clive, and that translated to his being more difficult when it came to the project.

Clive called us and said, "I'm not approving Tom." And how do you tell the biggest movie star in the world that? But we didn't have to. Things were dragging so much that Tom had kind of lost interest. Now we were back almost at square one. We still had Penelope but we'd been through Hugh Jackman and Tom Cruise and still didn't have the male lead.

Matthew McConaughey's team was still calling weekly. We knew that Matthew had flown out to meet with Clive on his own, before we had become involved with Clive. Clive was unsure about Matthew, as there had been some negative publicity around Matthew for playing the bongos in the nude in Texas. Also, Clive felt Dirk Pitt needed to have dark black hair. One day Karen and I were flying back to the east coast on a late flight that was totally empty in first class except for us, Matthew McConaughey and his friend and manager Gus Gustawes. I'll never forget it — and looking back, I realize it was very similar to accidentally meeting Phil David Fine on that flight to the WHA meetings 40 years earlier. We had never met Matthew, so we introduced ourselves and we all got along for five hours on that plane. That flight led to Matthew getting the part of Dirk Pitt. Matthew was totally dedicated to the role, and we could not have made a better choice. His persistence and passion were admirable and have served him well — as is illustrated in the remarkable work he did in *Dallas Buyers Club* and other films subsequent to *Sahara*.

Sahara was our biggest movie to that point, with a huge budget of $150 million. We got a big chunk of money, about $25 million, from what they call the U.K. Sales Tax Lease-Back. To get it, we had to employ a British crew. We filmed that movie in a lot of places, starting at Shepperton, the big studio in Surrey. Then we moved way out into the Sahara desert in Morocco, but the deal still applied because we carried the UK crew with us. Then we went to Marrakesh, and then to Spain for two or three weeks on a river — there's a great boat-chase scene in the movie — then back to Shepperton.

Clive's books always start with a historical piece. This one opened up with an ironclad battleship from the Civil War era being fired upon as it goes up a river. We had to build the boat in the studio and then add huge shock absorbers to get the rocking effect and the whole river feel. When you were inside it, you really felt like you were in an ironclad.

The movie did well in the theaters but not great. It opened as number one in the U.S. with $18 million at the box office in its first weekend. It did however have an amazing DVD life — it was the largest-grossing DVD for Paramount in 2005.

By the time *Sahara* opened, Karen and I had decided to leave Crusader and go it alone, forming Baldwin Entertainment Group. In addition to business considerations, we both had families back east and we wanted to go back and spend time with them.

We left on completely good terms with Phil Anschutz. Phil had two different companies — Crusader Entertainment and Walden Media, which was really into making only family G-rated movies — and he wanted to merge the two. I just felt we could never make it work. So Karen and I put our own banner together in 2004.

Three months before *Sahara* was released, Clive Cussler sued Phil because he felt we hadn't given him the script approval that he wanted. Between when the suit was filed and when it went to court, Karen and I had gone off on our own, but we felt an intense loyalty to make sure Phil won the lawsuit. Clive was being totally out of line.

Karen had been the producer in charge of creative on the film, so she was on the witness stand for three weeks, and she was great. The story was on the front page of the *L.A. Times*, in one form or another, every day during those three weeks.

It took two years for the decision to come down, and Phil won. There were subsequent judgments and appeals, but ultimately Phil prevailed.

Mr. Hockey

Going out on our own with the Baldwin Entertainment Group was a tough but rewarding experience. The business had changed, and it was getting much harder to get the financing for independent films because of the way banks had stopped lending. More equity money was needed to get films made, and the bottom had fallen out of the foreign sales market. Despite that, we were able to do a film in 2007 with Hyde Park Entertainment, *Death Sentence*, starring Kevin Bacon and directed by James Wan, and then we were able to bring a project to completion that had long been close to our hearts: *Mr. Hockey*. We had always been determined to tell the story, in film, of Gordie Howe coming out of retirement to play with his sons Mark and Marty. Too many people, even hockey fans, don't truly understand what an extraordinary story it is. If it were a work of fiction nobody would believe it.

It's safe to say that it will never happen again. This was just not any hockey player, hanging on by his fingernails to spend a nostalgic year playing with his sons. There isn't any question that Gordie is the Babe Ruth of hockey.

When Gordie retired from the NHL's Detroit Red Wings in 1971, he assumed he would never play again but that he would have a meaningful position in the Red Wings' front office. Gordie has more hockey knowledge in his little pinky than most hockey people, then and now, accrue in their whole lives. Gordie was given a corner office with few responsibilities other than to sign an autograph from time to time.

In 1973, during the second WHA draft, Bill Dineen, who was then the GM and coach of the Houston Aeros, made a very bold move and selected Mark and Marty Howe, then excelling in junior hockey for the Toronto Marlies. Nobody thought at the time that the Howes would actually sign, and certainly nobody thought that Gordie would come out retirement at the age of 45 to play for the Aeros with his sons. But, unbelievably, he did. The whole event was orchestrated with Dineen by Colleen Howe, Gordie's wife, the mother of their boys and the family business manager.

The signings of the Howes rocked the hockey world. Of course, the NHL hierarchy made fun of it and treated it as a "carnival event." Wouldn't you know, that first year, Gordie finished third in scoring and was the MVP of the league, Mark was the rookie of the year, and also made the WHA Second All-Star team. And as icing on the cake, the Aeros won the Avco World Trophy that year, too.

We wanted to tell the story of the Howes' unlikely first year in the WHA through a theatrical release film, but when we were in a position to try with Baldwin Entertainment Group, it was difficult getting *any* project made — but financing for period-piece hockey films had become impossible to secure. The project sat for six or seven years, but we remained committed to getting it made.

Mike Ilitch Jr., from the family that currently owns the Red Wings but did not when Gordie played there, joined Karen and me as a producing partner, which was value-added but still not enough to get us set up. We then met a company called Brightlight Pictures out of Canada, and they were able to work with us and get a deal at the CBC to make the story for television. So in 2013, nearly 40 years after the Howes came to Houston, *Mr. Hockey: The Gordie Howe Story* was released. It stars Canadian actors Michael Shanks as Gordie and Kathleen Robertson as Colleen, and it was shown on the CBC in Canada and on the Hallmark Channel in the U.S.

It was personally moving for us to finally bring the story to the screen, but the greatest satisfaction we had from the project was how positively the family felt about the end result. Karen and I have always felt very strongly about Gordie and his family, and in particular the late Colleen Howe. We were very pleased that their family story could be memorialized for the public.

Star Power

Because I've spent much of my working life in both worlds, people often ask me to compare the hockey and movie businesses.

There are many similarities, which is why athletes and actors often gravitate toward each other. They live in a fishbowl, their life work is very public and they trigger outsized emotions, both positive and negative, in their fans.

Like hockey, the movie business sells its employees' accomplishments to the masses. Both businesses soar and dip with public perception. They both market products which derive from universal pursuits: storytelling and playing games.

There are significant differences, though. From an ownership or management standpoint, one of the biggest is that when you own a hockey team and it doesn't open the season well, you still have 40 home games left to try to fix it. But if you release a movie and it doesn't open well, you don't have any more time. You're done.

The salary structure is also different in movies than it is in sports. Sometimes when they're justifying their clients' huge salaries, hockey agents will make the comparison to the top movie stars of the day. But there is a direct correlation between the movie star and the success of the movie he or she is in. There really is not the same provable connection in hockey.

As we know, most fans cheer primarily for the sweater of their favorite team. The player they like best is usually with that team for more than one season. But if you sign up to do a movie —

unless you're signing up for a series, and there aren't a great number of those — it's that movie, and that's it.

If you're one of the top two or three players in a movie, and it's a good movie, you will make big bucks. For the rest of the people in the movie the wages are good, but not great. Yes, actors can make $15 to $20 million from one movie if they're great, but you can count those actors on one hand.

There aren't many hockey players who can put fans in the seats in the same quantifiable way that a top movie star can. Mario could do it, Gretzky and Messier too. Sidney Crosby and Alexander Ovechkin can do it today. But there aren't many others.

That is why I want, and have always wanted, more star power in hockey. As with film, in sport, the more marquee value you can give your audience, the better. In my opinion it is important to differentiate between the local sports eye — whether it be in person or over the air — and the national sports eye. The national sports eye will, by and large, root for the sweater, no matter who is in it. This particularly holds true in hockey. Hockey has intensely loyal and dedicated local markets.

PART SIX

Our Final Chapter in Hartford, and Beyond

The Connecticut Whale

Although we hadn't been involved in the city since 1988, when the Whalers were sold, Karen and I always continued to pay close attention to Hartford and its hockey fortunes.

Ever since the Hartford Whalers moved to North Carolina and became the Hurricanes in 1997, we had felt a desire to go back to Connecticut and do what should be done for that market and its fans.

In 2009 we decided to take a break from the film business, return to the East Coast and spend time with our families. We also felt that it was an opportune time to try to do something good to reinvigorate the Hartford hockey market. We put together a select group of very strong and committed partners and formed a company to operate the New York Rangers' American Hockey League franchise in Hartford. The deal was that we would operate the team but not buy it. The easiest way to describe the arrangement was that we essentially leased the team, paying the Rangers an affiliation fee, and if there were profits they were ours, and if there were losses they were ours too.

Twelve years earlier, the New York Rangers had moved the franchise from Binghamton, New York, to play in the Civic Center as the Hartford Wolf Pack, but the team wasn't doing well at the gate or in sponsorships.

Some people might wonder why I would want to get involved in a market that lost its NHL team and was not responding to the AHL team (in 2009–10, the season before we took over, the Wolf Pack averaged 4,188 fans per game, 18th in the league).

There were a number of reasons why we wanted to return, but first and foremost was that the Whalers were the team that I started. I felt a loyalty to the city.

There are very few people who have given birth to a franchise and then carried it through the way I did with the Whalers. Ed Snider has done that in Philadelphia, the Wirtz family has done it in Chicago, the Knoxes have done it in Buffalo, and there has been perhaps a small handful of others. It was natural that I would want the success to continue after I left, but it hadn't. The Whalers had moved, unjustly in my opinion, because the governor and Peter Karmanos, the team owner, just locked horns.

It was a good marketplace with loyal fans, and to this day I think it still is.

Hartford was where I met Karen and where I raised my children. I had very strong feelings for the former Whaler players, and for the significant moments in the history of the franchise. That team meant a lot to a lot of people, and it still does. It's a team that doesn't even exist, yet it has a huge cult following.

We started negotiating with the Rangers in September of 2009 and got to the five-yard line, but couldn't go any further until we arranged an arena lease in Hartford. AEG had the arena management rights from the state until the end of the 2012–13 season, but they were having some issues with their partners, Northland Investment, a local real estate company. This caused significant delays in our lease approval. It is important to emphasize that AEG was on the front lines of any and all negotiations, but the

City and the State were calling the shots. To clarify, when we refer to AEG, we refer to it as the representative of the City of Hartford and the State of Connecticut. AEG didn't cause us any problems; it had its own problems with the City and the State.

It was July of 2010 before AEG told me they had worked things out with Northland and were ready to deal with the lease. I pointed out that it was now so late that I didn't know if we could make much of a difference in the team's situation for the season which would soon be opening. But they insisted that they had been counting on us. So, my heart being bigger than my brain, I went ahead and did a lease deal with AEG that I knew was the worst in the American Hockey League. We signed a three-season deal for $25,000 per game. It was a complete gouging. Dave Andrews, the excellent commissioner of the AHL, was very helpful to me through the process, but he thought I was crazy for agreeing to the deal. The next-highest rent in the AHL was about $15,000 per game, but the average would have been more like $9,000 per game. And we didn't get a dime from concessions. Nothing.

Why did I do it? Because I felt that once we got in there and proved our point that this was a good market, everybody would adjust. I could not have been more wrong.

Then the Rangers had their turn to gouge. For their affiliation fee — essentially the price for them to take care of the hockey aspects of the business — they got $1.35 million per year from us, one of the highest fees in the league.

That's where I was stupid, and I'm not afraid to admit it. I should have just walked away. But I cared about the market and I cared about doing the right thing. And I kept believing that people would step up and help, as everyone had done in Hartford in the 1970s and '80s. Plus, as you know by now, I hate to give up.

We started this venture with absolutely everything going against us. The Northlands delay, along with the Rangers delay, created a situation whereby we did not take control of the team until September 20th. The season began on October 6th.

Since AEG had anticipated consummating this deal with us early in the spring, it had essentially stopped operating the team.

So, our organization had less than three weeks to sell season tickets and sponsorships prior to opening night. That has to be a record in pro sports. To top it off, we received zero financial consideration from either MSG or AEG in respect to the delay that they caused. To add insult to injury, the schedule we inherited was heavily loaded with weeknight games in October, a graveyard time for AHL attendance. In the key month of February — hockey's bestselling time — we only had two home games at the XL Center, and one of them fell on Super Bowl Sunday.

The crowning blow was that this delay caused by MSG/AEG forced us to begin the season as the Hartford Wolf Pack. For legal reasons, we couldn't use the name Whalers, so we ended up renaming the team the Connecticut Whale to re-establish the connection with the WHA and NHL eras. In those days most people referred to the team as "the Whale" anyway. And we changed the uniform color scheme from Rangers red, white and blue to the green and blue of the Whaler days. But we couldn't rebrand to the Connecticut Whale until November 20th. Of course as soon as we did rebrand, we had over 13,000 fans attend.

On a Saturday in August of 2010, we held a Summer Fest, which attracted 5,000 people to meet former Whalers like Ronnie Francis, Kevin Dineen, Andre Lacroix and Gordie, Mark and Marty Howe. We followed that with a Winter Fest that went for 10 days at the football stadium in early 2011 and featured about 120 hockey games of every level — college, high school, boys' and girls' minor leagues — played around the clock.

We played an AHL game too, between the Whale and Providence, Boston's farm team. The Rangers weren't exactly cooperative, and they wouldn't let the game be played in the afternoon, because the team was coming back from a road trip, which shouldn't have mattered at all. It turned out to be the coldest day in the last 50 years and we had to play at night in the perishing cold. But the head count was still 23,000. If we'd played in the afternoon when it was more comfortable for fans, we felt we could have drawn about 35,000 people.

For both Fests, we had reached out to the State and to the City but we got zero help from either of them, which was typical for our entire tenure.

My son Howard Jr. was in charge of all business aspects of the team overall, and he worked very closely with Mark Willand on all ticketing and marketing for the Whale. They should get all the credit for raising attendance from 18th in the AHL the season before we took over, to 12th in our first year in the league, and for increasing the season ticket base by 250 per cent in our second year. For those two years we also won the AHL award for the greatest increase in overall revenues. In the second year we tripled sponsorship levels and in the third year of the contract we would have quadrupled them, and we would have been among the top three or four in the AHL.

But there was to be no third year.

We had no chance of breaking even with the exorbitant lease and affiliation fees we were paying, so we didn't have the income to properly market the team. In the middle of our second year, we went to Civic Center management and asked for a contract extension of five years. We made it clear that we weren't asking for a renegotiation of the remaining third year. We said we would do the last year under the onerous terms but we wouldn't go beyond that unless we renegotiated a new rental deal. In order to continue to put capital in the company, we needed to know that we'd have a business plan that went beyond one more year.

For reasons unfathomable to me, we received zero support from the City and the State. We were therefore unable to reach a reasonable deal for the Civic Center for the future. It became a very political issue with the State and City — it was almost as if they were punishing people like us for coming into the state and trying to do something good. We didn't want to be throwing good money after bad in the third year, and we were forced to walk away. It was heartbreaking.

The arena management company did get every single dime they were owed from us, and the Rangers got 80 per cent of their money for that second year. If everyone had worked together and agreed to extend the lease, enabling us to recapitalize our company, it would have greatly benefited not only the Rangers but the Hartford hockey market.

Since we left, sponsorships have fallen back to the bottom of the league, as has attendance. At the end of the season, AEG did not have its management contract renewed. Global Comcast took over managing the arena and the hockey team, whose name went back to the Wolf Pack.

Sadly, the expensive and harsh lesson that I learned was, "You can't go back. Don't try to recreate the past. Instead focus on the future." Our dear friend Chris Berman of ESPN fame would always joke with us, and referred to me as Don Quixote: always fighting windmills. Sometimes you have to know when to stop.

The entire experience accentuated what had worked so well in the '70s, when we had a corporate community working closely with city and state government for the betterment of all. You just had to walk down the streets of Hartford in the late '70s and '80s to feel the enthusiasm and energy of the city, thanks in large part to the hockey team. There was something to do, and to be proud of. Now when you walk on the streets of Hartford, there is nobody else on them.

The corporate community today isn't working toward the betterment of Hartford, and the City and State have their own agendas. Honestly, I haven't yet figured out what those agendas actually are, nor do I care to at this point.

In the 1970s we had leaders like Arthur Lumsden, head of the Downtown Chamber of Commerce, who was constantly pulling people together and trying to do the right thing for the city and state. Now, they have a thing called the MetroHartford Alliance that is run by Oz Griebel. To this day, I'm not sure what that is, but suffice it to say, in my opinion it's not very effective.

The media support was, by and large, okay, but not one media organization was really willing to roll up its sleeves and work. They were quick to criticize but not inclined to explore the problems more deeply. They all took the easy way out, which was to criticize us when all we were trying to do was bring some life back into the city.

The city wanted its major league team back but was unwilling to pay the price that needed to be paid, to take the steps necessary to rebuild the market.

The fans were great. They cared and responded. I think the fans understood and were prepared to do what had to be done, but the powers-that-be squashed it. They didn't get it . . . and still don't.

The people who run the NHL aren't sitting in New York City scratching their heads to think of other markets that may be suitable for the NHL. They aren't saying, "Gee, we have to go to Hartford, Connecticut." The people in leadership positions in Hartford need to be reminded now that the NHL didn't elect to come to Hartford in 1979, they came there because it was a solution to a problem: the war between the NHL and WHA. If it weren't for that, Hartford may have never been part of the NHL.

Hartford needs to put itself in a position whereby it is "all dressed up and ready to go." It needs to become a viable solution and a logical location for an NHL franchise, whether it be through league expansion or the transfer of a team. It needs to take a page out of Winnipeg's book. Winnipeg was led by Mark Chipman, who put an AHL team into a newly built arena, thereby keeping the market enthusiastic for hockey and keeping the market on the NHL radar. And, lo and behold, when Gary Bettman had a problem in Atlanta, he solved it by moving the team to Winnipeg.

The Guardian Project

Today, Karen and I reside in Los Angeles and are working diligently on our film company as well as the very exciting Stan Lee/NHL superhero project. Sports is still in my blood, but now finds its outlet in the superhero project and some of our movies. Running NHL teams is for younger people.

Just as *Sudden Death* and *Mystery, Alaska* and *Mr. Hockey* brought together my love for movies and for hockey, the Guardian Project is a perfect opportunity to blend the entertainment and sports worlds.

In 2010, Mark Terry, a friend of ours from the film business, introduced us to the Guardians, designed by the brilliant Stan Lee of Marvel Comics. Stan is the mind behind such graphic and memorable super-heroes as Spider-Man, Iron Man and Captain America. For the Guardians, he created one of his distinctive stylized superheroes for each of the 30 NHL teams, with complete back stories encompassing the lore of the individual teams and the cities they represent.

Pittsburgh's Guardian, for instance, is the Penguin, "who can project missiles from his hand, and travels on a frozen ice sheet."

Philadelphia has the Flyer, "a master of telekinesis and mind control" with wings, while Toronto is protected by the Maple Leaf, a walking, talking maple tree, "an immovable object which can grow exponentially larger at will." San Jose has the Shark, a really cool surfer who "controls an army of sharks to help him in battle."

Karen and I were blown away by the project. It was a well-thought-out business plan designed to bring the massive Stan Lee audience to the sports world with merchandising, gaming, TV, video, film and apps components. Mark, knowing our relationship with the NHL, suggested we show it to them.

We flew to New York for lunch with Gary Bettman, showed him the idea and the materials, and he immediately "got it." Gary was as enthusiastic as we were, and we eventually made one of the first joint venture deals the NHL has done with an outside company. The partners in the Guardian Project are the NHL, Stan Lee/POW!, Comcast, Domani Ventures and our founding group.

We all feel the Guardians has huge potential for NHL teams, will provide growth for the league and will become a solid profit center for all the partners involved. And it enables us to work with our friends in both the NHL and entertainment worlds.

The blending of sport and entertainment is the wave of the future, and the Guardians is the vehicle in which we are riding on it.

Entertainment Value in Hockey — You Didn't Really Ask, But ...

Here is one man's opinion — mine — of a few things that could be done to make hockey more entertaining in the future.

Offence: Star Power Created by Statistics

All the meaningful statistics in sports are offensive statistics. In hockey, when we think of the great stars we think of Wayne Gretzky, Gordie Howe, Mario Lemieux, Rocket Richard and Bobby Orr. Although Bobby Orr was a defenceman, he created his greatness through offence.

It is my belief that the NHL is in danger of becoming a low-scoring defensive league, thereby eliminating almost all the stars. The league must get its brightest minds (and there are some good ones) together and not be afraid to make the changes needed so that offence can rule the day. You just need to look at the goaltenders of today to see that they look like characters out of a *Transformers* movie, padded to the hilt.

We have to accept the fact that the human body is bigger, stronger and taller today than ever before. As well, the equipment is better and bigger. Yet the ice surface remains the same size: 200 feet by 85 feet. There is no longer the room to move around to create plays, so the sport has become so much clutch-and-grab and not the beautiful display of skill and finesse that we know hockey can be. It seems sad to me that I can name just as many NBA stars of today as I can NHL stars.

One idea that might create more scoring would be to have four-on-four hockey all game, thereby opening the ice up a lot more. Then, if there was a penalty, one team would get to add a player, rather than the offending team having to subtract one.

Four's a Crowd

I would have only the two referees on the ice, with the two linesmen sitting in the stands. If you're a tennis judge, you're sitting on the line, but if you're a hockey linesman you're moving up and down the ice and constantly looking at other things. You're never right on the line, even though you may think you are. Why not have a linesman 10 rows up from the ice on the blueline? I have a hunch very few calls would be missed then.

There Is No Point to a Tie

Nobody should be satisfied with a tie. We are rewarding mediocrity by awarding a point for a regulation-time tie. Games are played to be won or lost. If you win a game with a shoot-out, you gain two points, but the other team should get *nothing*. You shouldn't get a point for losing a game.

If you don't have that point available to you, you're going to go balls-out to try to win the game and not count on sudden death and the shootout. The way it is now, weaker teams will often times play for a tie on the road, particularly in the second half of a game, when they think they may get at least one point. Therefore the customer is cheated. It becomes a giant "snore." Whereas if there was no reward — i.e., no point given for a tie — that team would have no choice but to play its hardest to try to get a win. In a sporting event you either win or lose — there is no tie. There is no tie in baseball or basketball. In football you have one tie every few years.

Fighting is Bad Business

In the mid-'90s, at the annual meeting in Tampa Bay, when I was governor of the Penguins — I forget who was with me on this — we suggested to the other governors a vote on abolishing fighting. Needless to say, it failed. People felt fighting was important to the game. Many thought of fighting as a logical outlet for frustration that might prevent violence. Others felt that it was a bonus for the fans.

We have to reach a bigger audience in hockey to generate the electronic revenue that the other three major leagues get. Your hockey audience will say you have to have fighting because most of that hockey audience loves fighting. I think they do, and frankly, I understand why. But if we're going to broaden that audience, bring it into the average household with children, where there's a great resistance to the violence in hockey, we can't have fighting.

I also feel that players today are so big, so strong and so powerful, and we do have a responsibility to these young kids to make sure that they have a life after hockey. Just four or five games into the 2013 season, the fighting was vicious. Believe me, in the 1970s and '80s I saw some intense ones, but the fights now seem really mean to me. There was almost a joy to the fights in the '70s and '80s. Now they're vicious — players are really trying to hurt each other, and I think we have to do something about that. Right now, the whole issue of concussions is bringing this to the fore, which is a good thing. Keep in mind that the NFL, NBA and Major League Baseball all have their occasional fights as well, but those leagues just don't condone it the way the NHL does. If you fight in those other sports, you are out of the game immediately.

Location, Location, Location

The NHL has three big events a year, four if you count the Awards night: the draft, the All-Star Game, and the Stanley Cup final. I would suggest that the NHL consider doing what the other leagues do, which is to have the draft in a major media market every year. In the NHL's case, that would be Toronto, Montreal, New York and maybe Los Angeles. This would attract greater media interest. The bigger the market, the larger the advertisers and the more attention is paid to hockey.

If the NHL wants to move the All-Star Game around to help markets, fine. But let's have the draft in a major market each year. Why does the NFL always do the draft in Radio City Music Hall every year? *Duh.* The NHL is already doing that with the awards in Las Vegas, so now do it with the draft.

As for the Stanley Cup finals, of course those games have to be hosted by the cities that are actually in the finals. But if anybody tells you that the league office doesn't go to bed at night and pray the final includes at least one major market, don't believe them. I hope the day is coming soon when a European champion will play the Stanley Cup champion. When this does happen, let's make certain that the final is in a major media market, whether it's in North America or overseas.

Honoring the Past

As I reflect on the past, one of my hopes is that the current ownership and leadership, both on the player side and ownership side, won't forget those players, coaches, front office executives and others who took the leap of faith and moved from a well-established league into what was considered to be a "mighty risky venture," a.k.a. the WHA. Players such as Larry Pleau, Tom Webster, John McKenzie, Ralph Backstrom, Bobby Hull, the Howes, Dave Keon, Rick Ley and many more all had good NHL jobs and bright futures there and opted to take a chance and jump leagues. Of course, there are coaches and executives who took the leap as well, such as Jack Kelley, Terry Slater, Glen Sonmor, Harry Neale, Bill Dineen and many more.

It is only really in the last 15 to 20 years that salaries for hockey players, coaches and general managers have caught up to the other three professional leagues. I believe that the average NHL salary at the time of the formation of the WHA was about $18K per annum. Coaches and general managers were fortunate enough to make $30K to $35K per year. Today, players average almost $2.4 million per year and almost all GMs and coaches are in the seven-figure range. The entire budget for the first year of the New England Whalers was $700K — all in. Right now that is just a bit over the NHL minimum salary for just *one* player.

I point all this out only because in this world of "today" we tend to forget about those people that did so much with so much less to make the sport what it is today. One of the many things I love about hockey as a business is that the people in it have always been so great. They are the kind of people you would be proud to bring home to meet your family. Let us not forget our roots. There is nothing worse than being forgotten.

Epilogue

I t has been tremendous fun working on this book, because it has forced me to go back to recall certain events, people and experiences, almost all of which are extraordinarily positive memories.

Over dinner one night, my good friend Tom Reich looked at me and said that there were plenty of things we could have done that might have made us more money, but we sure wouldn't have had as much fun.

I am very proud of the fact that I came up "through the ranks" in professional hockey. I was never given anything — I had to earn it. One of the criticisms I have heard about me is that I work with OPM — other people's money. That is only partially true. Karen and I have invested significant sums of our own money into our film business, and we have invested money in sports as well. The fact of the matter is that when I got into sport, I didn't have the money to make a meaningful investment. If I had had it, I would have used it. When I finally was in a position to do so — I did.

Both businesses — hockey and film — take passion, commitment, and dedication. They are like any other business in that you will not succeed unless you persevere. But the key difference with the things that I have chosen to do in my working life is that in film and sports everything is visible, laid out in plain sight for public viewing. Early on in my career, I couldn't imagine anyone ever saying or writing anything disparaging about me, but over the years I have learned that you had better be able to take the good, the bad and the ugly, and not let any one of those three affect you. I have pointed out the portion of my career in Hartford when I did let it affect me and it created an environment in which I made some bad decisions.

When we left Pittsburgh amid considerable controversy, I made up my mind I wasn't going to talk to a single member of the media about the fact that I felt I was right in what I had or hadn't done. I knew that for myself, and it was enough for me. I have respect for most members of the media. I have always been honest with them. But what they think about me and about what I have done is their issue, not mine.

As I write these words, I think how extraordinarily lucky I am to be able to say that I have worked directly with the likes of such owners as Ed Snider, Bill Wirtz, Jeremy Jacobs, Phil Anschutz, John Bassett, Ben Hatskin and many others. I have had the honor of working with commissioners Ziegler and Bettman as well as other extraordinary hockey executives such as Jack Kelley, Emile Francis, Harry Neale, Ron Ryan, Larry Pleau, Colleen Howe, Craig Patrick, Scotty Bowman, Bill Dineen and others. Then when I think of the players who have played for me over the years — such as Gordie, Mark and Marty Howe, Ron Francis, Mario Lemieux, Dave Keon, Jaromir Jagr, Bobby Hull, Paul Coffey and anyone else who ever put on a Whalers or Penguins uniform during those years — I am humbled.

In terms of partners in hockey, I couldn't have asked for better ones: John Coburn, Bob Schmertz and the Hartford corporations, in particular the Aetna, led by Don Conrad. Then of course there is my partner, Tom Ruta, who has been with me in every deal I have ever done, and my San Jose/Minnesota/Pittsburgh partner, Morris Belzberg. I also feel fortunate to have been able to work with my son Howard Jr. as a partner during the Connecticut Whale experience.

In film I have been blessed with some terrific partners as well, over my several decades as part of the creative community. My first film partner, Bill Minot, a dear friend who recently passed, gave me my introduction to film. Richard Cohen was my partner for 10 years on nothing more than a handshake deal, and he was a wonderful friend and partner to both Karen and me. I am pleased to have done a few film deals with Richard's son Andy as well, continuing the legacy. Many of the films we did in our partnership with Phil Anschutz were nominated for awards, including the highlight, *Ray*, which was nominated for every single prestigious award that Hollywood has to offer, culminating in the two Academy Awards and the Golden Globe. *Ray* would never have been made if it weren't for Phil Anschutz. He had the courage and commitment and passion to fund 100 per cent of its production. This is rarely, if ever, done in Hollywood. There are a lot of people who claim some of the success for *Ray*, and frankly, many deserve accolades, but at the top of the list should be Phil, and Stuart Benjamin, who shepherded the project for 13 years.

We currently work with a third partner, Bill Immerman, who served with us in the Crusader years. In keeping with the six degrees of separation theme, we actually met Bill at a hockey game. Bill and his wife Ginger are major Kings fans, with seats near the player bench and the glass. During our film tenure we have also had the fun of hiring and working with young executives Todd Slater, who is the son of the late Terry Slater, who coached the WHA LA Sharks and the NCAA Champion Colgate hockey team, and Nick Morton, who is the stepson of John Picket, former owner of the New York Islanders. We hired Simon Fischler, son of the great hockey writer

Stan Fischler and Shirley Fischler, who were also the first broadcasting team in the New England Whaler years.

We have had the privilege of working with many film personalities over the years — actors, directors and writers. Many have become close friends. Several we have worked with more than once. To list them all would be impossible, as there are so many, but one just has to look at our résumé of films to see the talent we have had the opportunity to work with. We have also been blessed with good working relationships with the talent agencies in Hollywood, in particular with Jack Gilardi at ICM, with John Levin at CAA, and more recently with Sean Barclay at Gersh.

From a legal representation standpoint we have been lucky enough to have Jake Bloom in our corner. Jake is way more than a lawyer — he is practically our "Yoda." He and his wife Ruth are wonderful friends as well. Jake is one of the top attorneys in this town and we have benefitted greatly from his expertise and advice.

Then there's Karen, my partner in film and life. One could not ask for anything more. Karen is brilliant with a script, and one of the things she is proudest of is a note from Taylor Hackford, the director of *Ray*, who made it clear that the script wouldn't have been what it was without her dedication and persistence in working on it and fighting for the changes that needed to be made.

In reflecting, I realize how lucky I am to have such a wonderful family and such great friends. One could never ask for a better friend than Tom Ruta, who has stood by my side through all the crazy deals I have done — and the not-so-crazy ones too! Tom loves to wear suits with suspenders. I will never forget the scene after we won the Stanley Cup. There was chaos, and we were surrounded. I have a distinct memory of Tom in his impeccable suit and tie looking dazed as champagne was being dumped all over us. I remember giving him a hug and saying, "Tom, do you realize we just won the Holy Grail — Lord Stanley's Cup?" Tom's brother

Nick has also worked for us, loyally and tirelessly, in sports and film for over 30 years. Bob Caporale, my first real lawyer in the business world and to this day one of my dearest friends, has gone on to form Game Plan with former NFL wide receiver Randy Vataha, and they have brokered some of the biggest sports deals ever done — including a few for me.

My three children, Scott, Rebecca and Howard Jr., have given me great joy and pride and seven wonderful grandchildren, whom Karen and I enjoy spoiling along with their grandmother, Anne, a great friend of both of ours. My children were very patient with my compulsive business behavior, the constant phoning and all the other distractions. I remember the wonderful times my kids and I would enjoy together on various road trips with the hockey teams. On one road trip to Minnesota, wouldn't you know, my son Scott won the lucky number draw and had to go on the ice between the first and second periods to try to shoot a puck through a small hole in front of the goal, with the odds of achieving it about 1 in 1,000. When Scott was introduced he was booed, but he proceeded to line up the shot and *in it went!* His prize? A bag of groceries. My daughter Becka was the only female on the Watkinson School hockey team. I remember after one game I asked her what the other players (all boys) were saying to her when she faced off against them. (Keep in mind, her long blonde hair could be seen flowing out of her helmet.) She replied, "Dad, if I tell you what they say to me, you won't let me play anymore." And Howard Jr. grew up in the locker room. There are so many stories about "Bubba," as he is known in NHL circles, that I will leave them for his book, but he has been in and out of hockey with me, and we have had a wonderful time working together. Howard Jr. worked in the Whalers locker room until we sold the team, and then worked briefly in the San Jose Sharks and Philly Flyers locker rooms before joining me in Pittsburgh and subsequently in Connecticut.

Special thanks to House of Anansi led by Sarah MacLachlan and Matt Williams and their wonderful staff who worked tirelessly with us on this book to bring it to fruition.

Special thanks to David Andrews, President of the American Hockey League, who kindly provided the initial introduction to House of Anansi in Toronto.

Special thanks to Steve Milton for spending hours with us transcribing all the stories, and for researching and writing this book with me.

Special thanks to Mark Willand for working so hard on the marketing and for being a true fan.

Special thanks to my wife, Karen. She has put as much work into this project as anybody — including me.

Thanks to God for the gift of life and health and all of life's experiences, and the faith to pursue my dreams.

I love my brothers, their spouses and their children, and now grandchildren — Chelsie, Gage, Taylor, Gabby, Chris, Nick, and MacKenzie Rose. My brother Ian and his wife, Margo, have enjoyed a very successful career in publishing in Vermont with their company, Chelsea Green. My brother Michael and his wife, Margie, reside in Marion, Massachusetts, where Michael has an extraordinarily successful investment banking firm and is dedicated to his foundation, the Marion Foundation, a charitable organization dealing with key world health and environmental issues. My brother Philip and his partner, Monica, reside in Paris and are considered one of the top glass blower/designer teams in the world. Their work is extraordinary and is featured in top galleries and museums around the globe.

Karen's family has been wonderful to me and my children and grandchildren. When Karen and I met, we knew that if we were to have a relationship it wouldn't be easy because of our age gap and the fact that I had been married once before. Mary Jane and

Jim embraced the relationship, and once Mary Jane finally bit the bullet and sent out the wedding invitations, it was smooth sailing. Karen's sister Kristen and her brother Jason have always been devoted friends to me — and now with spouses and children of their own, that circle of devotion has widened.

Many people will look at Karen and me like we are nuts and wonder how we work together and yet stay so happily married. It is a fair question. We met each other in the workplace and we both love the same things — film and sports, and each other. My father would always say that in order to really succeed on the journey of life, you need a sense of humor. Karen and I have that in common.

Finally, I think of my parents.

My father had us on skates as soon as we could walk. He loved the sport of hockey and was a highly skilled player. The passion that I had for the sport emanated from him. Dad also taught me and my brothers the real values that enable one to succeed in life: loyalty, integrity, common sense, a sense of humor and kindness.

Speaking of kindness, one of the kindest people I have known was my mother, Rose. I am not sure I would have ever written this book if it wasn't for my mother. Particularly in her later years, she would love it when I would come to visit with Karen and tell all my old war stories. After each story she would say "Howdy, dear — you must write a book." She would constantly ask, "When are you going to write that book?"

Our family was blessed to have had both parents live well into their later years. My dad died in June of 2001, at 88. Three days prior to his passing, we shared a wonderful conversation about sports, and his frustration with the Red Sox, and his joy at watching Tiger Woods play golf. My mother died in March of 2013, at 95. She was sharp as a tack and focused up until the very end. In fact, the night before she passed she had a glass of wine and some oysters from the bay that she loved to sail upon, and was telling my daughter Becka about her escapades at school.

So, Ma, here it is. I hope everyone has had some fun reading it and maybe learned a little about me in the process. I sure have. I look forward to the chapters that are still unwritten.

Index

Howard Baldwin is a sports entrepreneur and film producer. He was co-founder of the New England Whalers, president of the WHA, and chairman of the Pittsburgh Penguins, and is now CEO of RSVP Entertainment. He lives in Los Angeles, California with his wife and business partner, Karen, who worked closely with him on this book.

Steve Milton has thirty-five years' experience as a sports-writer and writes for *The Hamilton Spectator*. He has won numerous Ontario Newspaper Awards and has been both a Gemini and National Newspaper Award finalist. He is the author of more than twenty books, including *Tessa and Scott: Our Journey from Childhood Dream to Gold*. He lives in Toronto, Ontario.